More Praise For
Just Get Serious® About Success

"Read this book and take action. You will not be disappointed. Donna's personal insights and concepts will inspire you to move ahead to create the life you want."

DR. SHIRLEY GARRETT, Speaker, Author & Coach

"If you have been stuck in the Land of Say Everything, while sitting on the Stool of Do Nothing, you need to read this book. It will get you motivated and moving! Do yourself a favor purchase it and follow through with pursuing your dreams."

PATRICIA WILLIAMS, M.A., Professional Counselor

"I love this book! Donna has created the ultimate step-by-step guide for those who are serious about finding their passion, while creating a successful career and personal life."

CARL S. MCNAIR, President, McNair Achievement Programs

"A valuable and illuminating book! The stories, practical advice, and thought-provoking exercises guide readers to 'Just Get Serious' about their goals. Feeling there may be more to life than what you are currently experiencing? If so, this is a 'must read' book."

ANDREA ROSENTHAL, M.S., Career and Business Strategist

"Donna weaves her personalized web of encouragement and spirit of motivation until the last word is read. Get ready to be moved to Just Get Serious."

RAYMOND E. BROWN, President
Atlanta Association of Insurance Professionals

"If readers of this book take advantage of all the exercises, they will feel as though they have their own personal cheerleader and life coach."

MONICA MILLINES, County Government Employee

"Donna Satchell is a dynamic speaker and success coach who can help you to grow and go to the next level. Just Get Serious® About Success is Donna at her best. This book will empower you to make massive steps and progress on your goals and dreams."

WILLY JOLLEY, CSP, Best Selling Author & Media Personality

"I cannot wait to make this book a vital part of the message I share with thousands across the globe. Its chapters are riveting. Those who read it will forever be inspired and catapulted into dimensions beyond belief."

KEITH L. BROWN, "Motivator of the Millennium"

"Many of us have forgotten what it was like to 'live our dreams.' The chapter on pursuing your passion serves as an inspiration to re-connect with those dreams and finally enjoy them. Don't skip that chapter."

ANWAR WESLKEY, Writer

"Whether you have entrepreneurial, workplace, professional, or personal aspirations, you will find this book invaluable. Donna shares priceless tips and techniques. Read it and make serious progress on your goals and dreams."

NIKKI SWEET, President, Customer Service University

"All readers of Donna's new book will gain from the valuable lessons from her own life and the lessons she shares from the people she interviewed. This exciting book will help you reach your goals."

ROBERT ALAN BLACK, Ph.D., CSP
Creative Workplace Consultant

Just Get
SERIOUS®
ABOUT SUCCESS

By Donna "Serious" Satchell

Forewords by Les Brown and Dr. Marthenia Dupree

ISBN: 978-0-983-64970-0
Library of Congress Control Number: 2011908436

For book orders, quantity discounts, author appearance inquiries and interviews, contact the Publisher:

STARR Consulting & Training
P.O. Box 870067
Stone Mountain, GA 30087
770-498-0400

info@JustGetSerious.com
www.JustGetSerious.com
www.JGSBook.com

First Printing

Acknowledgements

Like life, *Just Get Serious® About Success* is a result of great teamwork. Without it, you would not be reading this book.

First and foremost, I thank my editor extraordinaire, Steve Cohn. Your advice, direction, and patience were priceless. I appreciate the endless phone calls, endless consultations, and the endless hours you spent editing and re-editing, as I made changes and added unplanned sections. I know you thought it would never end. I now understand the adage that books are not written, they are re-written (by great editors). Words cannot fully express my gratitude.

To Gracie White, Cynthia Amiger, Pia Forbes, and Melanie White, your proofreading skills and grammatical suggestions were invaluable.

Samantha Angeli of Pixelution Studios, thank you for the exciting cover. It is amazing how you took my few rudimentary thoughts and turned them into the final design. Your artistic abilities and your patience made you a joy to work with.

Arlene Cohn, thank you for the fantastic layout of the book. I appreciate all your creative ideas. Letitia Owens of R'tish Creations, thank you for the great photo. It still continues to serve me well.

Bob Thiele of the Small Business Development Center (SBDC), thank you for being a tremendous source of expert advice on everything from design to compelling copy. Reggie Muhammad, of First Degree Publishing, I appreciate your guidance. Your passion for book publishing caused me to raise the bar on what I was creating and what I plan to do with the book.

Les Brown and Dr. Marthenia "Tina" Dupree, thank you for the incredible forewords. I know you have extremely busy schedules, so I am honored that you took the time to read the manuscript and write your commentaries.

I thank those supportive individuals who wrote outstanding testimonials about the book: Andrea Rosenthal, M.S.; Anwar Weslkey; Carl S. McNair; Dennis Kimbro, Ph.D.; Dwayne G. Smith; Jewel Diamond Taylor; Keith L. Brown; Monica Millines; Nikki Sweet; Patricia Williams, M.A.; Raymond Brown; Rene Godefroy; Robert Alan Black, Ph.D.; Dr. Shirley Garrett; Susan Wranik, M.S.; and Willie Jolley, CSP.

Carl McNair, my accountability partner, thank you for your enthusiastic and helpful spirit. You kept me moving forward. Donna Lang, my business coach, you are a wealth of ingenious strategies. I appreciate you sharing so many of them with me.

Cleopatra Bell and Letitia Baldwin, I value the calls and meetings to keep me focused on the big picture and share your many excellent ideas.

To Lynda Shorter and Janet Saboor, your enthusiasm about the book kept me inspired. Your enduring friendships meant I always had someone to talk with about the challenges and to celebrate my progress.

Joanne Simmons, thank you for your faith in me and for purchasing the first copy of this book before it was printed. William Johnson, I appreciate the many ways you encouraged me during the many times I felt discouraged. All you did meant more than words can say.

I thank the following individuals for allowing me to interview them and share their stories in order to inspire others: Brad Crose; Carlos Barham; Cindy Cannon; Cindy Light; Daemoni Franklin; Daniel Carr; Derke Clements; Donna Lang; Dot Murphy; Edith Dean; Ellen Crooke; Gale Horton Gay; Geno Evans; Jackie Boards; Jacquelyn Payne; Jennie Campell; Joanne Smith; Jordan Dean; Karen Ervin; Linda Hall; Margaret Johnson; Pam Williams; and Selita Victoria. I know your stories will encourage and motivate my readers because they encouraged and motivated me.

Ray Brown, thank you for your brilliant idea of having a glossary and index as well as your other great suggestions.

To my fellow members of the National Speakers Association (NSA) and the Georgia Chapter of NSA, thank you for answering my many questions and providing me with your individual insights.

To my copy reviewers, thank you for the time you took to read chapters and give me your thoughts on what you found insightful and motivating, what was confusing, and what needed to be clarified or deleted. For your invaluable feedback, I thank: Andrea Frazier; Anwar Weslkey; Audrey Turner; Barbara Johnson; Bernice Randolph; Brenda Young-Hathico; Carolyn Hartfield; Cindy Beckles; Claire Goddard; Clarissa Mitchell; Claudia Coplon; Cleopatra Bell; Deanne Athias; Darrell Hazelwood; Diane Bogino; Dianne Hargrove; Diva Dex Day; Dot Murphy; Fran Mohr; Gayle Greene; Gina Gorby; Gloria Sylvester; Henrietta Turnquest; Holly Brack; Jackie Board; Jahi Muhammad; Jennifer Truell; Joanne Simmons; Joanne Smith; Joyce Dawson; Juanita Mitchell; Karen Gavin; Karen Jordan; Kim Gilbert; Kufre Eduok; Lina James; Linda Murphy; Liz Lieberman; Margaret Johnson; Marsha Clark; Michelle Famusipe; Monica Millines; Nikki Sweet; Noreen Henry; Octavia Powell; Pat Alston; Patricia Williams; Patsi Turner; Peggy Lumpkin; Robert Alan Black, Ph.D.; Rosemary Willingham; Sandra Russell; Susan Wranik; Tammy Walker; Terri Waller; Thelma Williams; Toni Stewart-Sales; Dr. Torri Griffin, LCP; and Twanna Brooks.

To my mother, thank you so much for your enduring love and support. I love and appreciate you more than I can express in words.

I hope I have thanked everyone who was connected with this book. If I have not, I sincerely apologize for my oversight. To anyone whom I may have missed, understand it was not intentional. Please let me know of my oversight and I will include you in the next printing.

Teamwork makes the dream work.
Thank you everyone!

Foreword One

Donna "Serious" Satchell, author, dynamic speaker, seminar presenter and coach, has written a book for people who are seriously serious about living their dreams. For many years, you've heard me tell you to, "Get out of your head and into your greatness." But what does this mean, and how do you achieve greatness? Dreaming a dream is a wonderful thing. However, without action, that dream will be nothing more than ashes in the furnace of your mind.

Let's be clear. Your dream is not really your dream. It is the calling on your life. For this reason, it is your responsibility to make it come true. Many of us put our dreams on hold because we are so busy making a living. We tell ourselves that we'll live our dreams when we have enough education, money or support from others, when the kids are grown, or when whatever circumstances we are struggling with are resolved. These are all excuses for inaction. They give us a reason to hide behind our fear and uncertainty. I sincerely believe that by living your making, your making will make your living.

You cannot wait until the time is right to live your dream because the time will never be right. You will never have all of your ducks in a row. That's just life. You've got to go right now! Time is slipping away each day! If you don't live your dream, we will all suffer, because no one can execute your dream like you can. No one can bring to the world what you can bring in the way that you can bring it.

So the question becomes, how do you go about living your dream? You may feel stuck, not knowing where or how to begin. In *Just Get Serious About Success,* Donna "Serious" Satchell reveals to you a complete plan for believing in, and executing your dream, whatever it is.

In this step-by-step guide, you will understand the nature and level of belief that you have in your dream, and you'll discover the secrets to maintaining and strengthening your belief system, thereby accelerating your growth potential and catapulting yourself into action. *Just Get Serious About Success* will also help you get seriously serious about achieving your dream.

In order for you to be successful, you must internalize the notion that your dream is not optional. It is mandatory. Donna Satchell will help you understand that nothing is as powerful as a made up mind. Once you decide that something must be done, you can and will move mountains to make it happen. With this mindset, seemingly insurmountable obstacles become opportunities for your success.

Let Donna show you how to make serious progress toward your dream. Use *Just Get Serious About Success* to help you learn how to build a network for positive support, deal with passive and pessimistic people, and get over the past so that you can drop the drama and be a positive person. Once you achieve these things, you can truly create a solid foundation for your success.

Les Brown, Master Motivator
International Motivational Speaker & Author

Foreword Two

I have known Donna for many years as a speaker and trainer. When she announced that she was writing a book, I was excited and wanted to be one of the first to read it. Because of my past experiences with Donna, I knew that her book would be great. She has far exceeded my expectations.

There are many reasons I believe you will benefit from this book and will want to buy copies for people you know who need help to get serious about their dreams and goals.

Donna guides you through a strategy for success in a unique well laid out format that is easy to read and incorporate into your life. Although there are many books about setting goals, living your dreams, and finding your passion, Donna takes a different approach. She gives you activities at the end of each chapter so that you, the reader, can reflect and act on the key ideas she has presented. This is not just another book of repeating what you have read in the past. Donna has included her unique insights and original thoughts and gets you personally involved through many exercises.

Another special aspect of the book that I really value is the stories of success from individuals Donna personally interviewed. Real life experiences of people I am sure you can relate to. In addition, Donna shares her own signature stories.

Sit down with a cup of your favorite beverage and begin reading this book. Once you start, you will not be able to put it down. You will be inspired, motivated, and energized. I know I was.

Dr. Marthenia "Tina" Dupree
President, Motivational Training Center
Founder, Professional Speakers Network, Inc.

Message to the Reader

Congratulations for moving forward on your journey to greater success! All success starts with one step. By investing in this book you have taken that step.

Now, how are you going to use this book? You can read it from beginning to end, or you can explore the chapters you think would be most beneficial to your personal growth and development. Whichever you prefer, I suggest re-reading the chapters you feel are of most importance to you. Often by reading material more than once, we get greater value from it because we see things we previously missed.

No matter how you decide to read this book, I encourage you to complete the end of chapter exercises. They provide you with opportunities to reflect on and write your thoughts about the ideas presented. In addition, the exercises will help you take action, which is key to accomplishing your goals.

When I conduct achievement programs for businesses and organizations, I tell the participants that I don't believe success concepts are "one size fits all." Therefore, if you read about exercises or actions that don't seem to fit you, feel free to adjust them to better suit your needs. Since you know what works best for you, I want you to take what you can use and make it your own.

The exercises are also available at www.JGSBook.com (click on JGS Club). You can download and update them as your life or circumstances change. This will allow you to stay on course.

The website also offers videos and additional information about the people featured in this book. Also, at the page titled JGS Club, you can sign up for a free teleseminar, a free assessment, and a free motivational newsletter designed to support and inspire you on your journey to achieve greater success.

I suggest you keep track of your life journey in a journal. If you do not have one, they are available at www.JGSBook.com. Writing can be valuable for two reasons. First, you have a record of your growth and accomplishments to review in order to inspire you to stay serious and keep moving. Second, in reviewing your journal, you can see when you were not completely focused on your goals and how that affected your progress. You can then decide to make changes to get you back on course.

The last chapter of the book is "Be Inspired." It consists of stories based on interviews I did with a group of people I call The Daring Dozen. These individuals are goal-getters, passion-pursuers, or difference-makers. This is a must read chapter that is sure to motivate you. Read about each person and be inspired to discover and pursue your passions, move forward on your goals, or make a difference in the lives of others.

Now, are you ready to Just Get Serious® About Your Success? Let's get started!

Wishing You Success
In All Your Endeavors

Donna

Table of Contents

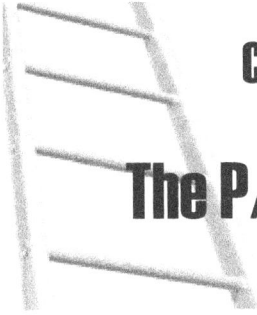

Chapter 1

The P/E Principle

Anybody who makes it, anybody who does achieve any level of success, that says to the rest of the world, "This is possible."
Oprah Winfrey
Business Magnate & Philanthropist

Over the years, many people have inspired me. Among them are well-known celebrities, local personalities, friends, family members, personal heroes and sheroes. They have included those who broke records, made contributions, and won awards. Some were the firsts in their fields, others did what many thought was impossible, and several bounced back from devastating losses. Their accomplishments have spurred me into action, kept me moving forward, or made me feel hopeful about my goals and dreams.

All around us are stories of achievement, even in today's challenging times. Success, triumph, or contribution is featured every Friday evening during ABC News' *Person of the Week* and on shows like Bravo's *Inside The Actor's Studio*, VH1's *Behind the Music*, TV One's *Unsung* and *Life After,* A&E's *Biography*, and special programs like CNN's *Heroes*.

We can read biographies or watch one-on-one interviews at Achievement.com, an online resource highlighting the lives of over 200 people whose accomplishments are having a major impact on the world. The range of individuals featured is incredibly broad, including Jonas Salk, developer of the polio vaccine; Johnnetta Cole, past president of Spelman College; Millard and Linda Fuller, founders of Habitat for Humanity International; James Earl Jones, award-winning actor and recipient of the National Medal of Arts; and Jeff Bezos, founder and CEO of Amazon.com.

If you go to YouTube.com and type "success" in the search field, you will find over 900,000 videos on the topic, including individuals describing their personal success stories, experts giving advice, and speakers motivating us.

There are hundreds of inspiring reality-based movies, such as *Pursuit of Happyness* (Christopher Gardner); *Music of the Heart* (Roberta Guaspari); *Men of Honor* (Carl Bradshear); *The Blind Side* (Michael Oher); *A Beautiful Mind* (John Nash); *Gifted Hands* (Dr. Benjamin Carson); and *Patch* (Dr. Patch Adams) just to name a few. There are far too many books on success and accomplished people to list here.

With all of this success around us, even in these challenging times, I have always wondered why more people aren't inspired and motivated to do more, have more, and give more. Personally, I have often questioned why my own feelings of "I can do it" have been high on some occasions and lower other times.

Studying my own thinking and listening to people talk about others' success led me to understand that we see achievement in one of two ways. I call the concept The P/E Principle.

Whenever we hear, read, or see evidence of someone's success, we gravitate toward one of two ways of thinking. Our choice determines how motivated or inspired we will be by that person's accomplishments.

On one side of the spectrum is "P" and other side is "E".

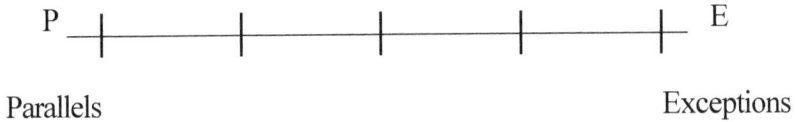

P ├──────┼──────┼──────┼──────┤ E

Parallels   Exceptions

The "P" represents parallels. Here, we see the similarities between us and those who are thriving. For example, hearing or reading about a successful person and feeling any of the following:

"She had financial challenges to overcome, and so do I."

"He made a lot of mistakes as I have."

"She had a learning disability, and I have one as well."

"People told her she was too short to pursue her dream and people say I am too tall."

"It took him years to achieve his goal, and it is taking me a long time."

There are always points of comparison if we take time to find them. This leads to thinking "It is possible for me to (your goal or dream)," "I have the potential to achieve more,", and "I see their success as a path I can take to my own success."

"P" reflects a statement made by Oprah Winfrey: "Anybody who makes it, anybody who does achieve any level of success that says to the rest of the world, 'This is possible.'" "P" thinking leads to our feeling positive, making plans and taking action.

On the opposite side of the spectrum is "E", representing exceptions.

It is seeing the differences between others and us, which leads to thoughts like:

"Those successful people have exceptional talents and abilities."

"They have extra things I do not have (like lots of money, supportive contacts, advanced education, great parents)."

"They have extraordinary traits (like attractiveness or height)" or "extraordinary circumstances allowed them to be successful (winning the lottery, marrying the 'right person')."

"They are in an exclusive group that I don't belong to."

"Their stories of success have nothing to do with me because we are different."

"E" thinking leads to excuses and inaction.

A couple of years ago, I had a memorable encounter with a woman and her "E" thoughts at a conference where I gave the keynote speech. I talked about going to college for the first time when I was in my 30s and how that decision opened the door for incredible opportunities for me. Toward the end of the presentation, I took questions from the audience. A woman, who missed the beginning of my speech, had several questions. Our conversation went something like this:

Woman: I work 9 to 5 every day. You weren't working full-time when you were in college, were you? (Note: Her tone indicated she had expected me to say "no".)

Me: Yes, I was working as an administrative assistant.

Woman: I'm 35 years old. That's kinda late to be starting college.
Me: I was 33 years old when I finally decided to go.

Woman: Were you married? Did you have any kids?

Me: No, I was divorced. And, no, I did not have any kids.

Woman: I got kids so I would never be able to go to college like you did.

Me: Oh, don't say that, I have read many stories about women with kids going to college. Don't let that stop you. Recently, I saw an article titled "Back to School at Any Age" and it included stories of women in their 30s and 40s with children who decided to go to college.

Woman: I work for a government agency, and they don't have tuition refund plans. (In my speech, I had mentioned a tuition reimbursement program helped me with my college expenses).

Me: Well, here in Georgia you can always look into the Hope Scholarship (a state-sponsored tuition assistance program). I have brochures about it at my table in the back. I also have copies of the article I mentioned.

Woman: I just don't have the time. I got kids and a husband and … I got some other questions, but I'll ask you later.

After my speech, I was selling books and many people came to talk with me, except the woman with all the questions and concerns. She never stopped by. I was there through the following morning, and we saw each other several times, but she did not approach me. I actually felt like she was avoiding me. I think she knew I would have answers for any obstacles she presented to me as questions. I believe she had already decided that the women in the article I mentioned and I were all "E" – being exceptions or having extraordinary circumstances that allowed us to pursue our goals and dreams. She had already formed all of her excuses and did not want to think differently.

How about you? When learning about the success of others, are you usually a "P" person, an "E" person, or somewhere in between?

P ———+————+————+————+———+ E

Parallels   Exceptions

As you read the insights, ideas, and stories in this book, I ask you to be aware of your thinking. If you find your thoughts drifting in the direction of "E", know you will probably take little action on what you are reading. For this book to have real value for you, I suggest you readjust your thoughts to be closer to "P." To do that, see the parallels you have with the people you read about. Focus on the similarities instead of the differences. Make a decision to be positive about the ideas. Think about all the potential you have. Consider all the unexplored possibilities in your life. Get serious by completing the end-of-chapter exercises and activities. Make a plan based on everything you have read. Then be proactive – move forward with purpose and persistence. By doing that, you will see great changes take place within you, because of you, for you, and for others as well.

Note: If you have not read Message to the Reader on page xiii and xiv, I suggest you do so before moving on to Chapter 2.

Chapter 2

Believe In Yourself

If you don't change your beliefs, your life will be like this forever. Is that good news?
Dr. Robert Anthony – Educator

Pay attention to what you are thinking, and then decide if those thoughts are creating the kind of life you want. If they are not, then change your thoughts.
Jill Bolte Taylor – Brain Scientist

Success is an inside job with outside results.
Donna Satchell

In the world of our goals and dreams, there are several roles we can play that produce little to no success for us. When we are in these roles, we are not making progress. We are:

1. **Waiters** – putting our plans on hold until the ideal time to move forward – such as when the kids leave home or when we have lots of money in the bank.

2. **Wishers** – always daydreaming about what we want; believing we could have it now while disliking the prospect of doing all that is necessary.

3. **Watchers** – looking at others and cheering them on as they go after their goals.

4. **Worriers** – agonizing over what will happen if we move forward and things do not work out.

5. **Wonderers** – always thinking about how to get started but not spending time to find out how or take any action

6. **Whiners** – constantly complaining about what is not working.

7. **Wounded** – hurting because we pursued our dreams in the past and things did not work out as planned.

Most of us have played some, if not all, of these roles; I know I have. Unknowingly, we occupy several at one time. We are *wishers*, wanting to be successful, while *wondering* how to get started. We are *wounded* by past disappointments or mistakes so we become *watchers*, rooting others on as they pursue their dreams. We become *waiters*, delaying moving forward, while *worrying* about things not working out if we do. We are *whiners* who are always complaining while *wishing* we had the time and energy to make our lives better.

What do these roles have in common? When we play them, we are stuck thinking instead of acting. I always say, "Success is an inside job with outside results." So getting unstuck or doing more begins within. It starts with that age-old question: "Do you believe in yourself?" But wait a second … is that the right question?

Over the years, I have been on a quest to understand success. I have read countless books, attended seminars, watched interviews of successful individuals, listened to people talk about their aspirations, and even examined my own thinking. In doing all of this, many thoughts came to my mind, the most prevalent being, "Is the question 'do you believe in yourself' the correct one?" I say, "No, it is not."

We need to go beyond such a simple question requiring just a yes or no answer. We human beings are much more complicated. Therefore, we need to dig deeper by asking a better question involving more thinking – "What is your *level* of belief?"

In life, we encounter ranges or scales. Whether school grades, credit scores, or movie reviews, there are levels from low to high, ratings from F (fail) to A (excellent), and ranking systems with words denoting where we stand. The same is true of belief, where I feel there are five levels:

1. Unbelief

2. Borderline Belief

3. Fluctuating Belief

4. Solid Belief

5. Bold Belief

How we move beyond being waiters, watchers, wishers, and the rest is by understanding our present level of belief and taking action to be at a higher one.

UNBELIEF

Since Unbelief is such a critical stage, I have devoted an entire chapter to examining it. I will cover levels two to five in the next chapter.

At the Unbelief level, individuals feel they cannot accomplish something they are attempting to do. For example, an employee may not think he is qualified to head up a special assignment his manager gave him. Consider a mother who has two small children and is saving to buy a house but doesn't believe she will ever have enough money for the down payment. Think of an aspiring entrepreneur starting a business during good economic times and, when times are uncertain, no longer thinking she can be successful.

> *Fearful unbelief is unbelief in yourself.*
>
> Thomas Carlyle
> Essayist, Historian

I believe many of us can relate to being at the stage of Unbelief. Think back to a time in school when you were faced with an extremely difficult subject. Maybe it was geometry, trigonometry, or calculus. Perhaps it was learning a foreign language or dissecting a frog in biology class without throwing up. For me, it was the first time I saw an algebra problem in a textbook. I freaked out. Seeing letters and numbers together in a mathematical problem, I immediately thought, "That's looks so hard. I will never be able to do that!"

So how do we move beyond the level of Unbelief? Here are seven ways:

1. Believe in the belief that others have in you.

My first experience with Unbelief was when I was about eight years old and I had a stuttering problem. I was embarrassed to complete a simple sentence. I would stumble over the words, have an incredibly difficult time pronouncing them, or would have to repeat the beginning of words over and over again. When teachers called on me to read a paragraph in class, it was a painful experience for both me and my classmates listening to me. I thought I was going to speak like that my entire life. I did not believe I would ever be able to talk like the other kids around me. Fortunately, at some point in elementary school, I was assigned to a speech therapist. Dr. Smith told me she strongly believed otherwise.

Dr. Smith would work with me using various techniques. She recorded my speaking with all my stuttering and then had me listen to it repeatedly. I clearly recall thinking, "How ridiculous! This will never work. I can only get worse by listening to myself over and over again." However, she believed differently and convinced me that it would help me improve.

I started to trust her and diligently complete the exercises she gave me. Slowly, I began to get better. Eventually, I could say an entire sentence and then several sentences without stuttering. In time, I could read a whole paragraph when called upon during class. I would read slower than the other kids, but I could finish the section without so many hesitations and stammers. Today, as I speak without stuttering, it is because of Dr. Smith's belief that I could do it.

In *Being Unstoppable*, three-time Olympian Ruben Gonzalez writes, "Sometimes we have to rely on someone else's belief (in us) until our own belief kicks in." He explains how four months before the 1948 Olympics, Bob Mathias was told by his high school coach, Virgil Thomas, that if he started training right away, he could possibly compete in the Olympics decathlon in four years. At the time, Mathias had never heard of the event.

> *My doctors told me I would never walk again. My mother told me I would. I believed my mother.*
>
> Wilma Rudolph
> Olympic Athlete

He had also never pole-vaulted, thrown a javelin, or run the 1500 meters, three of the ten activities in the decathlon. His coach saw his natural talents.

Based on his coach's strong belief, Mathias started training immediately. About a month later, he competed in his first decathlon and won first place. Several weeks after that, Mathias entered the U.S. Decathlon National Championship and won again. Amazingly, six weeks later he was competing in the decathlon at the 1948 Summer Olympics (four years before his coach's suggestion). Even more amazingly, Mathias won the gold medal, becoming the youngest person to win the decathlon. He repeated his win at the 1952 games. This happened because

Mathias believed in his coach's belief that he could do it.

The next time someone says how great you are at writing, singing, teaching, or anything they see you do, don't just shrug it off as a passing comment. Instead, value what they have said. Seriously consider the comment, and know the potential they see in you could take you far in life, if you recognize and pursue it.

> *Others can see in you what you cannot see in yourself.*
>
> Donna Satchell

2. Increase your awareness of your negativity and shift your thinking.

In their book, *The One Minute Millionaire*, Robert Allen and Mark Victor Hansen describe one of my favorite negativity-reducing activities. They suggest putting a rubber band on your wrist and slightly snapping it whenever you find yourself thinking or saying something negative. This alerts you to your pessimistic thinking and allows you to shift to a more positive thought. The authors suggest you do the exercise for 21 days, because it takes that amount of time to start to change a habit. Negative thinking is just habit we have formed.

I always tell my audiences that if they are really serious about changing their thinking and strengthening their belief system, they should go one step beyond what the authors recommend. Tell people you sincerely trust and who have your best interest at heart what you are doing. Then ask them to snap your rubber band when they hear you say something negative. Why? We don't always recognize our own pessimism. Other people can help us understand when we are being less than positive.

A few years ago, I was having dinner with a friend at the Cheesecake Factory in Atlanta. I was telling her about the great progress I was making in curtailing my negative thinking by doing the rubber band exercise.

When we began talking about my business, she suggested I try a new approach to marketing my services. I immediately started saying I could not do it because it would cost too much money. As she reached over to snap the rubber band on my wrist, I asked her what she was doing. She replied, "You are being negative," to which I responded, "No I am not, I am just being realistic." Later that evening, as I thought about our conversation, I realized "being realistic" can be just one step away from being negative. My friend helped me avoid confusing the two.

3. Use positive affirmations.

Affirmations are statements that we repeat in order to change our thinking. Repeating them helps create new thought patterns. Affirmations can be one sentence or several. For example, one of my favorites is, "I am happy, brilliant, and thankful."

I was in the audience when Keith L. Brown, a great speaker and a friend, made everyone repeat his famous affirmation, "I love myself. I believe in myself. I am proud of myself. I am a genius." He gave us a snappy beat and rhythm to use when saying it. His affirmation is one I repeat several times each morning.

> *Talk unbelief, and you will have unbelief; but talk faith, and you will have faith. According to the seed sown will be the harvest.*
>
> Ellen G. White – Writer

In her book, *On the Line*, Serena Williams writes about how she uses affirmations before all of her tennis matches. She keeps them in a small book she carries to her games. She calls them her "match book" entries. They include statements like, "You are #1. Play with a purpose. You are the best in the world." "Be strong. Now's your time to shine. Be confident." "Put your gifts to work. Endure. Persevere. Stand tall. You can endure anything." Serena Williams has been successful using affirmations for years. Why don't you try using them to see the impact they have on your success?

In her book, *You Can Heal Your Life*, Louise Hay recommends that you say your affirmations while looking at yourself in a mirror. She believes it increases their effectiveness and their impact. She also advises making affirmations in the present tense, such as "I am" or "I have" rather than the future tense of "I want" or "I will."

> *Our thoughts create our reality – where we put our focus is the direction we tend to go.*
>
> Peter McWilliams
> Writer

You can purchase affirmation cards at bookstores, online, or you can make your own. In the space below, write a positive affirmation that you want to repeat regularly. Later on, rewrite it on colorful paper, add pictures or symbols and post where you can see it often. Repeat your affirmation daily and watch your mind and life start to change.

```
- - - - - - - - - - - - - - - - - - - - - - - - - - - - - -

                        AFFIRMATION



- - - - - - - - - - - - - - - - - - - - - - - - - - - - - -
```

4. Listen often to positive and uplifting music.

Fortify your mind with music and song lyrics that motivate and inspire you. The repetition of a positive message can have the same effect as speaking positive affirmations.

Some of my favorite motivational songs include:

- "Dream Big" – David Cook
- "Get on Your Feet" – Gloria Estefan
- "Hero" – Mariah Carey

- "It's My Life" – Bon Jovi

- "Just Fine" – Mary J. Blige

- "Lovely Day" – Bill Withers

- "New Day" – Patti LaBelle

- "One Moment In Time" – Whitney Houston

- "Reach" – Gloria Estefan

- "Staying in Yes" – Jana Stanfield*

- "What a Feeling" – Irene Cara (from "Fame")

- "Where the Dream Takes You" – Mya

- "Win" – Brian McKnight

- "You Gotta Be" – Des'ree

- "You Gotta Want It" – Roberta Gold

I also suggest songs by Willie Jolley. My favorites are "It Only Takes a Minute," "It's All About Your Attitude," and "It's By Your Faith." Listen to his music and short motivational messages at www.WillieJolley.com.

Another terrific song is "Simply Ridiculous," written and performed by speaker and author Millicent St. Claire. Its repetitive message of "Let It Go and Move On" is energizing. You can get a free download from www.LIGMO.com.

Consider using an online service like Rhapsody, Pandora, or Last.fm to create your own CD or podcast of your inspiring songs. Play them often so you can begin to believe in yourself.

*If you have not heard of Jana Stanfield, check out her website at www.JanaStanfield.com and listen to a sampling of her songs. She describes her music as "psychotherapy you can dance to." I see it as being "dream and belief-affirming." Some other great songs by Stanfield are "Dare to Be," "Let the Change Begin (Within)," and "Get Happy."

5. Read motivational quotes and tips on a daily basis.

Sign up for daily inspirational quotations and tips from various websites that provide them for free or at a nominal cost. After reading them, take a few minutes to reflect on their meaning in your life. Print them and then read several times during the day to shift to a more positive viewpoint. There are many sites where you can read quotes, including mine at www.QuotesToMotivateYou.com

> *Quotes can be one of life's greatest sources of inspiration. They encourage you to live your dreams and become the person you always hoped to be.*
>
> Anonymous

6. Watch or listen to motivational speeches often.

You will find many inspiring speeches at www.YouTube.com by typing "motivational speech" into the search box. You can also type in the name of your favorite motivational speaker. I have three speeches on YouTube. Type in "Donna Satchell" and "motivational speech" to see them.

Also, go to my website (www.DonnaSatchell.com) as well as those of hundreds of other speakers, to watch and listen to their inspiring and motivating messages. My favorites include Les Brown, Zig Ziglar, Jewel Diamond Taylor, Tony Robbins, Cheryl Richardson, Willie Jolley, Rene Godefroy, Lisa Nichols, and Wayne Dyer.

7. Understand your past successes to believe you can be successful again.

I always say that success is not just what you have done; it's also how far you have come. For instance, if you are reading this book, you have been successful doing *at least* one thing in your life – you went from being a non-reader to a reader. While you may be thinking, "Everyone can read," there was a time when you could not. And millions of people cannot read at a functional level, if at all. Initially, none of us know everything we need to understand in order to succeed. We learn through books, classes, coaching, mentoring, and advice. And as we learn, we move forward.

My mother would say to my sister and me, "You will go to school and you will learn." And we did. How did we learn? By being open to the process, doing the work required, and repeating the topics we did not understand. We learned by raising our hands to ask for help or for the teacher to repeat something and by following one of my mother's cardinal rules: no playing until your homework is done. We can do similar things as adults. Right?

If I feel incompetent, I think of past success.

Og Mandino
Author

To be successful in today's world, we need to constantly learn, grow, and develop. If you become frustrated or doubtful with the process, consider your past successes, both large and small. See how far you have come and know you can be successful again by doing what is necessary.

On the next page is part one of an exercise to help you increase your belief in yourself.

Just Get Serious® About Success

Chapter 2 Exercise

LEVEL OF BELIEF ACTION PLAN (PART 1)

For this exercise, go to page 29 (the chart at the end of Chapter 3) and fill in only column #1, listing your goals, dreams, and the things you want to accomplish in life. For now, do not do anything with columns #2 and #3.

After you read Chapter 3 on the other four levels of belief, complete the chart by following the additional instructions on page 28.

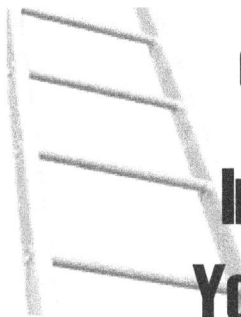

Chapter 3

Increase Your Belief

The story of the human race is men and women selling themselves short.
Dr. Abraham Maslow – Psychologist

Too many people overvalue what they are not and undervalue what they are.
Malcolm Forbes – Publisher

To be a great champion, you must believe you are the best. If you're not, pretend you are.
Muhammad Ali – World Champion Boxer

In Chapter 2, we explored Unbelief and how to overcome it. Now, let's consider the other four levels. As I describe them, think about what you listed as your goals and dreams on the Level of Belief chart on page 29.

1. UNBELIEF

Covered in Chapter 2.

2. BORDERLINE BELIEF

At this level, we have crossed over the border from the land of Unbelief. This is a critical stage because any negative comments, opinions, or feeling can easily push us back to where we were. Here's how to prevent that from happening:

a. Treat your plan, idea, or endeavor like mothers treat their newborn babies.

Mothers do not let just anyone hold or breathe on their infants. Have you ever watched a mother's reaction when someone who looks seedy, untruthful, or clumsy asks to hold her baby? Most mothers will freeze up or shake their heads no. Mothers carefully consider who they will let babysit for them. You want to treat your goals and dreams the same way. Not everyone knows how to hold and take care of a newborn baby, and not everyone knows how to talk to someone who has a dream or an ambitious goal. Be mindful of who you talk to and confide in.

b. Develop relationships with people who can give you the support you need.

We will often ask others "What do you think?" but we are not really looking for their opinions. Instead, we are looking for validation. And when we don't get it, we get discouraged, annoyed, or upset. If you want validation, find people who will give it to you. This reminds me of a statement that Life Coach Cheryl Richardson made in the movie *The Secret*. She said, "Don't go to the hardware store for milk." She explained that many times we continue going to the wrong people for what we want. If we want milk and find that a store doesn't sell it, it is a

> *There is nothing better than the encouragement of a good friend.*
>
> Katharine Butler
> Writer

waste of time or energy to keep going there. The same is true about people. If you want enthusiasm about your plans, go to individuals who can provide it. And just as we wouldn't fault the store for not carrying what we need, let's stop blaming people for not being who we need them to be. Instead, go elsewhere to find support and interest.

Often, we cannot go to the right people because we have not taken the time to develop new relationships. We would prefer our existing friends and colleagues to change into the encouraging people we need, but that is unlikely to happen. People change when it is in *their* best interest, not ours. So take it upon yourself to meet new people and foster new relationships by being the person you want to have in your life.

c. Get the information or knowledge you need.

Legendary tennis player Arthur Ashe said, "One important key to success is self-confidence. An important key to self-confidence is preparation." So take classes, read books, listen to audio programs, watch educational videos, and get coaching in the areas where you need help. Not only does it develop your skill set, but it also develops your mindset, which supports your belief system.

> *Life requires thorough preparation. Veneer isn't worth anything.*
>
> George Washington Carver
> Inventor

d. Take actions on a regular basis (preferably daily).

Actions lead to progress, and progress helps boost our belief system. Inaction can easily lead to slipping back into Unbelief.

About a year and a half ago, I began writing this book. Doing so took me away from the level of Unbelief where I thought, "I can't write a book! Who would buy it? What would I write about that is different from other authors? I don't have the time. It would take too long."

By shifting to more positive thinking, I finally got started. During the first month, I wrote every day for two to three hours. At the end of that month, I had written the equivalent of 90 pages! I was making great progress.

Suddenly, I was sidetracked with life issues so I spent less time writing. Next, I changed the direction I wanted to go with the book. Then I decided to take a break for a while. Without regular progress, I began to have my original doubts again and fell back into the stage of Unbelief. It took me many months to start again.

Don't let that happen to you. You can slow down, change direction, even try a new strategy, but don't stop moving altogether.

3. FLUCTUATING BELIEF

At this level, our belief rises and falls, resulting in inconsistent progress. Also, support from friends and colleagues begins to waver as they tire of the roller coaster ride of our enthusiasm.

Have you ever found yourself having strong belief in your aspirations at one time and then very little at another? When that happens, we need to identify what is triggering the drop and adjust our thinking and actions. The causes could be:

- Focusing on past failure by looking back instead of continuing to look forward
- Making mistakes
- Being afraid of new challenges we encounter
- Believing other people's opinion that what we're doing will not work
- Fearing making big decisions
- Seeing or hearing bad news reports that affect our disposition

■ Experiencing slower progress than anticipated

Some adjustments that can help us stabilize our thinking and actions are:

■ Staying focused on the future instead of the past

■ Seeing mistakes as a way to understand what works and what does not work

■ Viewing new challenges as opportunities for learning

■ Understanding that people's opinions are not facts

■ Getting the information required to make the necessary decisions

■ Limiting how much news we watch and listen to. Deciding to stay informed but not inundated

■ Realizing that success does not happen overnight. If necessary, set a new timetable

4. SOLID BELIEF

At this level, we believe we can achieve whatever we set out to do. We are unflappable when it comes to our goals and dreams. We are certain we can reach them because we have faith in ourselves and know others have done it or achieved something similar. We realize our accomplishments may take time, but we are certain that in the end we will be successful. We are confident, yet we are open to learning and getting valuable advice from knowledgeable people.

I am where I am because I believe in all possibilities.

Whoopi Goldberg
Comedian & Actress

What is most important at this stage is staying the course and not being deterred by lack of knowledge, people's negative opinions, limited resources, mistakes we make, or other things that may get in our way. If we find our belief slipping, we can undertake some of the activities or thinking found under Unbelief, Borderline Belief, and Fluctuating Belief.

By having Solid Belief in myself, I have been able to do many things. The list includes graduating from college with top honors, getting promotions at work, winning awards, overcoming my fear of public speaking, and starting a women's personal development group which celebrated its tenth year anniversary in June 2010. Having Solid Belief is the reason I can write this book.

Everything around us is the result of individuals having belief in themselves and others. Solid Belief is at the core of all work, business, and personal accomplishments. It is what achieved goals and dreams are made of.

With Solid Belief in your goals and dreams, you can create the life you desire. Everything we have covered so far is to get you to that place.

5. BOLD BELIEF

At this level, we believe in ourselves and our capabilities despite massive opposition, immense and widespread negative opinions, or the fact that others have not done it before.

I was living in New York City in the early 1990s. At the time, Donald Trump was the focus of every newspaper in the city (*The New York Times*, *The Daily News* and *The Post*). He was filing for bankruptcy, getting a messy divorce from his wife Ivana, and having an affair with Marla Maples. His life story was high drama being played out daily in the headlines.

> *Be bold.*
> *Be courageous.*
> *Be fierce.*
>
> Nailah Blades
> Life Coach

I did not know how Trump had enough belief to get out of bed in the morning. Yet he was trying to get loans to stem his bankruptcy and continue to build properties while all of this was going on. To many, his predicament seemed to be absolutely insurmountable; but he had Bold Belief in his ability to be a huge success despite enormous criticism and contrary thinking.

Before President Barack Obama won the presidency, he had a Bold Belief that he could achieve something never done before. At the beginning of his campaign, most people felt his election was impossible. On the day of his inauguration, millions of people around the world were thinking, "I never thought I would see a Black man become President of the United States."

People who exercise Bold Belief are often called arrogant, overconfident, or big headed. But actually, they are just driven and determined to realize their big dreams. The accomplishments of bold believers inspire and motivate us.

The firsts in any endeavor are people who epitomize Bold Belief. Along with President Barack Obama, this list includes individuals like:

- Sonia Sotomayor – the first Hispanic Supreme Court Justice

- Sally Ride – the first woman astronaut in space

- Dr. Benjamin Carson – the first African-American accepted into the residency program at Johns Hopkins Hospital and the first surgeon to successfully separate Siamese twins joined at the head

- Steve Fossett – the first balloonist to fly solo around the world

- Jim Plunkett – the first Hispanic NFL player

- Condoleezza Rice – the first female African-American Secretary of State and National Security Advisor

- Junko Tabei – the first woman to climb Mt. Everest

- Bernice Gera – the first woman professional baseball umpire

- Carlos Santana – the first Hispanic performer inducted into the Rock & Roll Hall of Fame

- Vernice "Flygirl" Armour – the first female African-American combat pilot

- Daniel Inouye – the first Japanese-American in the United States House of Representatives

- Ed Wang – the first Chinese-American NFL player

To this list, we can add individuals who are the first in their families to graduate from high school, go to college, start a business or undertake other work, business, and personal endeavors thought to be unobtainable.

How do you develop Bold Belief? You start with a goal others think is impossible because it has never been achieved by someone similar to you (with respect to: age, gender, race, national origin, abilities, etc.). Then you move forward with passion, conviction, and an unstoppable determination to do all that is necessary.

What is great about Bold Belief is that people who are the first to achieve incredible feats open the door for others to follow them. On May 6, 1954, Roger Bannister was the first person in history to run a mile in less than four minutes. Many others had tried, but none were successful. His record-breaking time was three minutes and 59.4 seconds.

You can change your beliefs so they empower your dreams and desires. Create a strong belief in yourself and what you want.

Marcia Wieder – CEO, DreamU

What he did was commonly believed to be humanly impossible. To understand how Bold Belief opens doors for others, another runner, John Landy, broke Bannister's remarkable record by a second-and-a-half just 46 days later. And within 12 months, hundreds of individuals ran a mile in less than four minutes. For them, Bold Belief was no longer necessary. They only needed Solid Belief because it had already been done.

I believe very few people have Bold Belief. But all of us can reach the level of Solid Belief and achieve great successes, many beyond our imagination.

Just Get Serious® About Success
Chapter 3 Exercise

LEVEL OF BELIEF ACTION PLAN (PART 2)

As I described previously, the chart on the next page is used for the exercise at the end of Chapter 2 as well as this chapter. Step 1 is to be completed after reading Chapter 2. Steps 2 – 3 are to be completed after you have read Chapter 3.

After Chapter 2
Step 1 – In column #1, write your goals, dreams, and the things you want to have and do in life. Do not do anything with columns 2 and 3 until you read Chapter 3 on the other four levels of belief and then continue with step 2.

After Chapter 3
Step 2 – Based on the information in Chapters 2 and 3, write your current level of belief for each item you have listed in column #1.

Step 3 – In column #3, list the actions you will take to increase or maintain your belief, using the suggestions you just read or ideas you think of.

Now you have a plan to strengthen or maintain your level of belief. Take action by adding what you listed to your daily routines or writing them on your to-do list. Consistently act on them so your level of belief increases to support your goals and dreams. Periodically revise and update this form as your belief level and/or dreams and goals change.

28

You can download a larger version of this form from www.JGSBook.com (click on JGS Club).

Column #1 Your Dreams, Goals & Plans (Short & Long-Term)	Column #2 Your Current Level of Belief*	Column #3 Actions You Will Take To Increase or Maintain Your Level of Belief

* Use the levels of Unbelief, Borderline Belief, Fluctuating Belief, Solid Belief, and Bold Belief.

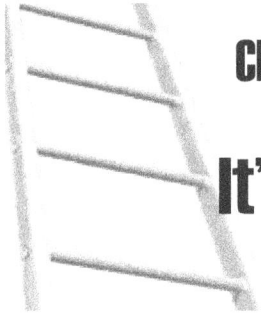

Chapter 4

It's Your Life ...

Part I: Explore the Past

There is a defining moment in every person's life. Within that moment, everything that person is shines its brightest.

Anonymous

The most important relationship you can have is with yourself.

Shirley MacLaine – Actress & Author

I think self-awareness is probably the most important thing towards being a champion.

Billie Jean King – Tennis Player

DEFINING MOMENTS

The above quote by Billie Jean King encourages us to take time to understand ourselves fully to be successful. One way to do this is to identify our defining moments.

Answers.com describes a defining moment as an "event, action, or decision that results in a significant change for a person, institution, community, country or the world." On a personal level, I think of them as events, people, and experiences that have shaped who we are today.

James DeBarge of DeBarge, a family singing group with short-lived popularity in the 1980s, talked publicly about a domestic violence incident he, his brothers, and sisters witnessed as children. It affected them in such a way that they eventually became heavily involved with drugs. That incident was a defining moment in their lives.

> *When a defining moment comes along, you define the moment, or the moment defines you.*
>
> Kevin Costner
> Actor

When Ellen Crooke was in college, her communications professor played the documentary, *Harvest of Shame*, produced by legendary journalist Edward R. Murrow. The film exposed the plight of migrant workers on American farms. Crooke said of the program, "I was so moved; that class changed my life forever. I found my passion for journalism." That was her defining moment. Today, Crooke is the Vice President of News for 11 Alive News in Atlanta.

We have both positive and not-so-positive defining moments in our lives. Do we know what these moments are? Have we acknowledged their impact? Mental health professionals can assist us in uncovering many of them; and I believe we can also discover some of the obvious and significant ones on our own.

Uncovering defining moments can be enjoyable, challenging, painful, or a combination of various emotions. Revelations about our past can help us realize what drives us, what holds us back, what causes us to treat others as we do. This awareness can help us better appreciate who we are, be more empathetic of others, and acknowledge what we need to change. All of these can be of value to us on our journey to success.

One of my defining moments occurred when I was living in New York. A friend and I went to see a Sunday matinee play. As I drove home after the performance, I decided to go to a favorite eatery to get a slice of cheesecake. I had plans of relaxing at home that evening, enjoying it with a cup of tea.

I parked the car and quickly headed for the restaurant. Suddenly, I heard a loud shrieking sound. I turned around and saw a truck run into my car, hitting the front driver's side. I stood there momentarily motionless. People quickly gathered around me and asked if I was OK, remarking how lucky I was since I had just left the car. Although seriously damaged, the car was still drivable. What shocked me was how close I came to being severely injured or possibly killed.

When I got home, I called my friend. As I explained what happened, Judy interrupted me, screaming in disbelief, "Your car was in an accident! But I just left you two hours ago." We talked about how quickly events can happen which change everything. I realized life is indeed precious and just as tomorrow is not promised, neither is the next hour. Since that incident, I live with that thought in mind. It has caused me to avoid hesitating to show people I care about them and to say encouraging words to others freely. It is also one reason I often move forward on ideas I have without the appropriate amount of planning. So the event has had both positive and not-so-positive effects on me.

Sometimes a defining moment is the result of what happened to someone else. Karen Ervin, a business colleague, described to me one of her life-changing events. She had traveled to New Jersey to plan the funeral of her cousin, Margie, who passed away at 55 years of age. As Karen sat in Margie's house, going through her financial papers and diary, she found out about her recent challenges and unfulfilled dreams.

Although Margie earned a six-figure income, she was fighting with the insurance companies and her employer to be paid for medical bills and time off. Karen read of Margie's plans to take a luxurious European vacation. She was considering remodeling her house and had been approved for an equity line of credit. Margie wanted to quit her job to start a business with her sister creating unique desserts. After reading Margie's diary, Karen decided to stop procrastinating about her goals and plans. Karen returned to Atlanta with a new sense of purpose, and within six months, she achieved every goal she set. They included republishing her book, *Live the Impossible Dream*, developing a website for on-line classes on entrepreneurship, and holding exclusive seminars and networking events for first-time business owners. She is now pursuing new goals.

> *Inspiration is the gift of those who have experienced life at its most defined moments.*
>
> Sasha Azevedo
> Actress, Athlete, Model

Defining moments come in all forms. Elijah Wood, the actor who played the hobbit Frodo in *Lord of the Rings* trilogy, spent 16 months in New Zealand during the making of the movie. He said the experience was "not just a benchmark in my career, but a benchmark in my life." At the time, Elijah was 18 years old, living on his own for the first time, making new friends, and having new experiences. Wood said of those 16 months, "It had a profound impact on me as a human being, and I did a lot of growing … that will always be a defining moment in my life, a defining time."

The exercise on the following page can help you explore your defining moments.

Just Get Serious® About Success
Chapter 4 Exercise #1

YOUR DEFINING MOMENTS

You can use a sheet of paper, your personal diary, or a page in your Just Get Serious journal for this exercise.

First, take time to think about the events, people, and experiences that have changed your perspective, challenged your beliefs, or given direction to your life. Then, list them.

Second, for each of your defining moments consider and answer the following questions.

1. What insights about life have you formed because of the experience?

2. How is the incident or insight affecting you today? Is it helping or hindering your success?

3. If it is helping you, have you been truly grateful for it? Are there people you need to acknowledge or thank? Also, consider how you can create a similar moment for others (without financial or personal gain for yourself).

– or –

If it is hindering you, are you taking steps to change the effect it is having? If you need ideas on how to do that, see the "Moving Forward" section in Chapter 16, "Moving Beyond the Past." Also, consider how you can prevent others from experiencing a similar moment (without financial or personal gain for yourself).

I encourage you to get in touch with your defining moments. Know what they are, recognize how they affect your life, and decide on the changes you want to make or actions to take because of them.

Part II: Understand the Present

Know thyself.

Socrates – Philosopher

If we recognize our talents and use them appropriately, we will rise to the top of our field.

Dr. Benjamin Carson – Surgeon

As you become more clear about who you really are, you'll be better able to decide what is best for you – the first time around.

Oprah Winfrey
Business Magnate & Philanthropist

PERSONAL INVENTORY

A major factor in being successful is understanding who you are right now. As reflected in Oprah's quote above, we are at our best when our actions and our plans for the future are based on that knowledge. When they are not, we can lose time, money, and energy pursuing endeavors that may not fully satisfy us if we achieve them.

When was the last time you did an inventory of *you*? If you have never done one, this is your opportunity. If it has been awhile, it may be time to do another one.

There are seven areas to examine. After reading about them, fill out the Personal Inventory form at the end of this section.

1. Strengths (Traits and Abilities)

Success is not about what you can do for yourself. Rather, it is about how you impact others. With that in mind, let us think about strengths as those things you do incredibly well that can be of value to others.

Think about Michael Jordan. He was a success on the basketball court because of his exceptional abilities and the impact he had on his audiences, thrilling them with his amazing feats. The same is true of other athletes such as Serena Williams, Lance Armstrong, and Michael Phelps. Other well-known successful people - Steve Jobs, Bill Gates, Quincy Jones, Barbara Walters, Russell Simmons, Radio One/TV One Founder Cathy Hughes, Facebook, Founder Mark Zuckerberg - have all had a tremendous impact on our lives by using their strengths.

> *Play to your strengths.*
>
> Dr. Faith Ralston
> Talent Consultant

Now consider people you personally consider successful (perhaps an influential teacher, an outstanding business leader or an excellent doctor). All of these people have at least one thing in common, they are using their strengths to be of value to others.

Understanding and utilizing your strengths is the key to your success. Marcus Buckingham echoes this sentiment in his books, *Put Your Strengths to Work* and *Now, Discover Your Strengths*. According to Buckingham, many major companies, including Toyota, Yahoo, Wells Fargo, Intel, Best Buy and Accenture, are successful by being strength- focused organizations. You can use the same strategy.

Strengths come in two forms:

- Traits – These are internal characteristics or qualities. They include behaviors and ways of thinking , including being creative, curious,

37

ambitious, friendly, helpful, agreeable, generous, forgiving, assertive, courageous, loyal, flexible, sociable, patient, logical, and energetic.*

One of my strengths is empathy. I can put myself in someone else's position and try to see the world through their eyes. As a result, I make an effort to make sure everyone is treated fairly. This strength brings value to the teams and committees I serve on as well as my clients and audience members.

- Abilities – These are innate or learned skills and proficiencies we exhibit. They include: writing, presenting, organizing, teaching, negotiating, painting, planning, performing, designing, analyzing, and speaking foreign languages.*

  Robin Williams uses his comedic abilities to bring value as laughter-filled performances. Dr. Benjamin Carson uses his surgical abilities to heal children. Michelle Shearer, 2011 National Teacher of the Year, uses her abilities to enhance student learning. What are your abilities?

If you are not sure what your strengths are, identify them by being extremely conscious of the things that come easily to you, the activities you love, the things you know more about than others, or what people say you do exceptionally well. In addition, you can take online assessments to help you identify your strengths. Google "personality tests," "personality assessments" or similar phrases for more information.

*For more examples go to www.google.com and type in "personality traits," "skills," or similar words or phrases.

2. Likes

What are your hobbies? What do you enjoy doing? What pursuits bring you pleasure? How often do you engage in these activities?

The last question is important because the benefits of hobbies are many, including:

- Making us feel good emotionally

- Providing personal satisfaction

- Developing new friendships

- Gaining and maintaining physical/psychological health

- Stimulating thinking

- Improving concentration

- Reducing stress

- Raising self-esteem

- Developing new abilities

A single hobby can provide many benefits. One of my hobbies is playing table tennis. The benefits include physical activity, better concentration, new friendships, and reduced stress. Some hobbies, such as jewelry making, photography and art, can be turned into moneymaking endeavors.

A hobby a day keeps the doldrums away.

Phyllis McGinley
Writer, Poet

If you do not have any hobbies, start exploring possible interests by taking classes or becoming involved in various activities. There are many categories and leisure pursuits to consider. Below are just a few:

- Sports (tennis, golf, bowling, basketball)

- Creative (sewing, painting, writing, photography)

- Education (reading, learning a foreign language)

- Health (hiking, belly dancing, yoga, jogging)

- Social (cards, games, movies, chess)

Most hobbies fall into more than one category. For example, golf could be in the health, social, and sports categories.

3. Passions

What are your passions? This is an important question to consider. I believe we can do good, or maybe even excellent work without being passionate about what we are doing. However, great achievements come from the investment of tremendous time, energy, and effort. That level of investment is easier to give when we are passionate about what we are pursuing.

> *Nothing great in the world has ever been accomplished without passion.*
>
> Friedrich Hebbel
> Poet & Playwright

When I ask my audiences about their passions, only a handful of people have answers. The others shrug their shoulders. If you are uncertain as they are, read Chapter 5, "Discover and Pursue Your Passions."

4. Weaknesses / Areas of Improvement (Traits, Abilities, Knowledge)

No one is perfect. We can be better in any number of areas in our lives. We cannot, however, get better until we acknowledge (at least to ourselves) what we need to improve. Let's face it; we will never take a class on time management if we do not think we have challenges managing our time. We will never take a class on being a better parent if we do not realize we need help in that area. Our weaknesses can thwart our chances for success when

> *The greatest of all faults is to be conscious of none.*
>
> Thomas Carlyle
> Essayist, Historian

they are traits, abilities, or knowledge required for a chosen endeavor.

How successful can salespeople be if they lack negotiation skills? How much success can a manager achieve if he cannot get along with people?

If you are not sure what your weaknesses are, you can identify them by being conscious of the traits and abilities you need for your success but are difficult for you to do, or what others say you could improve upon.

Remember, we all have weak areas. By being aware of them, we can take appropriate actions to become better. If you are an employee, consider taking classes in those areas required for your job, i.e., public speaking, managing people, or work-specific tasks.

For years, one of my weaknesses was giving presentations. I dreaded standing in front of a group to convey information. I always felt clumsy and rushed through presentations so I could sit down as quickly as possible. Knowing that skill was required for my job, every year I would take a public speaking class held at the company. I also joined Toastmasters, an international organization dedicated to helping people become confident and competent speakers.

> *You cannot fix what you will not face*
>
> James Baldwin
> Author

Consider areas where you lack knowledge or skills that could be holding you back. Then decide what steps to take to get better. You can become better by reading books, taking classes, getting a mentor, attending a teleseminar, listening to an audio program, or simply stepping outside of your comfort zone and doing it more often.

Pick the subject you need to focus on. Choose the method that will work best. Then, get started on your improvement program.

At this point, you may be wondering how to find time for this new learning. Here are some ways:

- Watch less TV.

- Turn your car into a traveling learning center by listening to audio programs on the subject in which you need to improve.

- Reduce the time you spend talking about unimportant matters to friends.

- Always carry a book or IPod to places where you know you will probably be waiting to be served (dentist's office, salon, Post Office) so you can read or listen.

- Relentlessly search for ways to have additional time. Consider taking a class on time management or technology (so you spend less time at your computer). If you are a business owner, think about outsourcing certain functions, such as maintaining financial records or promoting your services.

5. Dislikes (or Lack of Interest)

Simply because we dislike doing something doesn't always mean we can or should avoid doing it. Sometimes, not doing the things we dislike may prevent us from being successful. I once read that the great chef, Julia Child, disliked cutting up onions. Just imagine being a chef and not cutting onions! I also remember comments made by Sean Puffy Combs, the record producer, actor/singer and men's fashion designer. During an interview, he explained that in order to be successful he spends a lot of time working on things he would rather not do. It is important to identify our dislikes, determine if they are roadways or roadblocks to our success, and then decide what we will do about them.

Understanding what we dislike can also help us avoid being influenced by the media, our family and friends, and our own lack of thinking. Such knowledge allows us to make well thought-out decisions.

When I moved to Atlanta, I marveled at the beautiful homes with their lovely lawns and gardens of colorful flowers and well-manicured shrubbery. I imagined that one day I would own such a home. When I decided to purchase a house, I told the real estate agent I wanted a house with a large lawn and a nice deck overlooking the grounds. I imagined myself planting, cutting and taking care of my yard. I envisioned myself relaxing on the deck with a margarita in my hand after a long day at work.

The first summer in my new house, I went outside to work in my yard, and after a few hours, I realized it was not easy. In fact, it was hard and boring. When I was finished, I was hot, sticky, worn out, and did not have the sense of accomplishment I had imagined. I found I disliked "playing in the dirt." After a few more attempts, I gave up and hired someone to cut and care for the lawn. As for the deck, I used it more for entertaining family and friends than I did for relaxing or my own enjoyment. By the next year, I was rarely on the deck.

How did this happen? As I looked at my past and what I enjoyed doing, I realized I had never really spent a lot of time outdoors and rarely enjoyed tending to a lawn and flowers. (In fact, I had house plants that died from neglect.) For the 10 years prior to moving to Atlanta, I lived in a New York condo without a lawn and loved it. A failure to acknowledge what I liked and disliked led me to make an unwise purchase.

Here is another example of how not knowing yourself can lead to making questionable decisions. I have limited interest in monetary matters – insurance, stocks, and banking. So why did I end up spending years working for Mutual of New York, the American Stock Exchange, and Booz, Allen & Hamilton – all financial institutions? Instead of focusing on areas in which I had interest, like marketing and advertising, I focused on finding progressively better positions paying more money. Through a career assessment and consultation with a career advisor, I realized I was working in areas that did not interest me, something I could have identified on my own. Some of the jobs were exciting, but it would have been much better to work for companies where I was excited about both the job and the industry. I had that opportunity when I was hired to work at Clairol Inc.

Although my first position involved basic administrative duties, I loved being in the marketing/sales environment. I enjoyed reading company memos and newsletters about new product launches and advertising campaigns. Eventually, I was promoted to a job in the Marketing Department as an Assistant Product Manager; that led to other exciting positions.

Make sure you know what you dislike or have limited interest in. Then use that knowledge in making your important decisions.

6. Areas of Importance

What is important to you? Think about areas like health, family, friends, money, faith, personal growth, recreation, travel, career, business endeavors, education, personal development, sports endeavors, retirement, volunteerism and home ownership. Once you determine the important areas, you can set goals for them and be on the way to living a balanced life.

7. Aspirations

What do you want to be, do, and have? What do you want to accomplish in those areas important to you? I suggest you spend considerable time thinking about these questions. The answers will help you establish your goals. You can read about goal setting in Chapter 6.

Just Get Serious® About Success

Chapter 4 Exercise #2

YOUR PERSONAL INVENTORY

Based on what you just read, fill out the form below. When completed, use the information to guide you as you make decisions and plans about your life. Review this form to make necessary revisions at least once a year or more often if you have changes in your life.

1. Strengths
2. Likes
3. Passions
4. Areas of Improvement
5. Dislikes
6. Areas of Importance
7. Aspirations

You can download a larger version of this form from www.JGSBook.com (click on JGS Club).

Part III: Planning For the Future

Let us so live, that when we die,
even the undertaker will be sorry.

Mark Twain – Writer

I'm always relieved when someone is delivering
a eulogy and I realize I'm listening to it.

George Carlin – Comedian & Actor

I dream that long after I'm gone, my work will go
on helping people.

Isabel Myers – Creator of the Myers-Briggs Test

YOUR LEGACY

Years ago, I attended a funeral with a friend. Afterwards, as we had dinner, she asked me, "Who was that eulogy about? It certainly wasn't about Barbara?" I couldn't help but chuckle because I had to agree. The person described at the funeral was not the person I knew.

Will your eulogy be about you? Or will it be filled with kind words that could apply to anyone?

If you died today, what would people say about you tomorrow? Although it may seem morbid, this is an important question to ask ourselves. Thinking about it now allows us to live in ways we want to be remembered in the future.

Alfred Nobel, creator of the Nobel Peace Prize, learned the value of such thinking through a life-changing experience. Nobel was a Swedish chemist who made a fortune through his invention of dynamite, blasting caps, and other explosive devices. In 1888, his brother, Ludwig died. The day following his death, a French newspaper mistakenly printed an obituary about Alfred instead of Ludwig. The headline read, "The merchant of death is dead." The obituary continued with "Dr. Alfred Nobel, who became rich by finding ways to kill more people faster than ever before, died yesterday." Alfred was shocked and saddened when he realized people would remember him for inventing weapons of death. That insight led him to create the Nobel Peace Prize, which his estate has awarded annually since his death in 1896.

Nobel was not the only person to have a clear understanding of how he wanted to be remembered. The same was true of Grace Groner, a retired secretary. People who knew Groner described her as friendly, unassuming, gentle, witty, extremely caring, and always looking to help others. She probably knew people thought of her in that way. However, Groner also knew exactly what she wanted people to think after her death.

In 1935, she purchased three shares of Abbott Labs stock for $180. Over the years, as the stock split several times, she continued to reinvest the dividends. She was also not one to splurge. Groner lived a simple, modest life, in a one-bedroom house, all along planning how she wanted to be remembered. She died on January 19, 2010, at 100 years old and left $7 million to Lake Forest College, her alma mater. Everyone, including the

One way to evaluate your own reputation is to think about what would be said of you at your eulogy.

Brian Koslow
Author & Entrepreneur

college's president, was totally shocked. They had no idea the former student of the college and a former secretary of Abbott Labs had amassed such a fortune. Groner wanted to leave a lasting legacy, and she did. How about you? What will your legacy be?

Just Get Serious® About Success
Chapter 4 Exercise #3

YOUR LEGACY

Use the forms on the following page to write two obituaries about yourself. You can download the full-page version of this form from www.JGSBook.com.

1. Use the first form to answer the question "What would your obituary be if you died today?"

2. Use the second form to answer the question "What would you like your obituary to be if you died some point in the future?" You can decide on the time frame.

3. Now compare the two forms and consider the following questions.

   ■ How does your "current" obituary differ from your "future" one?

   ■ How do your current goals and life compare to your future obituary?

   ■ Do you need to make changes to your goals and your daily actions in order to achieve what you wrote in the second obituary? If so, what are they?

   ■ When will you start making those changes? (I suggest today).

You have just been given the same opportunity that Dr. Alfred Nobel received. You can alter how you will be remembered.

Now, if you think this exercise is morbid, let me share a thought with you: You are going to die one day. There will most likely be an obituary. Will yours be one you would be proud of or one you wished could be different?

The Present

Your obituary in tomorrow's newspaper

The Future

Your obituary several years from now

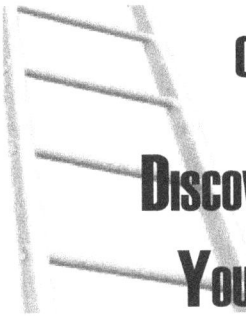

Chapter 5

DISCOVER & PURSUE
YOUR PASSIONS

*The only way to do great work is to love what
you do. If you haven't found it yet, keep
looking. Don't settle. As with all matters
of the heart, you'll know when you find it.*
Steve Jobs
Business Magnate & Innovator

*Ask yourself what makes you come alive.
And then go and do that. Because what the
world needs is people who have come alive.*
Howard Thurman
Theologian & Civil Rights Activist

In the last chapter, I posed several questions concerning knowing
yourself. One was "What are you passionate about?" In this chapter,
we are going to delve into the subject in detail.

I believe we can do good work and even excellent work without being
passionate about what we are doing. However, *great* achievements, which
lead to *great* success, come from knowing and pursuing our passions.

What are your passions?

Donald Trump is passionate about real estate and money. Beyonce, Celine Dion, and Usher are passionate about entertaining. Peter Max's passion is creating brightly colored paintings. Some people are passionate about being writers or athletes, while others' passions lie in serving their communities as firefighters, police officers, and teachers. Clara Hale, the Founder of Hale House, had a passion for caring for unwanted children and babies born addicted to drugs in New York City. Mother Teresa's passion was helping the poor, sick, and dying in Calcutta, India.

THE PASSION PURSUIT CYCLE

Passions take hundreds of different forms. What they have in common is people driven by intense interest, energy, conviction, and persistence. When pursued, passion makes things happen in five ways. You can think about it as the Passion Pursuit Cycle (PPC).

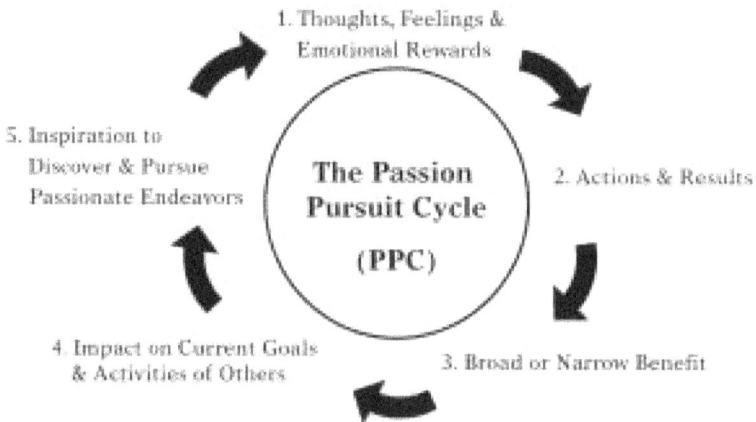

1. Thoughts, Feelings & Emotional Rewards

2. Actions & Results

3. Broad or Narrow Benefit

4. Impact on Current Goals & Activities of Others

5. Inspiration to Discover & Pursue Passionate Endeavors

The Passion Pursuit Cycle (PPC)

1. Thoughts, Feelings and Emotional Rewards

When pursuing our passions, we experience extreme pleasure and a sense of fulfillment.

For his book, *The Element*, Ken Robinson, Ph.D., interviewed or researched more than 70 people who are living or lived their passions. He wrote, "They feel like their most authentic selves. They find that time passes differently and that they are more alive, more centered, and more vibrant than at any other times."

His words echo the comments I heard during interviews I did with "passion pursuers." Linda Hall, a mixed media artist, told me, "When working with clay to make my jewelry, I experience the same feeling I have eating my aunt's homemade bouillabaisse. I am overjoyed and intensely immersed by the essence of color, texture, and spices serenading my taste buds. When I finish the first bowl, I want more."

> *When we are doing what we love, we don't care about time. For at least at that moment, time doesn't exist and we are truly free.*
>
> Marcia Wieder – CEO, DreamU

Joanne Smith, a jazz singer, said, "Once I got the high that comes from an audience's applause, I was totally hooked! A great performance has my adrenaline so high that I have to get 'talked down' after a show so I can go to sleep. I can't really think of any other way to describe the feeling. It's just the best feeling that I know."

In describing their passions to me, people commonly used words and phrases such as "absolute joy," "indescribable," "there is no other feeling like it," and "total bliss."

There are definite causes for these feelings. In *The Passion Test*, authors Janet Bray Attwood and Chris Attwood explain findings from studies conducted by neuroscientists Dr. Andrew Newberg and Mark Waldman. They found we are less likely to feel the negative emotions of fear, anger, and depression and more likely to feel the positive emotions of happiness, joy, and exhilaration when doing things we are passionate about. The neuroscientists told the authors that because of these positive emotions, "you get a release of dopamine, endorphins, and a variety of stress-releasing hormones and neurotransmitters. The more you focus on what you truly love, the healthier you are likely to be and the more you will feel the positive efforts of those stress-reducing neurochemicals in your body and mind."

> *Winning the prize wasn't half as exciting as doing the work itself.*
>
> Maria Goeppert Mayer
> Winner, Nobel Prize
> for Physics

2. Actions and Results

Because of these incredibly positive feelings, we are more willing to put in tremendous time, energy and money in pursuit of what we are doing. We are also more willing to engage in the learning, hard work, and serious commitment we need to succeed. Our can-do approach overrides our resistance to actions that could hold us back (such as trying new ideas, meeting new people, or using new approaches).

Ewa Laurance (aka "The Striking Viking") has been ranked number one in the world of billiards for years. According to her website, Ewa was 14 years old when, "she fell instantly in love with the game and practiced six to ten hours per day, doing her school homework between shots." The next year, she received her first Swedish 9-Ball title. That was the first of her many championships. Today, 30 years later, she is still competing and consistently winning at the sport of billiards. Because of her amazing abilities, Laurance has appeared on TV shows, such as *Late Night with David Letterman*,

> *Many people mistake my passion for discipline.*
>
> Luciano Pavarotti
> Operatic Tenor

Live with Regis and Kelly, and *Entertainment Tonight*.

When I took a painting class with award-winning artist, Charly Palmer, he said those who become great in the art field look at the world around them with the eyes of an artist. This meant they see things differently than non-artists. An artist looks at a tree and thinks, consciously or unconsciously, "How would I create the various shades of green in those leaves? What colors would I use to paint the bark of that tree or sunset?" Art is always on their minds, and it helps them do their best work. The same is true of any other field.

In his book *Inspired Destiny: Living a Fulfilling and Purposeful Life*, Dr. John F. Demartini, a leading authority on human behavior, writes, "When you do what you love and you love what you do, you have more energy that will constantly fuel you."

Pam Williams, 2011 Georgia Teacher of the Year, told me "I believe true success is achieved when people find their passions because then they will work harder, fight longer, and reach higher for the successes in that profession."

3. Broad or Narrow Benefit

Everyone is in this third stage, whether or not we are pursuing a passion. We have benefited from the endeavors of people like Bill Gates. His passion for computers, technology, and philanthropy has touched all lives. Whether pursued as a career, volunteer activity, business, or personal crusade, others reap the rewards of what the passion pursuers are doing or have done.

Nothing is as important as passion. No matter what you want to do with your life, be passionate.

Jon Bon Jovi
Musician & Singer

Consider how our society has changed because of Gloria Steinem's passion for women's equality, Ralph Nader's passion for automobile safety (seat belts), and Martin Luther King's passion for justice. Our lives have been enriched by Robin Williams' passion for making people laugh, Alex Haley's passion for writing about his family (in his book, *Roots*), and the passion of celebrity chefs like Emeril Lagasse.

We have benefited equally from the many unsung heroes and sheroes who contribute daily – dedicated parents, teachers, doctors, firefighters, public servants and others. Think about your state and community leaders, business people, volunteers, and working men and women who are passionate about what they do and how many lives they have touched and changed.

> *Find something you truly love doing and great things can happen.*
>
> Kirk Baxter
> Oscar Winner – Film Editing

A student said of Pam Williams, "Her enthusiasm and passion for the subject she teaches radiates throughout every word she speaks. Because of her class, I have learned more about the principles upon which our nation was founded, and I have become more involved in our government." That's the impact of passion.

Even if people's passions are personal hobbies, we can still benefit, because those people are more positive, relaxed, and/or enthusiastic about life. A message I read on an email says it best, "When you do what you love and you love what you do – you are a much happier person. And when you are a happy person, it rubs off on others."

So when you pursue your passion, others will benefit from your efforts.

4. Impact on current goals and activities of others.

As our enthusiasm grows, we overcome self-doubt, losses, tragedies, and other obstacles. Our efforts and achievements motivate other people to overcome the things that are preventing them from moving forward on their goals.

One of the best examples is the Olympics. Seeing the athletes compete and win, many people, including myself, feel a strong sense of "I can" about the things we want to accomplish. Then we go after them with a greater sense of commitment.

Former Dallas Cowboys player Everson Walls was motivated by Eddie Robinson, his coach at Gambling State University, to pursue a career in football. Robinson's passion for the game and for life is legendary. Because of it, more than 200 of his players played in the NFL. Hundreds of others were motivated to become doctors, lawyers and leaders in their communities.

Of equal importance is the impact resulting from the work and achievements of our personal heroes and sheroes, whether they are family members, friends, colleagues, or members of our community.

5. Inspiration to discover and pursue passionate endeavors

Beyond motivating people to make plans and reach goals, passion pursuers inspire others to discover and pursue their own passions.

Gordon Parks, award-winning photojournalist and filmmaker, inspired CNN anchor Anderson Cooper to be a journalist. Cooper said Parks "put the spark in me about reporting and about getting out there and seeing the world."

> *Passion inspires passion.*
>
> Daisaku Ikeda
> Writer, Poet, Educator

Princeton University President, Shirley Tilghman, said she is inspired by people "who have big ideas, and who are undeterred by all the obstacles that are in their path…by people who are able to see beyond the small details of getting through the day … and figure out how to execute a big idea."

Track star, Michael Johnson was inspired by distinguished athlete,

Jesse Owens, who won four gold medals for track and field in the 1936 Olympic Games. After his record-setting victories at the 1996 Olympics, Johnson said of Owens, "He inspired me to be a better athlete. … I can never be like him, but if I come close it's a great honor."

Legendary dancer, singer and actor, Fred Astaire inspired Michael Jackson, who dedicated his autobiography, *Moonwalk*, to him.

Passionate and inspiring people come in many different forms. Michael Gordon, producer of *Vidal Sassoon: The Movie*, described Sassoon as "an extraordinary inspiration to millions of people, reminding them what is possible with the right commitment and passion."

These individuals and thousands of others remind me of what Selita Victoria, owner of The Omni House, said to me: "Passion is not about you; it is about the universe and your impact on others."

So when you pursue your passion, you inspire people as well.

As new people are inspired to find and pursue their passions and the cycle begins again – they experience extreme pleasure and personal fulfillment. They do their best work, others benefit, and the sequence continues.

*   *   *   *   *

For years, I sat in audiences and heard speakers talk about how everyone knows their personal passions and should be pursuing them, and I would think "Everyone but *me*."

Do you feel that way? If you do, be assured you can discover your passions. In the following section, I will tell you how.

If you already know what your passion is, consider there are other things you love doing. For more than two decades, Madonna's passion has been performing for sold-out audiences around the world. Then at 43, she found something else she loved, writing children's books. Madonna said, "While I've envisioned myself doing many things in this life, writing children's books was never one of them." To date, Madonna has written 15 books for 9-to-12 year olds, (including *Friends for Life* and *Mr. Peabody's Apples*). If Madonna could find a new passion, so can you.

> *The more passions and desires one has, the more ways one has of being happy.*
>
> Charlotte Catherine
> Writer

Whether you want to discover your first-time passions or find new ones, you can look for them in three places: the past, present, and future.

THE PAST

When you look in the past for your passion, ask yourself, "What did I love doing as a child or young person? What did I dream of doing? What did I say I wanted to be when I grew up?" When you come up with answers, ask one more question: "Did I do it?" Many of us did not.

Maybe you got discouraged because family members, friends, or others said you couldn't pursue your desire because of your gender, race, or other personal characteristics. Maybe they pointed out your lack of resources or academic shortcomings.

> *Sometimes you have to find the passion. It comes from the inside. Everyone has to find it for themselves.*
>
> Candace Bushnell
> Author

Suzan Lori-Parks became the first African-American woman to receive a Pulitzer Prize in drama for her play, *Topdog/Underdog*. However, in high school, Parks' teacher dissuaded her from pursuing a career as a writer because of her low grades in English. Parks was good at physics; therefore, she decided to become a scientist instead. She went to college with that in mind. Eventually, she discovered her love for writing and majored in English and German literature. In an interview, she said, "What you love comes back to you. So I ended up in writing."

Whenever I talk about pursuing your passion, people tell me how, as children, they were discouraged from becoming artists, lawyers, chefs, police officers, and teachers. And I always ask them, "What is stopping you now?"

Last year, I received the following letter from Margaret Johnson, a reader of my newsletters. Her personal account shows it is not too late to move forward on your childhood dreams.

"When I grew up I wanted to be on the police force, be a firefighter or be in the military. But women were frowned on for doing those things when I was getting out of school in the 1960s. So I missed the boat for policing and fighting fires. And I remember all the ugly talk about women being in the military, including very negative comments from my parents. However, when I was 33 years old, I defied my parents and enlisted in the Georgia Air National Guard. I loved it! I served 18 years and 1 month and went into the ready reserves. When I turned 60, I retired from the National Guard with 26 years, 3 months and 19 days of service and started receiving my small retirement pay. I would not trade the experience for anything!"

I believe that people should do what they loved to do when they were 10, the age before you start caring what others think.

Joy Behar
Comedian, Co-Host TV Show

Read more about Margaret Johnson in Chapter 20 – Be Inspired.

If you have unfulfilled dreams, consider dusting them off and figuring out how to pursue them today.

Sometimes we cannot pursue our passions to the extent we would like. But, if we are determined, we can find ways to do something in our desired field. Dot Murphy, for example, had a passion for music and wanted to study voice and piano in college. But her father would only pay for college if she majored in education and became a schoolteacher. Since Murphy did not want to pursue that profession, she did not go. Instead, she had what she described as "a wonderful 52-year career as an administrative assistant."

> *If you feel like there's something out there that you're supposed to be doing if you have a passion for it, then stop wishing and just do it.*
>
> Wanda Sykes – Comedian

Murphy satisfied her passion for music by not only singing in her church choir, but also auditioning for and joining the Atlanta Christian Chorus (ACC), founded and directed by nationally known conductor and songwriter, Baynard L. Fox. With the ACC, Murphy performed in many venues throughout Georgia, including the famous Fox Theater. At 75, she has been in her church choir for 60 years and is still passionate about singing.

Maybe as young person, you did not know what your talents were, but others did. During an interview, award-winning comedian, Wanda Sykes said although she was funny as a child, she never thought about becoming a comedian. It was not something that even crossed her mind. Sykes finished high school, went to college, got a job and found she was bored with what she was doing. She started thinking, there has to be more to life. One day, Sykes was looking through her high school yearbook and began reading what classmates had written about her. There were comments like "You always have us laughing" and "You're so funny. You should be on stage." She thought, "I like comedy; maybe it is something I should try." And she did. She wrote a few jokes, went on stage at a local club, and found her passion.

Just think! Your yearbook may hold the key to your talents and passions.

If you have not looked at it recently, spend time doing so. You may be surprised at the insights your friends and others had about you. They could be worth investigating now. Also talk to teachers, coaches and family members to find out if they remember seeing a special interest or talent you had years ago.

Maybe it was not others who prevented you from pursuing your dreams but your own lack of drive or discipline.

Growing up in Australia, Glen Butler always wanted to be a jockey. He got his first job as an apprentice rider when he was in his twenties. However, by his own admission, he was not serious at the time . "The early mornings didn't agree with me, so I left. That was the biggest regret I've had in my life," he recalls.

Several times, Butler tried to get another job as an apprentice. On one occasion, he was too heavy. Another time, at age 30, he was too old. Over the years, the trade's regulations were changed and Butler began trying again. At age 42, Butler became the oldest apprentice jockey in Australia, and possibly the world. He won his first race. He decided to give it a shot after his wife said, "If you don't, you will regret it the rest of your life." Fortunately, that will not be the case for Butler. How about you? Don't let your childhood dreams pass you by.

As you move forward, do not overwhelm yourself and try to do everything at one time. As an adult, you may have many responsibilities, so pace yourself. If possible, do at least one thing regarding your passions or talents everyday. You may have to begin by saving money so you have the funds to pursue your dream. Or maybe you need to take a class, get a mentor, or read books on the subject. Whatever it takes, get started.

THE PRESENT

If the past does not hold the key to your passion, it could be in the present. Do you already know what you are passionate about and are pursuing it? If so, that's great. Congratulations! Keep at it. Don't let future obstacles get in your way. Stay the course. The following chapters will explain how to do that.

On the other hand, maybe you just need the confidence to get started. Many individuals don't think they can do it and have not even tried. Don't let your doubts hold you back any longer. Take measures to strengthen your belief (see Chapter 3).

Maybe you don't know how to begin. If that's the case, take classes or join an organization of people working in your chosen field. There are associations for every endeavor, including those for writers, singers, artists, electricians, lawyers, accountants, and teachers (just to name a few). There are subsets for women, minorities, and other groups. Don't let a lack of knowledge stop you.

In addition, don't let gender, race, or age stand in your way. Few fields have not experienced having their glass ceiling broken, or at least slightly cracked, by the first woman, first Hispanic, first African-American, first disabled person, and other pioneers. When Barack Obama was elected President of the United States in 2008, that glass ceiling was forever broken. If the glass ceiling of your particular field has not been broken, maybe you are the person to do it. So move forward.

> *When you reach that deep well where passion lives, nothing is impossible.*
>
> Nancy Coey
> Writer

Don't let a job stand in your way. Instead, be like Joanne Smith, a Senior Executive Administrative Assistant at The Coca-Cola Company. Smith shared with me, "Singing has been my passion since I was a little girl. In the past, I tried to stop because I knew I needed a steady income so I could provide a home for me and my family, so a full-time job was a must. But, I soon realized I have the music in me, and I couldn't stop performing. So I found a way to do both." Read how

Joanne did that in Chapter 20 – Be Inspired.

Charles Turner also decided to do both. From 9 a.m. to 5 p.m., he works for a financial services firm in New York City. On his train ride to and from work, as well as in the evenings, he was immersed in his desire to be a shoe designer. To pursue his passion, Turner took classes at Parsons School for Design, and enrolled in a two-day fashion designer/buyer internship through Vocation Vacations. In 2009, he launched his men's footwear line, Brown Luxe by C. Everette.

Like Smith and Turner, don't let a job stand in your way and don't let age do it either. In her 40s, Sara Walker founded the Madam C.J. Walker Manufacturing Company. Steadfast in her pursuit, years later, she became the most prominent businesswoman of her time and the first African-American female millionaire. In her 50s, Laura Ingalls Wilder started writing. Her published book, *The Little House in the Woods*, led to a series of books that were later produced for primetime television, *Little House on the Prairie*.

You may be thinking, "Donna, I am almost 60 years old" or "I am retired." If you are, then consider Morjorie Newlin.

A retired nurse, Newlin was affectionately known by many as Philadelphia's "first lady of fitness." At age 71, she began weight training and became extremely passionate about bodybuilding. She entered numerous bodybuilding competitions and won more than 40 trophies during a span of 15 years! Her appearances on *The View*, *The Tyra Banks Show*, and *Oprah* made many people rethink age. You can see videos about her at www.JustGetSeriousBook.com and www.YouTube.com

Our passions can keep us vibrant and excited about life even in our older years. Look at Tina Turner. At 68, she was still pursuing her passion, performing at sold-out concerts around the world. During an interview, she was asked how it feels to be getting older. Turner replied,

"That number doesn't mean a thing. It just doesn't."

Don't think that only celebrities feel that way. Check with people in your own family, and you just may find similar sentiments. My mother, Jennie Campbell, is 85 years old, and she has been passionate about sewing her entire life. She has always made her own clothes, including coats, suits, pants, and blouses. You name any outerwear, and she makes it. When I was with her last month, she was proudly showing me a dress and hat she made to wear to church the following Sunday. Again, my mother is 85 years old and would not even think about buying clothes because she is so passionate about making them. Read more about her in Chapter 20 – Be Inspired.

> *One of the true gifts that one can have is to find out what it is they truly love to do.*
>
> Keith L. Black
> Neurosurgeon

If you are a young person reading this book, do not think it is too early to start pursuing your passion. Do not think that people will not take you seriously just because you are under 21. If you are truly committed, they will take you seriously. We all know the Williams sisters (Venus and Serena) learned to play tennis at an early age. There is also Jyoti Guptara who, with his twin brother, finished the fantasy series *Conspiracy of Calaspia* at age 11. At 15, he became the youngest writer to publish in the Wall Street Journal. Do you think people like this are rare? Here are some more young people who did not let age stop them from pursuing their passions:

- Barrington Irving, at 23, was the youngest person to fly solo around the world. (He is also the first person of African descent to do so.) His interest in flying started at age 15. Go to www.JGSBook.com to see a video about his amazing feat.

- Boris Becker became the youngest male to win at Wimbledon at 17½.

- Hou Yifan, 14½, is the youngest female to hold the title of grandmaster in chess.

- Katie Spotz, 22, is the youngest person to sail solo across the Atlantic Ocean.

- Nathan Chen is considered the best 10-year-old figure skater in the United States. He is the youngest child to win the Novice gold medal at the U.S. National Figure Skating Championships.

There are also young people pursuing passions who have not gotten national or international attention or recognition yet.

Daemoni Franklin has a love for robotics. At age 12, he creates elaborate computerized structures, like roller coasters, and other automated objects, with many being over four feet in height and depth. Daemoni can easily spend four hours a day working on his LEGO Mindstorm projects because he says it "makes me feel smart." He has been on FLL (First LEGO League) teams with other youngsters that participated in both local and national robotic competitions. Daemoni wants to be a robotics engineer when he grows up.

> *The person born with a talent they are meant to use will find their greatest happiness in using it.*
>
> Johann Wolfgang Von Goethe
> Writer & Philosopher

At 9 years old, Jordan Dean started a dog-sitting business, providing a temporary home for pets whose owners are away. Today at age 12, her client list includes 16 dogs, ranging from a tiny Chihuahua to a huge Samoyed. Her business tagline, "Dogs are my passion, and I'm ready to take care of yours!" definitely describes her. Jordan plans to be a veterinarian. Read more about her in Chapter 20 – Be Inspired.

In the 4th grade, Daniel Carr started writing stories about dragons. Over the years, his fascination with the craft continued. At 13, he began working on a science-fiction/romance series and published his first book, *Iris Destiny* (a 300-page novel) at 18. It is the first in his eight-book series. He expects the second one, *Iris – Fate*, to be released by the end of 2011. Daniel finds writing to be therapeutic because he can transform his emotions to paper. He told me, "I'm in the zone when I am writing. It is something I will always be doing – writing stories, songs, plays, books." At college, Daniel will major in film so he can write screenplays to be made into movies.

If you are a parent, relative, or teacher of a child or teen who is exhibiting an intense interest in a particular area, encourage that young person with mentoring, classes, books, and anything else that would excite them and increase their knowledge. Within a short time, that interest can become a passion, which leads to his or her success.

Unlike Carr and the others described above, maybe you aren't sure what your talents are, but other people are. They have seen your special abilities and have mentioned them to you, but you have dismissed their comments, thinking, "Anyone can do that" or "Oh that's nothing special" or "You're just saying that because you're my friend." Whether you are an adult or young person, be open to the suggestions of others. That is how I discovered my passion for being a speaker, trainer, and coach.

For many years, I had a huge fear of public speaking. Whenever possible, I would take classes to overcome it, but I was not getting any better. So I decided to join a local chapter of Toastmasters International, an organization dedicated to helping people overcome their anxieties. A member of my chapter, Al Wiseman, was assigned to be my mentor.

A month after joining, with much apprehension, I prepared a seven-minute speech which would introduce me to the club. I went to Al's house to practice it and get his suggestions. I will never forget that day. I nervously recited my speech in front of Al. When I was finished, I was shocked when he said, "Have you ever thought about being a professional speaker? You are a natural." I thought, "This man must be crazy." It was the most bizarre thing that anyone had ever said to me. Me – be a professional speaker? I hated giving presentations for my job. Why would I choose to get up and speak in front of a group of people?" As outrageous as the idea was at the time, Al saw something in me, and he planted a seed in my mind.

After gaining a level of comfort with giving presentations, I phoned Al and said, "I want to be a motivational speaker. How do I get started?" That call was the beginning of my entering a field that I am truly passionate about.

My story is one example of how other people can see our talents and abilities before we can. Another is Cindy Light.

Cindy makes elaborate window treatments and customized clothing for clients. Some time ago, one of them said to her "You are the best image consultant." Cindy had never heard the term before and did not know what one did. After doing research on the field, she decided to pursue the profession. Today, Cindy is a certified image coach and is passionate about helping people dress for success.

> *Others can see in you what you cannot see in yourself.*
>
> Donna Satchell

So, be open to the insights others have about you. They can lead you to discover your talents or areas you could be passionate about.

THE FUTURE

If your passion or talent is not in the past or present, then it is in the future. Whatever it is, you have not done it yet. You may not even know that it exists.

In 2007, I realized just how limited many people's lives are, including my own. I was invited to speak to a group of women from Africa who are now living in Atlanta.

After my presentation, we gathered in the lounge area for refreshments. This group represented a broad cross-section of women (unemployed, support staff, stay-at-home mothers, managers, professionals). Nevertheless, all the women had one thing in common: they had lived in other countries before moving to Georgia. As we talked, one of the women asked me, "What other countries have you lived in?" I was surprised at the question because I had never been asked before. To my amazement, I found myself saying "Oh I used to live in New York." Clearly, New York is very different from Atlanta, but it does not qualify for being another country!

As they excitedly talked about the countries where they had lived, I realized there is a whole world out there I know little about. And it is not just countries; it is also professions, industries and fields. There are a lot I don't even know exist. I realized for many of us, including me, there are careers and areas we might enjoy or even love once we experience them. As passionate as I am about speaking and training, there may be something I would love to do as much.

This revelation brings Liz Mooney to my mind. She is a 30+ year-old critical care nurse, wife, and mother of two boys. After the birth of her second son, Liz wanted to lose weight. Her husband suggested she try a boxing routine. So she visited Rick Sweeney's gym in Delmar, New York. What started out as a workout to lose weight became her passion. She started boxing on the amateur level and decided to do it professionally at

> *Doing work you love is the dizzying path of saying yes to a brilliant, hidden self you do not yet know.*
>
> Tama Kieves
> Coach

the age of 35, when most boxers are retiring. What's amazing is boxing was something she had never done before or had an interest in until she tried it in her 30s.

In a similar way, at 56, Carolyn Hartfield had never hiked until she joined friends on a 5-mile trek through the woods. To her surprise, she loved being out in the nature, exercising her body, and "feeling free." Carolyn went with the group on their next several hikes. Then she found out about the Sierra Club, an organization dedicated to conservation and enjoyment of nature. Carolyn joined and became a certified outings leader through their program. Today, she is passionate about the great outdoors and organizes and leads day hikes and campouts through Hartfield's Hikers, a business endeavor she started several years ago.

Learn something new. Try something different. Convince yourself that you have no limits.

Brian Tracy
Author

An editor and writer for a local newspaper, Gale Horton Gay discovered a segment of her industry she did not know existed, and through it, she found a way to pursue her passion for travel. Whenever Gay read vacation articles, she would longingly think, "What a great job those writers have." She did not know how to enter the field, but Gay decided to find out.

Using her own money, Gay drove to a resort in Tennessee to write a story about it for her paper. By doing that, she discovered the exciting world of travel writing, where magazine and newspaper writers are often given free or discounted air travel, first-class lodging and meals, admissions to theme parks, shows, and tours. These complimentary trips are arranged so the writers can share information about the destinations with their readers. Over the years, Gay has traveled to numerous places, with her favorites being Quebec, Lake Tahoe, and Cancun. On these trips, she was introduced to exciting pastimes like dog sledding, snowmobiling, and zip lining. Gay's decision to venture into an unfamiliar segment of her industry has reaped great rewards for her. Now, she has a way to live her passion and experience new activities.

Today the world is changing rapidly and presenting opportunities for us to become intensely involved in brand new fields that did not exist five or even three years ago. Be willing to explore them using your current skills or interest.

For example, Donna Lang has always used a creative approach to pursue her goals. In college, she devised an ingenious way to get local tennis players to donate their time to teach her the game, and she became the youngest contestant to win her neighborhood's tennis tournament. While working in corporate sales, Donna created a new type of mastermind group for her division called "Armed and Dangerous." It resulted in higher sales and bonuses for everyone involved. When social media became the buzzword, Donna got creative again, using it to gain new contacts and opportunities. She meets new people around the world every day and converts them into friends, acquaintances, or clients. Today, her passion is creatively utilizing Facebook, LinkedIn, and Twitter to grow her business and teaching entrepreneurs her unique strategies.

Do not confine your passion search to traditional endeavors like painting, writing, and sewing. Look into the use of Internet and technology. There are people who are passionate about online marketing, website design, and blogging. You could end up being one of them.

In order to find your passion, you may have to change your current direction completely. That's what John Grisham did. He is the author of over 20 novels; all are international bestsellers, with nine being made into movies. However, his childhood dream was to be a professional baseball player. He played through junior college when he realized he did not have the skills he needed to play professionally. So he abandoned that goal to major in accounting and eventually went to law school to become a tax attorney.

Get passionate about finding your passion.

Donna Satchell

While in court one day, he overheard the testimony of a 12-year-old girl that led him to begin writing *A Time to Kill*. It took him three years complete the book. Although publishers were turning down the manuscript, Grisham had found his passion. The day after finishing his first book, he started writing his second one. After more than 30 rejections, a small New York publisher decided to take a chance on printing *A Time to Kill*. It became an international best seller, was made into a movie, and Grisham was on his way to undreamed of success.

About his accomplishments, Grisham said, "I never planned to write books … I thought I'd be a lawyer for the rest of my life … But life has a way of presenting opportunities that you don't really notice at first. Success, a lot of times, depends on whether you make a change and try something that you hadn't planned; something new."

That last statement by Grisham supports the question I have raised for years to people who tell me they don't know what they are passionate about. I ask them, "When was the last time you did something for the first time?"

Trying something new was what I did ten years ago. A friend, Lynda Shorter, approached me about the two of us holding a personal development book club meeting. I volunteered to host the first one at my house. About 15 women attended, and we have a great time discussing, learning, and sharing. After that, we continued holding meetings on a monthly basis. Eventually we named the group Women Aspiring Together To Succeed (WATTS).

There is no passion to be found playing small – in settling for a life that is less than the one you are capable of living.

Nelson Mandela
Former President of
South Africa

Lynda and I have done what we love, hosting over 95 meetings at no cost to the members and guests. Each gathering is a mini-motivational event centered on a personal developmental book, an exciting speaker, or inspiring video. There are no membership drives. In out early years, our attendance averaged between 10 – 12 women. Now, up to 45 – 50 women meet regularly. Our special, themed gatherings draw 80 – 90 women.

In June 2010, WATTS celebrated its 10-year anniversary and to my surprise, a group of women interrupted the program and showered Lynda and me with incredible gifts (video recorders, engraved silver bookmarks, custom designed jewelry, an exciting 10-minute DVD about the group's history and money!). They arranged for wonderful presentations featuring singers, praise dancers and a touching poem specifically created for us by spoken-word artist, Bernice Randolph. They wanted us to know

> *Chase down your passion like it's the last bus of the night.*
>
> Terri Guillemets
> Quotation Anthologist

how much they appreciated all we had done over the years, and we truly felt their loving gratitude. It was a phenomenal time. I realized through our discovery and the pursuit of our passion, women were truly benefiting from our efforts.

Lynda and I are not the only people who have decided to do what we are passionate about for free.

The Gesundheit Institute, founded under the leadership of Dr. Patch Adams, was a no-cost hospital operating 24/7 to serve the residents of Virginia. It opened its doors when 20 friends and three doctors converted a six-bedroom house into a facility to treat all types of medical problems. By working other jobs to support themselves, the staff was able to provide free services to the patients. Those who needed treatment beyond what the clinic could provide were referred to other facilities. Over its 12-year history, over 15,000 patients were treated. Dr. Adams describes the project as "truly ecstatic, fascinating, and stimulating."

Dr. Adams and his friends epitomize Dr. Ken Robinson's belief that "finding your passion changes everything". Robinson is a leading international authority of human potential and the author of *The Element*, a New York Times bestseller. What he believes is particularly true when people find their passion through tragedies or life-changing occurrences and it becomes their cause, calling, or life's work. Such individuals include:

- Candy Lighter – Founder of Mothers Against Drunk Driving

- John Walsh – Crime victims' rights advocate

- Judge Glenda A. Hatchett – Advocate for children and families

- Linda and Millard Fuller – Founders of Habitat for Humanity

- Hosea Williams – Founder of Hosea Feed the Hungry and Homeless

If you know of family members, citizens, and leaders in your community whose passions are driving them to improve the lives of others, you can add their names below.

_____

_____

_____

Now call or write them and let them know they are in "your book" and thank them for pursuing their passion to make a difference.

As you can see, discovering your passion can take many forms. I find it so important that I have summarized the key points along with additional tips. If you don't know what you are passionate about, then discover it by:

1. Trying things you have never done before. (Remember the slogan "When was the last time you did something for the first time?" and the stories about Liz Mooney and Carolyn Hartfield.)

2. Taking on new responsibilities on your job or for organizations you belong to.

3. Taking classes in an unexplored area that interests you.

4. Considering the suggestions of others about what they see you are good at doing (remember my story about Al Wiseman).

5. Revisiting your childhood and asking yourself, "What did you like doing, love doing, dream about doing?"

6. Looking through your high school or college yearbooks to see what friends and teachers said about you. (Remember Wanda Sykes). Also, check with family members and others to see what they remember you being good at doing.

7. Investigating segments of your industry or profession that are new to you (Gale Horton Gay).

8. Spending time with people who have found their passions, gifts and talents through books, audios, videos, and personal contact. Their amazing stories about how they discovered their own passions can inspire you.

9. Considering the following questions:

    ■ What would you do if you knew you could not fail?

    ■ Who would you love to spend an entire day with and why?

    ■ What type of people do you most enjoy spending time with? I am not talking about your friends or family members, but rather what kind of individuals feed your spirit (such as writers, teachers, artists, comedians, engineers, etc.).

    In his book, *The Element*, Dr. Ken Robinson calls this "finding your tribe." He says when we find the group of people we truly enjoy being around, it can connect us to our passions.

    ■ Are there any conditions or circumstances that you feel strongly about changing, such as, injustice, safety, inequality?

10. Being aware of your personal reaction to events and issues. This can lead to your discovering areas you are truly passionate about.

11. Trying your hand at activities connected with the Internet, such as blogging and social media with the thought that they could be of great interest for you (Donna Lang).

12. Believing that your passions and talents exist in one of three places and being determined to discover them in:

   ■ The past – It is something you did or felt as a child or young person. You need to rediscover it.

   ■ The present – You are in one of three situations:

       o You know what you are passionate about and you are pursuing it. If that is the case, congratulations to you – continue making progress.

       o You know what you are passionate about, but are afraid to move forward. If that's you, read Chapter 3 on increasing your belief and Chapter 8 on getting started.

       o Others see your talents and they are telling you how great you are at doing something; however, you do not believe them. If that sounds like you, strongly consider the compliments people are giving you, and decide to pursue your gifts.

   ■ The future – You have not done it yet. Maybe you are not even aware of it. Plan to be more adventurous. Try new things, from new hobbies, new roles, new tasks, and new classes.

       Also, be cognizant of your feelings about what is going on in your life and the lives of others. Is there something you feel strongly about changing to make your neighborhood, community, or city a better or safer place? If so, move forward to change that societal condition.

Once you have discovered your passion, then learn all you can about the subject and begin working at it. You never know where your passion can take you, how much pleasure you can get from it, and how much value you can be to others.

Consider pursuing what you are passionate as a new:

1. Position at your workplace or project in your department.

2. Task at community activities your employer sponsors.

3. Role in events planned by organizations of which you are a member, or a position on the leadership board or one of the committees

4. Occasional or seasonal business

5. Part-time business.

6. Full-time business.

7. Volunteer opportunity for hospitals, senior centers, nursing homes, any place that could use your services.

8. Hobby (e.g. writing, singing, baking) for the personal pleasure and satisfaction of doing it for yourself and those you love.

9. Endeavor you create and do free (remember what Lynda Shorter and I did with WATTS, also how Patch Adams and his friends formed The Gesundheit Institute).

10. Personal crusade – make your passion your cause, your calling, or your life's work. Get others involved in supporting your ideas and helping you bring about change.

These are not exclusive, so you can engage in more than one. For example, if you have a passion of photography, you could volunteer to take pictures at senior citizen centers, be the photographer for events your church holds, and have a part-time or seasonal photography business.

Once you have found your passion, know that pursuing it will take hard work, serious commitment, persistence and everything needed for accomplishing any goal. These areas are covered in the next chapters.

Whether you pursue your passion for several hours a week, a short time every month, or as a full-time job or business endeavor, know that others are benefiting greatly from your efforts and that you are an inspiration to many people.

*   *   *   *   *

Consider the compelling question and direction in the quote below by writer T. Alan Armstrong:

"If there is no passion in your life, then have you really lived? Find your passion, whatever it may be. Become it, and let it become you and you will find great things happen for you, to you, and because of you."

Just Get Serious® About Success
Chapter 5 Exercise

YOUR PASSION

To conclude this chapter, answer one of the following two questions:

1. Do you want to discover your passion, because you do not know what it is? If yes, re-read the section on the twelve ways to do so a few pages back. Then decide how you will get started finding it. You can detail your ideas below.

_____

_____

_____

– or –

2. Do you want to move forward on what you already desire to do? If yes, I suggest you learn as much as you can about your passion and then decide which of the ten ways you will pursue it. You can outline your plans below.

_____

_____

_____

3. Now, move forward enthusiastically on what you have written as an answer to question #1 or #2.

4. Write about your progress in your personal or Just Get Serious® journal.

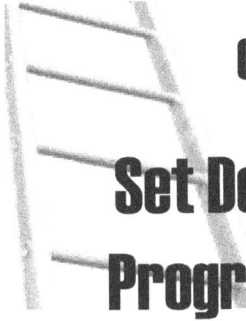

Chapter 6

Set Definitive and Progressive Goals

Written goals have a way of transforming wishes into wants; can'ts into cans; dreams into plans; and plans into reality.

Anonymous

Even if I don't reach all my goals, I've gone higher than I would have if I hadn't set any.

Danielle Fotopoulis
Soccer Player & Coach

Those who do not have definite goals they are working on are easily influenced by those who do.

Donna Satchell

During my years of reading personal development books and attending seminars, I have found that all the experts on success stress the importance of writing goals. Among them is Brian Tracy.

Today, Tracy is an internationally recognized business consultant, seminar leader, and achievement speaker. However, he dropped out of high school at 18 and, for several years, had menial jobs at factories, farms, and steamships. At 23, he got a commission-only sales position where he not only led his team in sales but also became the vice president of sales in charge of 95 people within two years.

Tracy attributes his success to his decision to write an ambitious goal to earn $1,000 a month at his job. When he actually accomplished that feat, he began to value goal setting, which led him to spend more than 40 years studying, researching, and practicing the concept.

Goals determine what you are going to be.

Julius Erving
Basketball Player

As a leading authority on success, Tracy has spoken to more than four million people through over 4,000 presentations, worked with 1,000 plus companies, and written 45 books. With his vast knowledge and experience, Tracy says if he had only five minutes to tell someone just one thing to do to be more successful it would be, "Write down your goals; make plans to achieve them, and work on your plans every single day."

That is exactly what former Notre Dame football coach Lou Holtz did 30 years ago when he was let go from his assistant coaching job at the University of South Carolina. Depressed and in dire need of encouragement, his wife gave him *The Magic of Thinking Big* by David Schwartz. After reading it, Holtz decided to follow the author's advice and wrote down the things he wanted to accomplish. He ended up with a list of 108 goals – many which were extremely ambitious. As of today, he has accomplished 102 of them, including dining at the White House,

You are never too old to set another goal or to dream a new dream.

C.S. Lewis
Novelist

meeting the Pope, being a guest on *The Tonight Show*, and being inducted into the College Football Hall of Fame. At age 70, Holtz is still setting, writing, and achieving goals.

Success through goal setting is not limited to the well known only. In an interview with me, Cindy Light explained how she wanted to move from China to the United States for the many opportunities this country offered. She relocated to Chicago having no job, knowing no one, and not being able to speak English. Once there, her first goals were securing housing and stable employment, learning the language, and acclimating herself to our culture. The latter two took quite some time, but she achieved them all. Then, having learned to sew as a child, Cindy's next goal was to start a business creating elaborate clothes and home fashions for high-end clients. With lots of hard work and commitment, she accomplished that as well. She then set her sights on working in the image-consulting field. Today, Light is a certified image coach, helping people enhance their appearance so they can become more successful. You can read more about Light's remarkable journey in Chapter 20 – Be Inspired.

My goals have included relocating to Atlanta, starting a part-time business doing art shows, winning analyst awards at work, becoming an achievement speaker and trainer, and writing this book. None of these were easy, but I accomplished each one (more on these later).

THE SMARTER FORMULA

I hope you are now inspired to set new goals or raise the bar for those you have already set. As you do, I suggest they reflect the aspirations you listed in your personal inventory on the last page of Part II of Chapter 4. In writing them, follow my SMARTER formula. It builds on the traditional SMART method used by others but includes what is necessary after writing your goals.

S – Specific

Goals should be as clear and precise as possible. A goal of "graduating with honors from New York University in 2014 with a Bachelors degree in Business Administration" is more definite and exact than "graduating from college in four years with a Bachelors degree." Including a specific college, "with honors," "business administration degree," and the year makes it very defined. We have a greater chance of accomplishing that type of specific goal than a vague one because our minds can focus better on targets with clear details. Make sure you have covered as many of them as possible.

> *People with clear, written goals accomplish far more in a shorter period of time than people without them could ever imagine.*
>
> Brian Tracy – Author

M – Measurable

Quantify your goals with definite numbers. A goal of making $100,000 a year is far better than a goal of making lots of money. This way, you can make adjustments if you find you are not close to earning that amount. Having a goal to buy a house in three years is better than making plans to buy one in the near future because we will be better able to evaluate our progress.

Even noble goals can be measurable. Taylor Mali is a high school teacher, slam poet, and voiceover artist. His objective is to have a positive impact on the lives of people by inspiring them to become teachers through his engaging, powerful spoken word poetry. Rather than "many," "several hundred," or "thousands," his goal is to inspire 1,000 people to become teachers. As of the writing of the book, 503 people have become teachers because of him since he undertook this project.

> *You have to measure what you want more of.*
>
> Charles Coonradt
> President,
> The Game of Work

A – Ambitious, Yet Achievable

I believe there is a huge difference between items on our "to do" list and real goals. The former are easily obtainable. The latter are challenging to reach and cause us to move outside of our comfort zones. A quote by Mary Kay Ash, founder of Mary Kay Cosmetics, reflects my feelings: "A good goal is like a strenuous exercise. It makes you stretch."

In *The Welch Way*, author, Jeffrey Krames describes former G.E. CEO Jack Welch's philosophy about company goals. Welch feels it is important to "reach for more than you think is possible. Don't sell yourself short by thinking that you will fail. It is better to reach for the impossible than to settle for just another lackluster performance." We can apply this same thought to our personal goals to make them ambitious ones.

The German philosopher and author, Johann Wolfgang von Goethe, wrote, "He who does not expect a million readers, should not write a line." His quote tells us if we are not planning to do something in a big way, we should not do it at all. This idea can be challenging for many of us because we've often been taught not to expect big successes. So we make comments like, "I'm going to write this little book" or "I'm going to start this little business." We apply for jobs we can easily get even though they are not the ones we truly want. We believe that if we lower our expectations, we can avoid the disappointment of failure and increase our chances of success. What we are really doing is setting a limit on what we will achieve.

> *Have the courage to dream great dreams. Who wants a dream that's near-fetched?*
>
> Howard Schultz
> Chairman of Starbucks

We should ask ourselves, "What is it that keeps us from thinking larger?" Is it fear? Is it lack of faith? Is it low self-esteem? It could be any one of these factors … or a host of others. For instance, when we have low expectations, we often surround ourselves with like-minded people who support our limited thinking.

Do we think we deserve *millions* of readers, *millions* of customers, and/or *millions* of dollars? Do we think we deserve an exceptional relationship, a great job, a beautiful home, and truly supportive friends? If we believe we deserve all these things, then we need to expect to have them.

When we expect great things, we operate at a different level. The and effort you put into searching for an average job will be different than what you expend when you are looking for a highly coveted one.

The energy and effort you put into a business that you think will eventually be worth thousands of dollars will be different than what you will do for one you believe will be worth millions. Likewise, the energy and effort you put into writing a book that will reach a few hundred readers is quite different than what you will do when you imagine your work will be a best seller and be read by millions.

> *Think BIG. There are unseen forces ready to support your dreams.*
>
> Cheryl Richardson
> Life Coach

Truly, Sidney Poitier's goal to be an actor was an ambitious one. He had only been in the United States for a short time when he decided that was what he wanted to do. By his own admission, he spoke and read poorly (at about the fourth grade level), had a thick Caribbean accent, and had no acting experience whatsoever. Ambitious goals require ambitious effort.

Poitier spent endless hours teaching himself how to read better. He constantly listened to the radio to practice improving his speech. In addition to working as a dishwasher, he took an unpaid job as a janitor at the American Negro Theater in exchange for acting classes. Despite his teachers' feelings that he would fail at acting, Poitier continued with the course work. His efforts eventually paid off when he got the chance to replace another actor in a play. His performance caught the attention of a director who was in the audience. He offered Poitier a small part in one of his upcoming productions. There were still many years of struggle ahead, but Poitier was on the path to fulfilling his ambitious goal. He went from achieving it to excelling at the craft, becoming the first African American to receive an Academy Award for Best Actor. He has received other prestigious awards including the Presidential Medal of Freedom.

When you are setting goals, think big, think bold, and think brilliant. By doing so, you set the stage for high expectations. Expectations set the stage for action, and action sets the stage for results.

It is important to understand that what is ambitious for one person may not be for another. For example, is it an ambitious goal to buy a $150,000 home? It depends on your income. If you are single, making $85,000 per year and have little or no debt, it is not. However, if you are a man or woman making $40,000 per year and have three children with no spouse to assist you, it would be ambitious.

> *Before you can make a dream come true, you must first have one.*
>
> Ronald E. McNair
> Astronaut

To determine if your goals are ambitious, ask yourself the following questions:

1. Are they difficult to achieve?

2. Will they require additional learning?

3. Will I have to ask others for help or assistance?

4. Do I feel a sense of trepidation?

5. Will they stretch me beyond my comfort zone?

6. When I achieve them, will I have a tremendous sense of personal satisfaction and accomplishment?

If you answered "yes" to all or most of the questions, you have ambitious goals. If you did not, I challenge you to consider revising them to those that will demand more of you, force you to reach outside your comfort zone, and help you grow and develop your skills, abilities, and talents. Those types of goals require us to raise our expectations of ourselves.

For me, writing this book is such an endeavor. In my wildest dreams, I never thought this was something I could do. In fact, when I become a speaker and trainer, colleagues were always suggesting that I do this, but I would not even consider the idea. At the time, it seemed like too big a project for me to handle on my own. Subsequently, I became one of the co-authors of various anthology books instead. Then a year and a half ago, I decided to take the plunge. As I look at the six questions above, I can answer "yes" to each of them. So this book is definitely an ambitious goal for me. How about you? Are your goals ambitious? If not, reconsider them.

> *You want to set a goal that is big enough that in the process of achieving it you become someone worth becoming.*
>
> Jim Rohn
> Speaker & Author

R – Real Aspirations

Be sure your goals reflect your own desires. You may be saying to yourself, "Well, that seems obvious. Why wouldn't they?" The answer is very simple. The impact of advertising, pressures from family and friends, as well as trying to keep up with the Joneses can cause us to want things we might not otherwise aspire to have. Just think about all the items you have purchased or things you have done that were not part of your original plans, did not satisfy you at all, or fulfill a significant purpose.

> *A successful life is one that is lived through understanding and pursuing one's own path, not chasing after the dreams of others.*
>
> Chin-Ning Chu – Author

Several years ago, I was presenting a program at Clemson University's Conference for Women. During lunch, I struck up a conversation with Vanessa, one of the attendees. I told her about my upcoming presentation in the afternoon segment. She said it sounded exciting, but she had to leave to go to class. I asked what her major was and Vanessa replied,

"Law." As we parted, I wished her well on her plans to be an attorney. Then she sighed and said something I found astounding: "Oh, I don't really want to be a lawyer. It is something my family wants me to do. That's the only reason I'm in law school. I really dislike being there." Then she walked away. Now, how successful will Vanessa be doing something she does not like? How will she be able to serve her clients and withstand the demands of that profession when it is not her real aspiration?

Vanessa is certainly not alone in having family pressures to pursue a career that she does not want. Differences between people's dreams and the plans their parents have for them are not new.

- Maria Montessori's father strongly objected to her desire to be a physician. But, with her mother's help, she went to and excelled in medical school. She became the first woman doctor in Italy. Her work with children led to the Montessori teaching method widely used today.

- Gordon Parks' wife and mother-in-law were against him pursuing his interest in photography, but he persisted. By seriously committing himself to his endeavors, he became an award-winning photographer, filmmaker, writer and composer.

- Amy Tan's mother wanted her to become a doctor. Defying her wishes, Tan became writer. She wrote *The Joy Luck Club*, which became an international bestseller and was made into a movie.

- James Cameron's father strongly disapproved of his dreams to be a director. In fact, Cameron felt he was waiting for him to fail so he could say, "You should have been an engineer." Still, he pursued his dreams, eventually directing *Titanic*, which won 11 Academy Awards, and Avatar, which was a huge success.

Parents, teachers and others may have our best interests at heart; however, they do not know what really motivates and inspires us to do our best work. The question of "real aspirations" doesn't apply only to our career goals but to other goals as well.

Think … do your goals reflect what you actually want to have, do, or be? Or are you being influenced to go after things that do not truly excite you? I suggest you carefully consider both questions. Be honest with yourself about the answers. And, if necessary, think about making changes to your goals.

> *My parents wanted me to be a lawyer. But I don't think I would have been very happy. I'd be in front of the jury singing.*
>
> Jennifer Lopez – Singer

Last, it is important to include plans to pursue your passions or talents. If you are not sure what you are passionate about, then include activities that can help you discover them. See the list toward the end of Chapter 5 for suggestions.

T – Time Based

Successful goals have a strong element of time. Know when you are going to start working on your goal. When will you review your progress? When do you plan on completing it? The answers to these questions are major keys to getting started and making progress.

At age 27, I said to myself, "I am going to go to college. I should have gone when I graduated from high school like my friends did, but I am going to go someday." Do you know what happens with "someday" goals? When I was 29, I was still thinking about college. At 32, I was upset and frustrated that I had not gotten started yet. When I was 33, I said, "I am going to be enrolled in college by the fall." I did not know where I was going to go or how I was going to pay for it. However,

> *A goal is a dream with a deadline.*
>
> Napoleon Hill
> Author

I wrote it down as a goal with the start date being September. That's when I finally went to college. Six years later, I graduated with top honors. So I know from experience the importance of writing goals and having a time frame.

E – Energize Your Goals with Action and Enthusiasm

Until you act, your goals are just ideas waiting to happen. Acting requires you to make a detailed plan of the steps and actions you will undertake on a regular basis, ideally daily, to reach your goals. For example, if you want to start a business, your initial steps include researching the product or service you plan to offer, talking to others who are already in the same or similar endeavor, writing a marketing plan, getting a business license, and possibly meeting with bank officials to secure financing. If your goal is purchasing a home, the early steps are deciding on the type of house (including location and price range), saving money regularly, finding out about loans, and meeting with real estate agents. For getting a promotion at work, you need to find out the required experience and qualifications, and then decide how you will get it.

Take action. Develop a sense of urgency in your life.

Les Brown
Motivational Expert

Once you have your plan, take action. Do not allow doubts to delay you. Do not let others dissuade with their negative remarks. Do not let distractions take you off course. (More on that in upcoming chapters). Stay focused on what you want and move forward through your actions. As you do, be enthused. Norman Vincent Peale said, "There is real magic in enthusiasm. It spells the difference between mediocrity and accomplishment." Bill Gate's quote, "We were young, but we had good advice and good ideas and lots of enthusiasm," signals the role highly tuned positive emotions played in building Microsoft. So be excited about your goals and they will keep you motivated. Enthusiasm will get people interested in helping you. And it will make others remember you.

Bear in mind you do not have to possess the outward zeal of Tony Robbins and many other high-energy motivational speakers to be excited. Having studied personality and behavior styles, I understand we have different levels of excitement and show it in different ways. You may have a quieter inward enthusiasm that propels you forward. So don't feel that you must be walking around shouting loudly, "Look at what I am planning to do!" Instead, be excited in your own way.

> *A mediocre idea that generates enthusiasm will go further than a great idea that inspires no one.*
>
> Mary Kay Ash – Founder, Mary Kay Cosmetics

R – Review Your Progress and Decide on One of the Four R's

Periodically examine your progress to figure out what is working and what is not working. Then you can choose from four types of action:

- Repeat – We keep moving forward because things are going as we planned.

- Rearrange – Sometimes we have to reorganize certain aspects of our lives so we can make progress on our goals. For example, we may need to spend less time holding idle conversations with friends, watching TV, or going to the mall to shop. By cutting back on these types of activities, we can have more time and energy for our goals.

- Rewrite – Be willing to rewrite your goals if necessary. We might need to revise our goals because unforeseen circumstances have surfaced. Or maybe we need to re-evaluate our goals to determine whether we set the bar too high or too low. Maybe your initial target should be increased or decreased. Maybe your time frames need adjusting. Maybe you can finish your endeavor sooner, or maybe it will take more time. It is alright to make changes after you have given the situation careful consideration.

When I decided to go to college, my initial goal was simply to graduate, but that quickly changed. During my first semester, I got a B+ and an A. The next semester, I got the same grades again. The following semester, I got two As. Then I started thinking maybe I could do better than "just graduate." If I worked harder, maybe I could graduate with honors. So I raised the bar and set a new goal. I did everything possible to get only As in all my other classes. That meant many nights staying up late to do homework, using vacation time to study for finals, missing many social activities, and getting a tutor. As I mentioned earlier, six years later I graduated with honors (summa cum laude) and received a bachelor's degree in Business Administration.

- Release and Replace – We may no longer choose to pursue our original goal. Maybe we have lost interest in it or perhaps circumstances in our lives have changed so dramatically that we must put the goal on hold indefinitely. Give yourself permission to let go of a goal once you have made a sincere and persistent effort to achieve it. If you find that you must do that, replace it with a new goal. Keep in mind the quote by Dr. Benjamin E. Mays, former President of Morehouse College, "The tragedy of life doesn't lie in not reaching your goal. The tragedy lies in having no goal to reach."

Over the years, I have pursued various endeavors and released some of them for legitimate reasons. With each one, I learned valuable lessons, gained great experiences, or developed incredible friendships because I undertook them. Deciding not to continue with a goal does not mean you have accomplished nothing.

In the past, I started a part-time art business, setting up shows in people's homes. I would invite local artists to participate, give presentations about collecting art and then sell the paintings and prints I had on display. I loved the business, but my workload as a category manager increased dramatically, and I found myself constantly exhausted. I eventually stopped the art show endeavor. However, because of it, I developed a friendship with Janet Saboor, one of the gallery owners I partnered with on several occasions. We have gone on vacations together to Japan, Brazil, and Jamaica. We are still the best of friends today.

Although I released the art show goal, I ended up with a great new friendship. So I gained something valuable in the process. As you think back on your previous goals, I am sure you will find the same is true for you. So even if you don't reach all your goals, they can still help you live a richer life.

Make sure you have goals for all areas that are important to you. For example, if one area is education, have written plans for going beyond your current level of learning or knowledge. For most of us, health is of major concern, so have goals for that area. In Chapter 4, you identified areas of importance on your Personal Inventory. If you have not completed the form, I suggest you do it now. Then, write your goals accordingly.

Plan to look at your goals several times a day to keep them in the forefront of your mind. I suggest writing them on index cards and carrying them with you. Not having our goals with us is like walking into a supermarket or grocery store without a shopping list. Without it, we purchase items we did not intend to buy and do not truly need. The same thing happens when we go into the "Mall of Life" without our written goals. We can spend time doing things and going places that are not connected with what we truly want in life. Don't let that happen to you. Regarding our goals, I feel we should follow the famous slogan from American Express, "Don't leave home without it."

The previous chapters (Knowing Yourself, Increasing Your Belief, Discovering Your Passions) and this one were all written to lead you to do one thing: take consistent action. To do that, you may need a Goal Achieving Partner (GAP). This is someone who also has goals. The two of you contact each other regularly to make sure each person is moving forward. A GAP can help you make progress because you have someone to whom you are accountable. This is particularly important if you are working by yourself and not in a group.

In selecting a GAP, find someone who is positive, motivated, and determined in addition to their having goals. Over the years, I have had several GAP arrangements. Some have been extremely valuable, and others worked marginally well. I suggest starting as a temporary arrangement to make sure your personalities are compatible and each person feels he or she is benefiting from the interaction. Before setting up anything definite, talk with each other about what you want to accomplish from the arrangement. If you decide to move forward, here are some guidelines to consider:

1. Plan to talk on a regular basis (weekly is best).

2. Schedule the conversations for the same time (i.e. every Monday at 9:00 a.m.; every Thursday at 8:00 p.m.). If one person needs to change the time because of an unexpected event or project, still speak sometime that week if possible (even if it needs to be for a shorter period of time).

3. Share the time. Make sure one person does not dominate the conversation. In the beginning, you may want to actually divide the time and keep track of it so no one feels he or she was short-changed.

4. Agree that all conversations are confidential. (I have found the trust factor develops over time.)

5. If the person is someone you do not know well, then act as you would with any new relationship. Do not immediately divulge confidential or personal information until you know the person extremely well.

6. Be as interested in hearing about the other person's progress as you are in talking about your own.

7. Be a good listener and be considerate. During the conversations, avoid taking other calls unless they are crucial (consider disabling "call waiting"). Also, do not engage in "side-line" activities (surfing the Internet, texting, watching TV). Act as if the person is in your physical presence.

8. See this arrangement as a valuable investment of your time and energy and that of the other person. Do not take it for granted.

9. Decide what would work well for both individuals, but be open to changing to a different format if it might be better.

    For example, Dawn and I initially agreed to talk weekly for 30 minutes (15 minutes for each person). Then we changed to an hour with one of us getting 15 minutes to give her update and the other having 45 minutes so we could brainstorm on ways she could approach or solve any challenges she was having. We would alternate the 45-minute slot each week. We found that worked a lot better for us. Be creative so each person's needs are met.

10. Decide to hold the conversations on a trial basis for a set period (i.e. a month). At the end of that time, the two of you can decide if the calls are working well for both parties. If they are not, you can discuss changes that could make them better or you can discontinue the arrangement. Agree in advance that no one will take it personally if the latter is the case. That happened when I realized another individual and I had different life philosophies, which interfered with us being supportive partners. Since we did not take ending the endeavor personally, we are on good terms today.

Remember, a GAP is not necessary. It is an arrangement to consider if it makes sense and works for you and the other person. For information about other supportive relationships you can consider pursuing, see Chapter 10 – Build a Positive Network of Support.

The next chapters will show you ways to stay focused while moving forward; but first complete the exercise on the following page.

Just Get Serious® About Success
Chapter 6 Exercise

YOUR WRITTEN GOALS

Use the forms below and on the next page to write out your goals with the steps and actions necessary. Use one form for each goal.

Goal*	Steps (Optional)	Actions	Time Frames
Write name of goal vertically			

You can download this form at www.JGSBook.com (click on JGS Club).

Goal*	Steps (Optional)	Actions	Time Frames & Frequency
Write name of goal vertically			

Goal*	Steps (Optional)	Actions	Time Frames & Frequency
Write name of goal vertically			

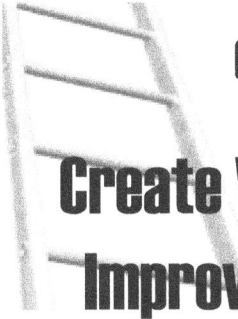

Chapter 7

Create Visual Goals to Improve Your Focus

The most pathetic person in the world is someone who has sight but has no vision.

Helen Keller – Author & Activist

Before you can do something that you've never done, you have to imagine it's possible.

Jean Shinoda Bolen, MD – Psychiatrist

You've got to think about big things while you're doing small things, so that all the small things go in the right direction.

Alvin Toffler – Writer & Futurist

Do you have a vision board? If you do, that's great. I hope this chapter gives you several creative ideas to consider for your next one. If you do not, I encourage you to make one. It is a great way to stay focused on your goals and dreams so you can reach them.

I was introduced to the concept of visual goals in the 1980s through *Creative Visualization*, a book written by Shakti Gawain. She is one of the pioneers in mental imaging and brought the idea of vision boards to the attention of millions of people through her writings. This interest in visualization resurfaced in the mid 2000s because of the film, *The Secret*, and the book, *The Vision Board,* by Joyce Schwarz. Both stressed its importance in creating success in our lives through creating vision boards (also known as treasure map, dream board, and life map).

A vision board is a collage of pictures, slogans, and words which represent what you want to see happen in your future. Vision boards answer the question, "What would make you feel successful?" I think of them as visual representations of our written and unwritten goals and dreams.

Having a marketing background, I like to compare them to TV and print advertising. Why do we buy most of the things we purchase? We see them over and over again in commercials and magazines, and they stay in the forefront of our minds. The impact of advertising and frequently viewed images in movies and TV shows has been thoroughly documented in books such as *Can't Buy My Love: How Advertising Changes the Way We Think and Feel* by Jean Kilbourne; James B. Twitchell's *Twenty Ads That Shook the World: The Century's Most Groundbreaking Advertising and How It Changed Us All*; and *The Hidden Persuaders* by Vance Packard.

> *A vision is not just a picture of what could be; it is an appeal to our better selves, a call to become something more.*
>
> Rosabeth Moss Kanter
> Professor, Harvard Bus. School

I see vision boards as having the same effect as advertising. The more we see the images of our goals and dreams, the more likely we are to focus our time, talents, and energy in their direction. Then, using the five A's of **Attention**, **Affirmation**, **Attitude**, **Action**, and **Attraction**, we are able to make progress on and eventually achieve our aspirations.

- **Attention** – Placing the board where you can see it several times a day will direct your attention to what you desire. What we see consistently has a strong influence on what we think and eventually do. We can think about the board as "selling" ourselves on our goals and dreams.

> *You must structure your world so that you are constantly reminded of who you are.*
>
> Na'im Akbar
> Psychologist

- **Affirmation** – Saying positive affirmations to yourself several times a day strengthens your belief system, boosts your confidence, and propels you to action or keeps you moving. (See the "Using Positive Affirmations" section in Chapter 2.)

- **Attitude** – Creating and looking at our boards can help us feel optimistic about the future since they represent where we want to be, not where we are now or where we have been. Best-selling author John Maxwell says, "When there is hope in the future, there is power in the present." Hope-filled thinking creates a focused and enthusiastic person who moves forward to make things happen.

- **Action** – Acting on our goals and dreams results from looking at our boards several times a day. The more we act, the more likely we are to achieve results.

- **Attraction** – The more we act, the more we attract the people, opportunities, and things we need or desire. The novelist and philosopher, W. H. Murray, described the law of attraction when he wrote, "The moment one definitely commits oneself, then providence moves too. All sorts of things occur to help one that would never otherwise have occurred."

Since 2001, Lynda Shorter, a colleague, and I have held annual vision board making events for Women Aspiring Together To Succeed (WATTS), a group we co-founded. When we held our first vision board meeting in 2001, 20 women attended. The number increased to 30 the next year. In 2003, 40 women came out. By 2010, over 70 members and guests attended the event! Every year, returning women talk about the successes they had in previous years because of their boards.

I have facilitated vision board sessions for youth groups and women's events. The concept is part of the goal achievement programs I present for corporations and government agencies. I have seen hundreds of boards and heard stories of incredible success individuals have realized, including getting married, securing promotions, acquiring major tangible possessions, taking wonderful vacations, and meeting people who helped with work-related opportunities and business endeavors.

You can create vision boards on a variety of flat surfaces, including large poster boards, small note cards, various-sized books, and even computer monitors (in the form of screen-savers). The types I am most familiar with are made on poster or canvas boards. On the surface, you paste inspiring pictures, motivating words, and encouraging quotes taken from magazines and other printed materials, as well as the Internet. To personalize and enhance your board, you can add photos of yourself and others, decorative lettering, and various embellishments, such as shells, stars, etc.

Let's suppose you want to have a prosperous career as a well-known writer. Your board could have pictures of people reading books, lots of money, a fancy sports car, and a beautiful house. You may include pictures of yourself typing at a computer or writing. You could add slogans like, "Write Your Way to Success" and "Write Now – Your Future Depends on It," motivating words, such as *Dream, Dare, Achieve* and your favorite success

Dreams are extremely important. You can't do it unless you can imagine it.

George Lucas
Director, Screenwriter

quotes. If you have a business card for your writing business, you can include it, along with a mock-up cover of your book or just the title written in bold letters.

Once your board is completed, hang it in a place where you will see it several times each day (your office, bedroom or exercise room). Some people prefer to place the board in a private place where others cannot easily see it. They do not want people asking them questions and then adding their not-so-positive comments, like "Why would you want to do that?" "You don't have enough money (or experience) to pursue that goal," or any other disparaging comments. If you would find such questions or remarks discouraging, find a secluded place for your board.

> *The future belongs to those who see the possibilities before they become obvious.*
>
> John Scully
> Corporate Executive

Other individuals want people to know what their goals and dreams are, so their boards are in a more visible place, such as a living room. I know people who have them in their offices at work. Wherever you choose, you need to look at it regularly so your mind can be focused on what you want to accomplish.

There are countless vision board success stories, including:

- Julia Mancuso, gold medal Olympic skier. As a child, she created a poster of herself winning medals at the Olympics. Her board and her success are featured in a VISA commercial. It can be seen at www.JGSBook.com (under "Videos").

- Lisa Nichols, author of *No Matter What*. She created a vision board featuring herself as a guest on *The Oprah Winfrey Show* and actually showed it to Oprah when she accomplished her goal.

- Jim Carrey, comedian and actor. He used the vision board concept as a struggling young comedian. In 1987 he wrote a check to himself for $10 million for "acting services rendered" and carried it in his wallet for years. By 1996, he was one of Hollywood's super-stars, earning $20 million a movie.

- Bruce Lee, martial arts expert and actor. In 1970, he used the visioning concept by writing a letter to himself stating, "By 1980 I will be the best known oriental movie star in the United States and will have secured $10 million." Three years later, Lee accomplished international acclaim and success before his untimely death in 1973.

It is interesting that Carrey and Lee wrote specific amounts of money they wanted to be paid for their services and it was the same figure – $10 million. Remember what I covered in Chapter 6 about making our goals specific. They were both following that principle.

If you think children can be too young to create a vision board or use visualization techniques, think again. At 7 years old, Farrah Gray began carrying business cards that read "Future 21st Century CEO." Between ages 8 and 12, he started several businesses, including the KIDZTEL pre-paid phone. At 14, he was a self-made millionaire. He is the youngest person to have an office on Wall Street and was the youngest person invited by former President Bush to be a member of the African-American Leadership Roundtable. Today, Dr. Gray truly represents the business card he carried at 7 years old.

Although my successes are not as huge as Dr. Gray's, I can personally attest that vision boards work. I created my first one years ago when I decided to become a motivational speaker. In my collage of pictures, slogans and words, I pasted photos of internationally renowned motivational speaker Les Brown and Jewel Diamond Taylor, leading keynote presenter and life coach. I hold them in very high regard. At the time, I did not know either of them personally.

Since I was always looking at my board, I focused on doing things to move forward on my goals, one being staying in touch with people. I believe it is crucial for success, so I would often talk to people I had worked with at Clairol. One of these individuals is Stephanie Townsend, a former sales analyst. I would tell her about my passion for being a speaker and the challenges I was having. After many months of having these conversations, she ran into Les Brown at the airport in Atlanta. Stephanie told me as soon as she saw him, despite some hesitancy, she felt compelled to tell him about me because of my excitement about speaking and training.

Les Brown called me immediately, and our conversation led to the great working relationship we have today. I have shared the platform with him on several occasions, and we recorded a CD together. One of the highlights of my speaking career was when four other speakers and I put on a two-hour motivational event and Les Brown was the Master of Ceremonies.

Having Jewel Diamond Taylor on my board sparked a conversation in which I found out a friend knew her. Because of her association with Jewel, she arranged for her to be the speaker for meeting held in my home. Taylor was in my living room giving an incredible speech to 40 women. Immediately above her was my office where my vision board (with Jewel's photo) was hanging on the wall. Then as happened with Les, I found myself presenting on programs with Jewel.

What is amazing is the impact vision boards can have on other people besides their creators. When I first talked to my friend Janet Saboor about vision boards, I knew she would be eager to make one because she is an imaginative, creative, right-brain individual. Her husband Lonnie is more of an analytical type left-brain person who would not have such an interest, or so I thought.

Vision is the art of seeing what is invisible for others.

Jonathan Swift
Essayist & Writer

Janet created a striking board she hung in their bedroom. One weekend, Janet went out of town on a business trip. When she returned, she called me and frantically asked me, "Do you know what Lonnie did with my vision board?" "Oh, no," I replied as a dreadful thought of him taking it off the wall or doing something worse entered my mind. Janet continued, "He made one!" I was shocked because it was the last thing I would imagine him doing. Lonnie told Janet that just seeing her board was so inspiring he had to create his own. His board included pictures representing him winning Toastmasters speech contests – which he accomplished the following year.

Keep in mind that a vision board is just one form of what I call a vision collage. Others include pictures placed on vases, mirrors, and similar items. Linda Hall is a mixed media artist and jewelry designer who has created interesting collages on a variety of objects. I asked her to tell us about "moving beyond the board."

Donna: Linda, the first time you attended the annual vision board event at my home, you created a "vision vase." How did that happen?

Linda: As I was collecting magazines and items to bring to your house, my mind kept percolating with the idea of creative pieces you could view as functional art. I believe everyone is unique, so I was motivated to show everyone that we don't all have to use boards. In fact, over the years, I have never worked on one.

Being a mixed media artist, I love to repurpose items, so I have used paint cans, vases, Styrofoam™ head forms and tabletop "Lazy Susan" servers to create my vision collages. I have even considered using clocks. It is all about being open and tapping into your imagination. For me, I may hear a phrase and my creative muse leads me to an object to consider. For example, the creation of my *Yes I Can* collage is based on President Obama's *Yes We Can* speech. I thought how great it would be for me to focus on what I can do to make my life more fulfilling. That led me to use a metal paint can.

I use lots of color in my mixed media creations, so I covered my paint can completely with beautiful pictures and vibrant words. I keep my *Yes I Can* collage in my art studio filled with colored pencils and markers. It inspires me to stretch my imagination. I also like the portability of my collage. I can place it in any room. Most people see it as a piece of art, but I know its true meaning.

Donna: How would non-artists, like myself, create their version of your *Yes I Can* paint can?

Linda: You would need the following supplies:

- Magazines
- Scissors
- An empty pint or quart size metal paint can (from Home Depot or Lowe's)
- Glue
- Foam brush (arts and craft store)
- Modge podge (arts and craft store)
- Clear polyurethane varnish (Home Depot or Lowe's)

First, you decide what you want to accomplish in your life. Next, cut out pictures, phrases, and words that represent those things. Glue the pictures on the entire can while leaving no space uncovered. Last, use a foam brush to cover the entire can with modge podge, a clear drying glue that is used to seal and finish projects. Let it dry for 24 to 48 hours. In warm, humid climates, the modge podge may feel slightly sticky. To fix this, apply a clear varnish over the product.

Donna: Is there anything else we need to know?

Linda: That's it. You can use the same materials and process for most objects. I encourage you and your readers to begin with an open mind and think "beyond the board." Consider things you enjoy doing. Think about your hobbies. Let your imagination direct you. You would be amazed at what ideas will come to you. Then, think about how you would add pictures to create something unique and representative of you. Envision yourself being an artist opening the door to all kinds of possibilities by creating an interesting collage of your goals and dreams. After making your creation, look at it several times a day to stay focused on the prize!

*   *   *   *   *

If you are more motivated by words than images, do not think a vision board or collage is something you cannot create. Carolyn Hartfield, a participant in one of my vision board classes, made a beautiful board of mostly words and phrases. You can see it and Linda's creative collages at JGSBook.com (under JGS Club) and then select "Vision Boards, Books & Collages."

You can also make your vision portable by creating a vision book or using movement and music to produce a vision video. Monica Smith, EDS, teacher and the head of the Science Department at Champion Elementary School in Daytona, Florida, has created both of these. I asked her to tell us about her approaches to making and using them.

Monica: I have been creating vision books for many years. I actually call them my CANI books – CANI standing for Constant And Never-ending Improvement. I heard Tony Robbins use the term years ago, and I love it.

The process of creating a CANI book is very easy. You need:

- Magazines
- Scissors
- Glue
- Card Stock
- Pencil or pen
- 3 ring binder (your size of choice)
- White or colored paper (the size of the 3-ring binder)

- Protective sheet covers (optional)

- Photos of yourself (optional, but makes the book more personal)

When I create a CANI book for clients, I set it up as a template. There are seven sections, each representing different key areas of life.

1. Family and Friends

2. Finances

3. Spiritual

4. Health

5. Education

6. Recreation

7. Workplace or business

Following each section, I place blank paper for pictures and goals. Next is the journal area. I find it helpful to write in here every day about what I did to get closer to achieving my goals and what I will do tomorrow. There is no right or wrong way to write. It is just a daily practice of self-reflection.

Once I set up the books and give them to my clients, I encourage them to go through each section and paste pictures, words or phrases that inspire them. I remind everyone not to worry about the pictures making sense to other people. It is only important that the owner of the CANI book understands the significance of the images and words he or she has chosen.

I look at my CANI book at least twice a day. I begin my morning with a brisk 30-minute walk. After it, I sip a cup of hot green tea while I read my CANI book and listen to soft music containing subliminal messages about success. I also read through my CANI book before I go to sleep every night. There is a lot of research about how important it is to read or listen to something positive before sleeping. I believe that conditions the subconscious mind.

Donna: What successes have you achieved because of your book and your daily practices?

Monica: I have accomplished so many goals. The major ones are:

- Obtaining my master's degree in a year with a 4.0 GPA

- Getting a specialist degree in a year with a 4.0 GPA

- Receiving from my husband a three-karat diamond ring as a 10-year anniversary gift

- Being offered a teaching position at a school near my home

- Traveling to Europe for a predetermined price

I have achieved all of these things! In addition, I continue to update the goals section in my CANI book on a regular basis so my accomplishments will continue.

Donna: I understand you have started creating vision videos. What made you decide to do that?

Monica: The inspiration came from a short video I saw on the website for *The Secret*. I found it very interesting. But since I was not in the video, it was hard to see myself achieving the things shown. So I decided to create a video with my face, my desires, my goals, my affirmations and music that was uplifting to me. After making it, I realized it was too much work for me to view it regularly as a DVD. So I decided to put it on my iPod. That way, I easily carry it everywhere I go. I listen to it in the morning when I am taking my walk and after I read my CANI book. With a quick switch of the menu, I can view my vision video. I created my video in a software program called *ProShow Gold*. I am sure there are many others you can use. The key is to find one that is compatible with your mp3 player or iPod.

Donna: Do you use the book *and* video in your daily visioning routine?

Monica: Yes. After reading my CANI book, I watch my vision video. Then I spend 10 minutes in meditation. I try to see myself as if I have achieved my goals already. I even try to see myself in color and hear my own voice speaking about what I have accomplished. Since I carry my iPod with me everywhere, I take it out and watch my vision video as many times a day as possible. Sometimes, we get so caught up in our day-to-day activities that we don't realize how much down time we actually have. My son takes piano lessons, plays soccer and is involved in many activities. I spend many hours each week sitting and watching or listening to him play. If he is just practicing, not competing or performing, I use that time to read my CANI or watch my vision video. There is always time if you make the time.

Donna: How does someone decide whether to create the book or the video?

Monica: I think it depends on your lifestyle and your beliefs. I have a friend who is on the go and is not an early riser. She asked me to make a vision video for her because she wants something she can watch in just a few minutes. She is very busy, is late for everything, and does not believe she has time to review her goals every day.

The CANI book has a lot of details, so it takes a little longer to review. I spend about 15 – 20 minutes reading through my book. I believe very organized people can easily incorporate the CANI book into their daily routines.

Over the years, I have found putting pictures and words down in some form and then regularly reviewing them is the best way to stay focused on one's goals and achieve them.

*   *   *   *   *

You can see an example of a vision book at www.JGSBook.com (under JGS Club) and then select "Vision Boards & Collages."

At the end of one of my speeches, I was asked, "Does Oprah have a vision board?" I answered, "No. During one of her shows, I remember her saying she had never created one." I went on to explain I think of Oprah as being extremely disciplined and focused. And being that way, she would not need to make one to be as successful as she has become. Comments she made during an interview proved I was correct.

When Oprah was on *The Larry King Show*, she said, "I read *The Color Purple* and then went out and got books for everyone I know. I was obsessed about this story, obsessed about it. I ate, slept, and thought all the time about *The Color Purple*." She talked about how her "obsession" led to her being in the movie.

I see obsessed as being extremely focused. Many times, we are not obsessed about our goals and dreams; we are transitory. Today, we are interested in doing something, tomorrow we have moved on to something else. That is being unfocused, uncommitted, and unserious.

Early in my speaking career, I was told in order to be successful as a motivational speaker, I must make it my magnificent obsession. In other words, you must be extremely focused and committed to the endeavor. And that magnificent obsession does not just apply to being a speaker, it applies to any endeavor you want to pursue and achieve. A vision board, collage or book can help you get and maintain that extreme focus. Create one and see the results for yourself. On the next page is an exercise to get you started.

Just Get Serious® About Success

Chapter 7 Exercise

CREATING YOUR VISION

Your Vision Creation Blueprint

■ First, think about which one you want to create – a vision board, collage, or book. (You may want to review the details you just read).

- Decide what pictures would represent the things you want in life and draw them on the previous page. Don't focus on making perfect images since this is only a preliminary blueprint. If you cannot draw the pictures to your liking, then write a description of them (e.g. "a beautiful house by the lake"; "a navy LS 10 Lexus"; "masters degree"). Also, think about inspiring words or motivational quotes you want to use and jot them down as well.

After drawing your blueprint, you are ready to make your vision creation. Here are the steps:

- Schedule a personal appointment with yourself for working on your creation. Make it a time when you are least likely to be interrupted.

- Get all the necessary materials you will need in advance, including magazines and any personal photos. You may want to re-read the sections on the type of board you plan to make.

- Think about the atmosphere you want for working on your creation and then decide how to arrange everything for it. Let's imagine you desire relaxing ambiance – create it with soft jazz, inspiring spiritual/Christian music, or classic romantic songs; scented candles; and your preferred drink in a beautiful glass. If you want a more upbeat setting, have R&B/hip-hop, rock, Latin or country music playing; a colorful decorative bowl of delicious snacks on hand; and a pitcher of your most liked beverage available. These are just two examples. Consider what would make it a special time for you and create it.

- Make this project your personal priority. So keep your appointment with yourself. If something pressing comes up, then reschedule it. But plan to get it done within a week or so. Do not do what I did. I learned about vision boards while I was in college and did not create my first one until many years later.

- When the time comes for you to work on your creation, take a few minutes ahead of time to clear your mind, become relaxed, and put yourself into an optimistic mood

- Once you have finished, re-read the section on where to place your creation (see page 103).

- If you have any questions, please feel free to contact me at Donna@JustGetSerious.com. I have been making vision creations for years and would be happy to answer any questions you have.

Lastly, a vision board-making event is a great way to bring friends and family members together to talk about and focus on their goals and dreams in an exciting, creative, and motivating way. Why don't you consider having one? If you want details on how to plan and host such a get-together, please email me. I have been hosting annual events for years and would enjoy sharing what I know. Also, if you need a facilitator for your event, I am a Certified Vision Board Counselor and would enjoy helping you out any way I can.

Once you have completed your personal inventory (chapter 4), written your goals (chapter 6), and finished your vision creation, you can use the concepts, ideas, and insights in the rest of the book to move forward in your journey to success.

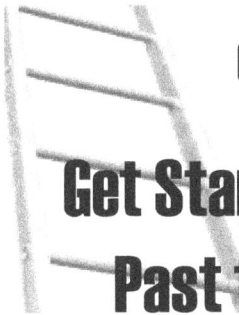

Chapter 8

Get Started and Move Past the D-Blocks

I want people like me to see that they shouldn't let a disability get in the way. I want to raise awareness – I want to turn my disability into ability.

Susan Boyle
Singer, "Britain's Got Talent" Semi-Finalist

Don't wait until everything is just right. It will never be perfect. There will always be challenges, obstacles, and less than perfect conditions. So what? Get started now.

Mark Victor Hansen – Author

GET STARTED

Often, we see obstacles in our way even before we get started. Sometimes, they are all in our minds. Sometimes they are enormous. Sometimes we are simply making a mountain out of a molehill. Whatever they are, others have moved forward despite them. Knowing that can inspire us to do likewise.

At 20 years old, Tiffara Steward is only 4 feet 6 inches tall and weighs 90 pounds. She is blind in one eye and partially deaf. Scoliosis left one of her legs shorter than the other, and some of her vertebrae are not fully developed. It would be understandable if she felt sorry for herself, lacked drive, and had no interest in sports. But those assumptions are far from true. Tiffara loves basketball and had an ambitious goal to be a college basketball player. Doing so meant overcoming what many people would call major obstacles. Yet she achieved her dream.

Tiffara is the shortest person to ever play college basketball, but don't let her height deceive you; she can definitely play the game. In 2009, she was the starting point guard and star player at Farmingdale State College in Long Island, New York. In a *USA Today* interview, her coach, Chris Mooney, said, "She's our best on-ball defender. She's a really good three-point shooter. She's a great example of what people can do when they're determined to do something they love. I really enjoy watching her. She's a very talented athlete." See a video about Steward and her incredible basketball abilities at www.JGSBook.com or www.YouTube.com.

> *You may be disappointed if you fail, but you are doomed if you don't try.*
>
> Beverly Sills
> Operatic Soprano

Because of Tiffara's determination and playing abilities, she was featured on CNN, where she talked about never thinking she could not do something. Tiffara said, "If you want to do it, go out and try it. If you try it and can't do it, try again. Maybe you will get it the next time." Sounds like great advice from a 20-year-old.

WHAT IS STOPPING YOU NOW?

Age?

The number of people overcoming age as an obstacle is endless, including the well known and the lesser known. Here are just three of them.

Growing up, Virginia Hudson wanted to be teacher. Instead, she got married at 20 years old and started a family. Twice divorced, she worked as a clerk and receptionist to raise her three sons and put them through college. Then at 53 years old, she decided to pursue her childhood dream. With her sons financially supporting her desire, Hudson enrolled at Miles College to major in education so she could become the teacher she always wanted to be.

Age is an issue of mind over matter. If you don't mind, it doesn't matter.

Mark Twain
Writer

Some people start on their dreams late in life, while others continue pursuing them. Award-winning actor and director Clint Eastwood is not letting age define him. At 79, Eastwood directed *Invictus*, a movie about Nelson Mandela and the South African rugby team. The film garnered Oscar nominations for Best Actor (Morgan Freeman) and Best Supporting Actor (Matt Damon), as well as a nomination for Best Director at the Golden Globes.

Being able to swim is the result of Ada Gibson's late-in-life decision. In an interview for NHS Choices, she said, "I used to be petrified of water. But when I reached 75, I said I wanted to do things I'd always been scared of doing." So she learned to swim. Gibson developed a passion for the water and says "I won't give up swimming until my body tells me it's time to stop." At 92, Gibson is still swimming.

Race? Gender? Other Traits?

The list of those overcoming barriers of race, gender, sexual orientation and other traits is long enough to inspire all of us to engage in the bold belief, hard work, and serious commitment we need to get started and keep moving. They include:

- President Barack Obama – the first African-American President of the United States

- Connie Chung – the first Asian American woman to anchor a major news program

- Mae Jemison – the first African-American woman in space

- Diane Crump – the first woman to ride in the Kentucky Derby

- Roberto Clemente – the first Latino inducted into the National Baseball Hall of Fame

- Annise Parker – first openly gay mayor of a major U.S. city (Houston)

- Cathy Hughes – the first African-American woman to own a radio and TV station

- Cynthia M. Trudell – the first woman to head a US car company (Saturn Corporation)

- Johnathan Lee Iverson – the first African American and youngest ringmaster for the Ringling Bros., Barnum & Bailey Circus

- Antonia Novello – the first Latino and first woman Surgeon General of the US

- E. Lynn Harris – the first openly gay African-American best-selling author

- Eugene Chung – the first Korean-American player in the National Football League

There are the hundreds of others on this growing list.

Money?

Quiana Childress was a homeless 16-year-old girl living in her car, going to school, and working two jobs just to survive. In May 2010, she graduated from University of Arkansas at Pine Bluff with plans to continue studying to become a doctor. First Lady Michelle Obama, the college's commencement speaker, said, "I want you to tell yourself that if Quiana Childress can go from being homeless to graduating with the highest GPA, not just in the biology department, but in the entire School of Arts and Sciences, then surely you can overcome whatever adversity you face in your own life."

> *Lack of money is no obstacle. Lack of an idea is an obstacle.*
>
> Ken Hakuta
> Creativity Advocate

Time?

Quiana Childress got up at 3:00 a.m. in the morning to study. Be willing to get up early.

Health Concerns?

Beginning in the sixth grade, Cindy Cannon's life was transformed into a continual series of hospital trips, daily pain, endless doctors' examinations, Valium and other painkilling medicines, and numerous misdiagnoses lasting for over 25 years. The medical nightmare finally ended when Cannon was correctly diagnosed at age 40 as having Idiopathic Eosinophilic Enteritis, a rare stomach disease. Despite her years of unimaginable pain, 15 operations, and continuous medical challenges, Cannon excelled in college and at every job she held. Cannon became the top staff recruiter for a national employment firm before starting her own business. Read her remarkable story in Chapter 20 – Be Inspired.

What is stopping you now?

Just Get Serious® by acting on the plans you wrote about in the exercise at the end of Chapter 6.

DEALING WITH THE THREE D-BLOCKS

As we move forward with our goals and plans, we will want to find ways to get past what I call, the three D-Blocks that can delay or diminish our progress. They are Doubts, Disruptions, and Distractions. Let's examine each of them.

1. Doubts

In Chapter 2, we looked at negative self-talk as keeping us at the level of unbelief and inaction. However, even after we begin to believe and move forward, that same negative self-talk can raise its ugly head again as doubt – doubt that we will be successful. There are two types:

Inner Doubt – This is a conversation that starts within your mind with thoughts like:

- I'm not smart enough

- I'm too old

- I don't have enough money

- I'm too young

- I'm a woman (or man), so I can't

- I don't know the right people

- I don't have enough time

On the TV show *Behind the Music*, Jennifer Lopez talked about how even though she had achieved great success as a dancer and actress, she was still plagued with doubts about being a singer. When recording her first album, *On The 6*, Lopez struggled with singing *Mahogany*, the classic by Diana Ross. She felt, "Who am I kidding? I can't match her." Album producer Corey Rooney helped Lopez overcome her doubts by telling her, "Don't worry about Diana Ross. Express this song as it feels and means to you." Those are great words for all of us to remember when we start to compare ourselves to others and have doubts about our abilities.

Each of us is unique. There is no one just like you. No one thinks just like you, speaks just like you, or behaves just like you. Value your individuality and move forward to express it in as many ways as possible. This is essential not just for ourselves, but for those around us because our doubts can prevent others from experiencing our unique gifts and talents.

In 2007, Paul Potts was one of the performers on *Britain's Got Talent,* the equivalent of *American Idol*. As he walked on stage for his first audition, the television audience saw a very shy, insecure man who visibly lacked confidence. When he announced to the three judges (including Simon Cowell, from *American Idol*) that he was going to sing opera, they looked at each other as if to say, "He must be kidding." When Potts opened his mouth to sing, it was an incredible moment because he sounded like Pavarotti, the world famous tenor.

> *You'll never do a whole lot unless you're brave enough to try.*
>
> Dolly Parton
> Singer & Actress

I have seen that audition. Although Potts is singing "Nessun Dorma" in Italian, a language I do not know, his performance brings me to tears every time I hear it because his voice is so beautiful. The transformation between what you see and what you hear is indescribable.

During his performance, the audience appeared frozen, as they were so captivated. Afterwards, they burst into wild applause and cheers. The judges looked stunned and amazed. Potts went on to win with a final performance that was breathtaking.

Despite his incredible singing abilities, Potts had extreme doubts about both his talent and entering the competition. On his website, he describes how he got the application online and then lost confidence to fill it out. "I got a ten pence piece out of my pocket and thought, 'Right, if it lands on heads I'm going to submit it, if it lands on tails I'm going to delete it.'" Obviously, it ended up heads.

Doubt can only be removed by action.

Johann Wolfgang von Goethe
Writer

You can watch Paul Potts' amazing performance at www.JGSBook.com (video page). After seeing it, I am sure you will understand why I feel it is critical for us to shift our negative self-talk to more positive. We can then move forward with our talents and people can benefit from them. My thoughts echo similar sentiments expressed by Marianne Williamson in her book, *A Return To Love: Reflections on the Principles of A Course in Miracles* - "Your playing small doesn't serve the world." I see "playing small" as having doubts and thinking so little of our talents that we do not develop and pursue them. Don't let that happen to you, move forward despite your uncertainties.

Many times, we see our doubtful thoughts as representing reality. Instead, let us see them as pessimistic ideas preventing us from taking action or limiting those we do take. As I stated earlier, one of the "cures" for negative inner dialogue is to increase your awareness of your doubts and shift to more thinking that is positive. Using the rubber band exercise described in the "Increase Your Awareness of Your Negativity" section of Chapter 2 can

What is being realistic costing you?

Marcia Wieder
Founder, Dream U

be a powerful way to help you do that. Other techniques are also listed in Chapter 2.

Outer Doubt – This initially starts outside of our minds. Someone makes a disapproving remark about us and we "swallow it, hook, line and sinker" by completely believing them. We don't question their opinions or judgment; we simply think they must be right. A few years ago, I was having lunch with another speaker, Sandy, and I asked her how she got started writing articles. I will always remember the story she told me.

Sandy had written her first article and was proudly showing it to a group of colleagues. One of them was a gentleman she greatly admired because of his reputation as an exceptional speaker and years in the business. He read the article and privately told Sandy he thought it was poorly written and not good at all. He suggested she focus on speaking and leave writing alone until later. Once home, she filed the article away, deciding not to pursue getting it published based on his comments. Several months later, a colleague who was helping Sandy organize her office came across the article, read it, and asked, "What magazines do you plan to submit this to?" Sandy replied, "Oh, I really meant to throw that out. It is not very good". Her colleague argued back, "It is great. I am sure magazines would be interested in it." With much reluctance, Sandy submitted the article to several magazines and one of them decided to publish it.

If that was the end of the story, it would be a good lesson for us, but it is not. Weeks later, the gentleman who dismissed the article as being poor saw Sandy and excitedly announced, "I see you got published in …" (he named the magazine) adding, "Great article. Congratulations! Keep up the good work."

I asked Sandy, "How could he say that after the discouraging remark he originally made? Do you think he was purposely misleading you?" She answered, "No, not at all. I think he forgot seeing the article and now was simply telling me what he thought of it today." Sandy and I went on to talk about how often we take someone's comments as being a fact (or as my grandmother would say being "the gospel") when it is merely their opinion at the time.

When confronted with negative remarks, we can decide to be like former Vice Presidential candidate Sarah Palin. During an interview with Barbara Walters about her book, *Going Rogue ... An American Life*, Barbara mentioned the disapproving comments being made about her. Walters said, "McCain's senior advisor said publicly and I quote, 'She would not be a winning candidate and if she was, the result would be catastrophic.'" Palin replied, "I guess I really disappointed him. Everyone is entitled to their opinion. I know the truth – I am fine with who I am and where I am." Regardless of one's political views, what a great way to handle criticism expressed by others. When necessary, consider using similar thinking for yourself.

2. Disruptions

There always seem to be individuals or events that prevent us from doing what we intended. They come in the telephone calls, emails verbal requests, emergencies, invitations, and so much more. Some are unavoidable. Some we welcome. Some are great opportunities. Some are a nuisance. Disruptions can be time-consuming; continuous disruptions can be draining.

Except for emergencies or activities that you immediately know you want to do or must do, it is best to think through requests for help, invitations to events, lunch engagements, favors for friends (or relatives) and other "opportunities." Not doing so has cost me time, money and energy doing things while my goals sat on a shelf. I have had out-of-town guests stay for weeks instead of days. I served on committees that ended up requiring much more time and work than I thought would be required. I

> *You must learn to say no when something is not right for you.*
>
> Leontyne Price
> Opera Singer

have spent hours on phone calls, at social activities, and helping others. In all these cases, my goals suffered from lack of attention.

How can we deal with the disruptions that come into our lives? First, decide if you definitely have an interest. If you do, then say "yes." However, in most cases it would be best to use what I call the D & D response, standing for *delay* your answer and get all the *details*.

Many times, we feel we must reply immediately. We say "yes" when we could have said, "I need to check my calendar" or "Let me get back to you." Whenever possible, one of the latter statements should be your first answer.

Next, ask about the details before making a decision. Imagine being in the checkout line of your favorite store. A store rep walks up to you and explains a great new product that appears to be very exciting. He hands it to you and asks, "Wouldn't you like to buy this?" What would be your first response? You'd probably ask, "How much does it cost?" You need to decide if you have enough money.

You need to make a similar decision when you are in "The Mall of Life" and someone asks, "Can you help me?" "Can you attend my party?" "Can you be President of our chapter?" "Will you buy a ticket to my group's luncheon?" Before you decide if you have the time, energy, and money, get as many details as possible. Ask questions like "How long will it take? Exactly how much money will it cost? What is required?"

Recently, my friend Tonya called me to complain about proofreading a document for a colleague. She had agreed to help when the friend asked if she could review it and make the needed changes. Tonya said she was shocked when she opened the email attachment and found a 50-page document! She assumed it would be about 8 – 10 pages. Don't let something similar happen to you. Get all the particulars.

Once you have the details, you can make a knowledgeable decision and say "yes" or use one of the four responses below.

"No" with limited information – There is a line I often hear that goes, "No is a complete sentence." I say, "No is a complete sentence most people cannot or will not say." Many of us, including me, at times, have a problem with being direct so we end up committing one of the cardinal sins of poor communication – TMI (Too Much Information). We just can't seem to resist the impulse to offer more details than necessary. We say, "No, I can't help you today because I have a meeting downtown at 2:00 and I am sure it will not be over until 5:30 and then I need to rush home to fix dinner." The person asking the favor can then respond with, "Well, if you can just come over at 11:00 or 11:30, you can leave by 1:00 to go to your meeting." Now that's a fine plan, if it is something you want to do. If not, you have to come up with another reason why you cannot help or you end up saying "OK" when you don't want to. But few of us are good at saying "No" or even "No, I cannot help."

The solution is "no" with limited information. Your response would be something like:

- No, I already have plans for Saturday.

- No, I will be studying for a test.

- No, I will be busy over the weekend.

- No, I am working on a project.

- No, that's not in my budget.

Now the person with the request has no information to use to try to rearrange your day so you can do what they are asking. Some people find it necessary to add, "I am sorry" between the "No" and the limited information. An apology is not necessary, but if it works better for you, use it. For example, "No, I'm sorry; I already have plans for Saturday."

A few years ago, I was taking a class on stress management where they introduced the idea that "plans" can be *anything* we are planning to do. Keep in mind that plans don't have to be just tasks, like going to the dentist, working on a theme paper, or attending a meeting. Plans can include staying home to relax, playing with the kids, or having some "me time" to unwind.

"Not now" or its equivalent – This is particularly useful for phone calls, activities, and requests demanding our immediate attention. When confronted with a situation that has you thinking "Not now!" consider saying:

- I can't talk with you now; let me call you back later.

- I will not be able to do that right now. But I can get to it tomorrow.

- Right now I can't help you. But I can later this evening. How's 7:00?

If you prefer using the affirmative first, think about replying:

- I will call you later on. Right now I can't talk.

- I can do that later today; now I must finish an important project.

- I can help you later this evening. Is 7:00 good for you?

"Maybe next time" – This reply is good for invitations, requests for donations, and for those interactions that are truly optional. It sounds like:

- Maybe next time I can go.

- Maybe next time I will be able to serve on your committee.

- Maybe during your next fundraiser, I will be able to contribute.

If you would like, you can add an opening phrase like, "thanks for (asking … inviting … or suggesting)" to your response. It now becomes "Thanks for inviting me to the banquet, maybe next time I can attend."

"Let's make a deal" – Here you discuss what you *can* do, which may be less or different from what was asked. You negotiate the terms of the request by offering, "I can help you for two hours rather than all afternoon;" "I can talk right now for about 15 minutes and call you later on;" "I would like to donate $25 to the organization instead of purchasing a $50 ticket for the banquet," or "I am willing to serve as Director of Events, but not Vice President".

As we use any of these strategies, it is important to understand that at some point we will need to ask for help, a favor, or assistance in some form or fashion. We will have an event that we want friends and colleagues to attend. We will have a cause we would like people to support. We will need someone to watch our children, work with us on a project, or help us get something accomplished personally or professionally. We will need favors in the form of someone's time, talents, money, or energy. As others are with you, we can become disruptions in people's lives. Do what you can to help, attend, and support others when possible; just make sure it is a definite decision you have made and not a knee-jerk response that you will regret later.

Last, when you are asking a favor or making a request, be willing to accept a "no", "yes", or a response that is less than what you wanted to hear. In the case of the latter two, be considerate of the person's time and be appreciative of their efforts. And don't forget the two words most of us learned as children – "please" and "thank you".

3. Distractions

Disruptions are interruptions by others that keep us from being focused. Let's think of distractions as our not staying focused on our goals and dreams. We have a lot of distractions in today's world. We are constantly bombarded by commercials. They are no longer just on TV; they are everywhere. We are liable to see commercials when we are in line in WalMart, when we are walking in the aisles of stores, or when we are pumping gas. No wonder we become distracted.

You can always find a distraction if you're looking for one.

Tom Kite
Golfer

How can we reduce some of the distractions? I tell my audiences to think about their goals and plans as American Express tells you to feel about their card – "Don't leave home without it." Have them with you at all times and review them regularly so they are in the forefront of your mind, and therefore, in the forefront of your actions.

I have written my goals on a bright pink index card. On the reverse side, I created a mini-vision board. I look at both of them several times a day. I have found doing that keeps me more focused.

Surprisingly, when I am doing a program on goal achievement and ask how many people have their goals with them, only about 5% of the hands go up. Think about what happens when you go into a grocery shop or supermarket without your shopping list. For most of us, we buy more than we intended because we are distracted by the "Buy One Get One Free" sales, the new products in brightly colored packages, and the items with the "Improved – Better Tasting" signs.

When we go into "The Mall of Life" without our goals, we can easily get distracted by everything else we could be doing with our time, money, and energy. We find ourselves making plans to go on vacation when that is not one of our goals. We end up going to the movies when we intended to spend time writing a marketing plan for a new endeavor or studying for an exam. We volunteer for a project when we already have too much to do.

> *Being distracted can be devastating.*
>
> Avi Greengart
> Research Specialist

This happens because we did not consult our goals before making a decision about what we should be doing or planning to do. This does not mean that we should not take vacations, go to the movies, and volunteer. Rather, whenever possible, they should be undertaken when directly or indirectly supporting our goals. For instance, spending time with my mother is one of my goals, so taking her to the movies fulfills one of my important goals. Helping friends is important to me so I will assist them after getting all the details about how I can be of value to them.

You now have several tips and strategies to deal with the three Ds: Doubt, Disruption, and Distraction. So don't let them delay or diminish your progress any longer. Get started … keep moving!

Just Get Serious® About Success
Chapter 8 Exercise

THE THREE D-BLOCKS

First, put a check next to the area(s) you plan to focus on.

Doubts

__ Inner Doubt – Monitor your negative thoughts and shift to more positive ones by using the rubber band exercise and other techniques in Chapter 2.

__ Outer Doubt – Maintain your belief by being confident and believing in yourself.

Disruptions

Unless you have an immediate interest, plan to manage requests with the D & D strategy (*delay* your response; get all the *details*) and then decide to say "yes" or, depending on the request, use one of the following:

__ "No" with limited information

__ "Not now" or its equivalent

__ "Maybe next time"

__ "Let's make a deal"

Distractions

Look at your goals at least three times a day by having them with you.

___ In your wallet / Day-Timer

___ On cell phone / computer

Second, focus on the areas checked and document your progress in your personal or Just Get Serious® Journal.

Chapter 9

MAKING SERIOUS PROGRESS

You don't make progress by standing on the sidelines, whimpering and complaining. You make progress by implementing ideas.
Shirley Chisholm – Congresswoman & Author

You have an obligation to face whatever life throws your way with confidence and with hope.
Michelle Obama – First Lady of the United States

You have gotten started on your goals and dreams – that's good. You have moved past the three D's of Doubts, Disruptions, and Distractions – that's great! Now, in order to make serious progress, you will want to focus on moving beyond your C-zone, becoming inversely paranoid, getting help, celebrating your progress, and bouncing back from losses you encounter. Let's examine each of these areas.

MOVE BEYOND YOUR C-ZONE

C stands for *comfort, confining, crippling,* and other similar words. These C-zones are those areas of our lives where we feel comfortable, relaxed, and not anxious. Now, no one wants to feel stressed out all the time. Nevertheless, these zones also *confine* our thoughts and behaviors to what is familiar. We become *complacent* and do not engage in new ways of thinking and functioning, and that can *cripple* our ability to achieve our goals. Many of us like to operate within our C-zones because then we do not have to meet new people, read new books, engage in new thinking, or do things in new ways. Newness can be taxing and frustrating and, many times, we prefer *convenience*. However, *convenience* is *costly*; the price is our inability to reach our utmost success.

> *Move out of your comfort zone. You can only grow if you are willing to feel awkward and uncomfortable when you try something new.*
>
> Brian Tracy – Author

There are many types of C-zones. Let's focus on three major ones: Mental, Functional, and Relational.

Mental C-zones are how we normally think about problems, situations, or ourselves. Sometimes these zones feature negative thinking. For that type, see Chapter 2. Let's examine another one – limited thinking.

Many times we don't realize how limited our thinking is until we meet someone who thinks bigger and bolder than we do. That is what happened when I met Jordan Dean. Jordan is a 12-year-old girl living in Atlanta who started a dog-sitting service when she was just 9-years-old. Now you may be wondering why someone so young would decide to go into business. It happened because Jordan, who loves pets, found out she had to be 16 to volunteer at her favorite animal shelter. Instead complaining about the unfairness of the rule, or just waiting around until she was old enough, she came up with the idea of dog sitting on the weekends (providing a temporary home for pets whose owners are away). Now, that's a creative solution! She started slowly with family friends and her business gradually grew. What was even more remarkable was the idea she thought of three years later. Her mother, Edith Dean, relayed to me the following story.

> *Think like a child – children have no limit to their thinking.*
>
> Paul Polak
> Social Entrepreneur

One night she told her daughter to turn off the computer and go to bed immediately because it was late. Jordan begged to stay up a bit longer, adding, "I'm waiting to hear back from Delta." Shocked at the mention of an airline, her mother asked, "Exactly what are you doing?" Jordan explained she was waiting for a reply to an idea she had just emailed Delta. When passengers bought a ticket, they would be asked if they had any dogs needing boarding while they were away. If they did, the airline would email them information about her. If they booked their pets, Delta would get a commission.

You are probably thinking, "Clever idea. But an airline would never partner with a 12-year-old girl." But Jordan did not think in such a limited way. She emailed them her idea and eventually got a reply back telling her to mail a letter to procurement. To date, she has not received a response. Jordan's way of thinking interested me so much I wrote about her inventiveness in my monthly newsletter and that resulted in her getting five new clients!

When I think about Jordan, I ask myself, "When was the last time I had a BIG out-of-the-box creative idea that I pursued?" Sadly, it has been a long time. How about you? Are you stuck in the land of routine thinking and not using your ingenuity?

I coined the acronym JDI (Jordan Dean Idea) to represent thinking big, bold, and brilliant. In other words, thinking like 9-to-12-year-old children who do not have the restrictive adult notions of "it would never work," "we tried that before," or "others will say we are crazy." In today's challenging and competitive times, creative thinking is necessary to stand out from others in order to get and keep a job, increase sales, and secure a contract. Also, such thinking can keep us excited about what we are doing because it is new or different.

> *Creative thinking empowers people by adding strength to their natural abilities.*
>
> Edward de Bono
> Creativity Expert

Below are seven ways to increase your creative thinking abilities and generate JDI. For others, read *The Power of Thinking Differently* by Javy Wong Galindo, MA, and *How to Get Ideas* by Jack Foster.

1. Believe in your creative genius. Belief is the foundation of all we think and do. Human beings have unlimited creative potential. The problem comes when we have creative sparks and we censor ourselves by thinking them impractical or illogical. Consider all the products and services people thought were absurd just a few years ago that today are an essential part of our everyday lives (cell phone, home computers). They exist because people believed in their ideas and pursued them.

2. Listen to classical music. Studies suggest music enhances creativity and learning. Research comparing the corpus callosum part of the brains of musicians and non-musicians point to a connection. It has been reported that when the famous physicist Albert Einstein had difficult problems to solve, he found playing music, particularly classical music, stimulated his thinking.

3. Brainstorm (by yourself or with others). Come up with a list of ideas without judging the value of them. Force yourself to disregard any tendency to think about the how's and why's, leaving those considerations to later. Once you have ideas, start to determine which ones to investigate. However, continue thinking creatively

so you do not select those that are more routine and familiar than others.

4. Change your atmosphere. Go to art galleries, decorative coffee shops, or other places that can have a strong visual impact on you. Looking at things you are not accustomed to seeing every day helps stimulate your thinking.

5. Move your body. Studies show that exercise stimulates the brain. Another benefit of movement is it allows you to get your mind off what you are currently focusing on and think differently.

6. Read science fiction or highly imaginative books or short stories to expose you to novel ideas. Get completely lost in the plots. Try to picture the settings and characters in your mind. There is magic in reading. It can take you to places you've never been before, and it can even return you to your childhood frame of mind, when you thought everything was possible.

7. Listen to and talk with creative people to stretch your thought process. This may mean expanding your circle of friends and colleagues. If you still have limited access to creative discussions, visit www.TED.com to watch videos of presentations involving new thinking. TED is an acronym for Technology, Entertainment, Design and the name of a foundation whose purpose is sharing innovative insights and ideas.

   TED's belief is "there is no greater force for changing the world than a powerful idea." I believe that is also true for changing our individual lives. So generate creative ideas and then act on some of them.

Functional C-zones are the ways of behaving that we are most comfortable with. Some of us like to be in the limelight, while others prefer being behind-the-scenes. Some of us take action immediately and others like to think, analyze, and plan before moving forward.

Some of us like to be in charge and give orders, while others prefer to be led and take direction. It is not a matter of which is right, wrong or better. Different goals require us to exhibit different traits, abilities, and behaviors to be successful. This may mean stepping outside of our C-zone and doing things differently.

To avoid the possibility of changing, people often will say, "I've been like this my entire life" or "I have always done things that way." The question for them is the same one Dr. Phil often asks the guests on his TV show: "And how's that working for you?" If it is not working very well or preventing you from reaching your goals, then it is time to step outside of your C-zone and change.

Over the years, I have found myself stuck in various functional C-zones. In many cases, I was forced outside of them because of people, projects, or life issues. In others, I literally pushed myself beyond them.

When I attended college as a part-time student, one of my goals was to have an academic experience rivaling that of full-time students. So I participated in as many extra-curricular activities as possible, something I normally would not have done. As a member of the Alpha Chi honor club, I was sitting in a meeting when the president announced, "Our upcoming convention will be in New Orleans. We are looking for a student to represent the chapter by going and giving a speech. Anyone interested?" Shocking myself, I raised my hand! As I was doing so, I was thinking, "Are you crazy? Have you gone insane?" Back then, just the thought of speaking to even a small group of three or four people made me

> *Most people are not really free. They are confined by the niche in the world that they carve out for themselves.*
>
> V. S. Naipaul – Writer

have sleepless nights, a queasy stomach, and become a "nervous wreck" for days.

Three months later, I was in New Orleans presenting in front of an audience of over 100 people. It was one of the most terrifying moments of my life. My speech was awful, filled with lots of "ums" and hesitancies. I was so nervous, I felt like I was going to pass out. But I survived, and by presenting, I had something impressive to put on my resume – I had represented the chapter of an honors organization at its national convention!

I did not let my C- zone hold me back. I suggest you do likewise. Your zone may have nothing to do with giving speeches, but whatever it is, step outside it and do the things necessary to help you reach your goals. I always say, "Get comfortable with being uncomfortable." You can do that by taking classes to prepare yourself, getting coaching, or venturing into areas that you usually dread on your own.

> *To the degree we're not living our dreams, our comfort zone has more control of us than we have over ourselves.*
>
> Peter McWilliams
> Author

Relational C-zones involve the kinds of people we are with most often. Are many of your friends just like you? Are most of them like each other? Having a limited range of relationships can keep us from having access to ideas and thinking unlike our own. Workplaces often force us to work with people who are different from us in age, race, gender, sexual orientation, abilities, and so on. We become comfortable with the various people on our team or in our department because we have to. However, seldom do most of us interact with new people until required to do so. Whenever I hold achievement programs for companies and organizations, I start out the session asking how many people are *purposely* sitting next to people they do not know. Rarely does anyone raise their hand.

I was like those seminar participants for years until I attended a Toastmasters International convention and attended a program presented by Dr. Terry Paulsen, a psychologist and expert on change. He asked an audience of over 200 people the same question I pose to my seminar attendees, "How many of you are *purposely* sitting next to people you do not know?" Only a few hands went up. Dr. Paulsen then asked us why we would sit next to people we knew already when there were people we did not know in the room. He said that showed our need to stay within our comfort zone.

Dr. Paulsen asked us to imagine how much more we would know if we had access to ideas unlike our own. New contacts can introduce us to fresh ways of thinking, approaching problems, and doing things. Hearing Dr. Paulsen's presentation was a life-changing moment for me. Since then, I have pushed myself to spend time with people I do not know at social gatherings, business meetings, and networking events. In the beginning, I felt awkward not being with my buddies. It has, however, resulted in my forming new relationships which opened doors of opportunity, introduced me to new ideas, and enriched my life in countless ways. I encourage you to broaden your circle of friends and colleagues; you too can experience the many benefits of doing so.

At a recent networking luncheon, my colleague Karen, and I decided to sit at different tables. While dining, I met two people who were interested in my speaking for their organizations. I am presently in contact with them about doing major programs in the coming months. Karen met Gail Margolies Reid, the author of *The Complete Idiot's Guide to Low-Cost Startups*. Within two months, they designed and co-presented a 90-minute seminar on "Publishing Your First Book." They are now working on a half-day workshop. Clearly, Karen and I would not have these opportunities if we sat together talking to each other.

> *Life begins at the end of your comfort zone.*
>
> Neale Donald Walsch
> Author

Bob Thiele, my business consultant at the Small Business Development Center and I are dissimilar in terms of gender, race, age, personality style, and business philosophies. During meetings with him, I am exposed to ideas I never would have considered. His suggestions have helped me stay in business and move forward. He offered ideas I would never receive from people who are more like me.

By moving beyond my relational C-zone, I have also made great new friends, been invited to wonderful events, and had incredible experiences. You can reap similar rewards.

If you are in the "world of work," you probably have immediate access to people who are different from you. That's great! Are you taking advantage of it? When was the last time you had lunch with someone you did not know? When have you asked for suggestions from employees who worked in different departments, had different jobs, or were in some way different from you?

> *Don't be afraid to expand yourself, to step out of your comfort zone. That's where the joy and the adventure lie.*
>
> Herbie Hancock
> Pianist & Composer

If you are an entrepreneur, when was the last time you spent time (on the phone or in person) developing relationships with new individuals you met at networking events, association meetings, or other functions who were unlike you? They can be a source of new ideas, new clients, and new friendships.

I know from experience meeting new people is not easy. We can end up trying to talk to people who are not open to interacting with us. Don't take it personally. If they seem standoffish, try again at a time that seems to be more convenient for them. If they are still not interested, approach other individuals. After all, it's a big world.

BECOME INVERSELY PARANOID

The term "paranoid" means believing everyone is out to *harm* you. Being inverse paranoid means believing everyone is out to *help* you. People who consistently practice the latter achieve remarkable success because of it.

One such individual is Paul J. Meyer, a top producing salesperson who founded the Success Motivation Institute, which has sold over $3 billion of resources in over 60 counties. In an interview, Meyer said the key to his success is believing "that everyone in the world is out to help me do whatever I want to do. I think everyone wants to be my partner; everyone wants to be my customer ... He not only wants to buy, he wants to be my friend." Now, that's inverse paranoia in action!

> *I've always been the opposite of paranoid. I operate as if everyone is part of a plot to enhance my well-being.*
>
> Stan Dale
> Transactional Analyst

Like Meyer, I have practiced the concept. I used it as a way to boost my confidence temporarily. I would walk into meetings thinking the people viewed me as a valuable team member or great presenter because of my past successes. When I thought that way, I found people were more receptive to my ideas, opinions, and proposals.

The difference between Meyer and me is I would think of concrete reasons why people felt highly of me. He always thinks that way, regardless of what he has or has not achieved. The other difference is I would sporadically practice the concept while he would do it all the time. No wonder he was able to produce tremendous successes in his life.

In his book, *The Success Principles*, Jack Canfield writes that his mentor, W. Clement Stone, was also considered an inverse paranoid. He said Stone influenced him to think similarly. Doing so led to Canfield's many successes, including the bestselling *Chicken Soup* book series.

As you encounter people in the future, gauge your immediate "knee-jerk" reaction. Do you find yourself thinking they do not like you, would not hire you or do business with you? If so, I suggest you QYA (Question Your Assumptions) by asking yourself why you think that. Do you have valid reasons, or are you imagining their feelings based on your predisposition. In the past, I have found myself assuming individuals disliked or were uninterested in me because they were not overly friendly or appeared to be more excited to talk with others. Through later conversation with them, I found out they were tired, shy around strangers, or thought I was not eager to interact with them. The same thing may be happening to you. Give people the benefit of the doubt. Practice inverse paranoia by constantly thinking, "They want to help me," "They like me," or "They want to do business with me." You can then see for yourself the results that kind of attitude produces.

GET HELP

If you read the previous chapter and are thinking, "Now Donna is suggesting I become a 'disruption' to someone's day or plans," you are right. Remember I wrote, "At some point, we will need favors in the form of someone's time, talents, or money." Achieving some of our goals, especially the ambitious ones, will depend on our getting help.

In her book *Mayday*, M. Nora Klaver states, "Asking for help is a universally dreaded endeavor. We often choose instead to continue on alone, struggling valiantly and often unnecessarily with day-to-day burdens or even with crises, convinced asking for help would exact

> *You've got to ask! Asking is, in my opinion, the world's most powerful and neglected secret to success and happiness.*
>
> Percy Ross – Businessman

an emotional price too high to bear." Does that sound like you or individuals you know? Why do many of us avoid seeking assistance? The reasons include:

- Being afraid we will hear "no"

- Not wanting anyone to know we need help

- Having been taught not to ask for help

- Not wanting a lecture about not asking earlier or hearing any comments that make us feel inferior

- Believing the problem will solve itself

Instead of focusing on our fears or reasons, let's realize that asking shows we are serious about our goals and dreams. It lets people know despite the obstacles, our embarrassment, or lack of knowledge or resources, we seriously believe in ourselves and what we want to accomplish.

That kind of belief compelled Michael Johnson to ask for assistance to achieve his dream of being the first man to win gold medals for both the 200-meter and 400-meter races during the same Olympics. Prior to the 1996 games, Johnson formally petitioned the International Amateur Athletic Federation (IAAF) to reschedule the dates for the 200-meter race and 400-meter race so he would have a day's rest between the two events. His request was granted. He won both races and the rest is Olympic history. Johnson was willing to ask for help to achieve his dream. Are you willing to do that?

Are you asking for enough help? If not, start doing so more often. Below are seven tips to keep in mind.

1. Select people who are knowledgeable about the subject and who would be in a position to assist or advise you.

2. Decide what you will say in advance. Plan to be as specific and concise as possible.

3. The more important the request, the more time you should take to think through everything.

4. Pick an appropriate time to talk with the individual. If necessary, schedule an appointment at his or her convenience.

5. Be polite, enthusiastic, confident, but not demanding.

6. If he or she agrees to help you, don't take the assistance for granted. Be thankful and communicate your gratitude.

7. If the person says no, don't take it personally. Thank him for considering your request. Find out if he can suggest other people you can approach and continue asking until you find someone who can help you.

CELEBRATE YOUR SMALL AND LARGE SUCCESSES

Success is a series of small accomplishments leading to slightly larger ones, which result in huge achievements. Overlooking our small successes may make us feel like we are not making any progress. Then we can become discouraged and eventually stop trying all together. Acknowledging and celebrating our progress will help us stay focused, positive, excited, and moving forward.

Getting together with friends can be a great way to celebrate. Therefore, plan to do so. But if you find that others are not readily available, do not become disheartened.

My mother is my biggest cheerleader. After my first major speech, I excitedly called her to suggest that we go out to celebrate my success. She already had plans for that evening. The following day, I was busy working on a project. The next day she had an appointment. We went back and forth like this several times trying to find a day that would be good for both of us. I remember thinking, "If I am having a difficult time trying to make plans with my mother, who is busy at 80 years of age, I cannot expect to easily get together with my contemporaries."

> *Even the smallest victory is never to be taken for granted. Each victory must be applauded.*
>
> Audre Lorde
> Poet

If others are available, make plans and have fun with them. If they are not, don't take it personally, and don't miss the opportunity to celebrate. Instead, do something by yourself or purchase something for yourself. Consider going to your favorite restaurant, getting a massage at a spa, or buying an inexpensive (or expensive) item you have always wanted. Whatever you do, mentally stamp on it "Congratulations!" Keep in mind – ABC – Always Be Celebrating.

BOUNCE BACK FROM YOUR LOSSES

Eventually it is liable to happen. You don't win …. You don't get selected … Your hard work is not viewed highly by others … Your best laid and executed plans do not succeed. What do you do?

I just knew I was going to be the winner …

For 18 months, I had worked on a first-of-a-kind analytical process to gain additional shelf space for Nice 'n Easy and other brands. It included test stores, before and after consumer sales analysis, a pre- vs. post evaluation and other analytical methods. My approach had not been used before for hair color. My manager and others were excited about it. I was even asked to present my concept at a national sales meeting. So you can imagine my shock when I heard the "Category Manager of the Year Award goes to" and the name that followed was not mine. I could not believe it. Even several of my close colleagues mentioned how stunned they were that I had not won.

> *Keep swinging. Whether I was in a slump or feeling badly, the only thing to do was keep swinging.*
>
> Hank Aaron
> Baseball Player

I just knew they were going to choose me …

My speech was really funny. I spent endless hours practicing. I went to various Toastmasters clubs and gave the speech to get suggestions about how I could improve it. I usually finished the speech in 7 minutes and 20 seconds. So during the statewide contest I was certain I had cleared the time requirement of 7 ½ minutes with 10 seconds to spare. When I did not hear my name announced for 3rd or 2nd place, I felt I had nailed it. I even smiled with anticipation. When I heard "the winner of this year's humorous speech contest is …" my smile quickly faded because my name was not called.

What do you do when you don't come in first, or even second place, don't get the job you interviewed for, don't receive the promotion you think you deserved, or don't get your prospect's acceptance of the new product you presented? Should you give up?

When confronted with a losing situation, whether it's work-related, business or personal, ask yourself, "What's preventing me from reaching my goal – a temporary stumbling block or a permanent one? You get to decide which one it is. Just like stubbing your toe on the corner of a cabinet or getting your hand stuck in a car door, stumbling blocks can hurt. But you can overcome them and here is how:

> *Being defeated is often a temporary condition. Giving up is what makes it permanent.*
>
> Marilyn vos Savant
> Columnist & Playwright

1. Do not mistake losing with being a loser. Losing is a temporary event which we can conquer. Being a loser is a permanent state and we should not think of ourselves in that way.

2. Stay positive. Avoid slipping into negative self-talk by thinking, "I will never win," "I'm not smart enough," "I'm too old to be trying" or other similar thoughts. Replace such feelings with positive ones like, "I've got what it takes," "I will try harder" or "I'll be better prepared next time." Constructive thinking propels us to take further action.

3. Ask yourself, "What could I have done differently?" and "What did I learn?" These are key questions because there is always something we can change. By honestly looking for ways to improve, we will be on our way to getting better results next time. Keep in mind the quote, "When you lose, don't lose the lesson."

4. Take the appropriate action. After you have decided what you want to do differently, move forward to make those things happen the next time.

5. Get positive support. We must associate with encouraging, helpful people. Avoid the naysayers and their dim outlook on your prospects. If you cannot avoid them completely, at least limit what you tell them.

6. Rely on your spiritual beliefs. Use prayer, faith, meditation, or whatever your practice may be. Engage in them fully. During challenging times, our beliefs can make all the difference in creating a better outcome in the future. So do not forget about them.

7. Celebrate your *efforts* to stay excited. Embody the quote by Sir Winston Churchill, "Success is going from failure to failure without losing enthusiasm."

Now, try again! Go on another job interview, apply for another promotion, and make more calls to potential clients. Whatever your goal is, go for it with more knowledge, better preparation, additional skills, and/or greater faith than the last time.

In the previous story about not receiving the category manager award, I decided to let more people know about my project. I became a one-person P.R. team for the work I was doing by sharing my strategies with other analysts. I also talked to my manager about what I needed to do differently and then followed his advice. The next year I asked him in advance if he thought I should be considered for the award and he did. I also checked to make sure the paperwork was submitted on time. That year, I won!

> *It's fine to celebrate success, but it is more important to heed the lessons of failure.*
>
> Bill Gates
> Co-Founder, Microsoft

In the case of the humorous speech contest, I realized I might have exceeded the time limit (there is no way to know since those details are not released). I decided that would never be a possibility again. The next competition I entered was the International Speech

Contest. I presented a story about being a cheerleader. I opened and closed my story by throwing into the air bright red pom-poms, matching my red jacket. It was quite exciting and I was sure I had a winning speech. Most importantly, I was ending it with 25 seconds remaining – perfect! I won the club, area, and district contests. At the next level, I competed against other speakers who were more creative than I was and I lost for a second time at the statewide contest. But that will not stop me from entering again.

> *Don't be discouraged. It's often the last key in the bunch that opens the lock.*
>
> Anonymous

If you succeed on your next attempt, have a celebration – you deserve it! If you fall short of your goal, ask yourself, "Do I still want to achieve this?" If the answer is, "yes" see steps 1 – 7 and start anew.

If you are hesitant about trying again, keep in mind that most people do not succeed right away, but positivity and persistence pay off.

Picture this … people noticing the great job you do and always giving you lots of praise. Now imagine being nominated year-after-year for an award that represents excellence in your field and you never win it. At what point would you become discouraged? How many years would it take you to feel unappreciated by the losses? When would you get so annoyed that you start doing less than your best? Would it be three years? Five years? 10 years? 15 years? How about 18 years? That's how many years Susan Lucci was nominated and did not win an Emmy for her role as Erika Kane on the daytime drama, *All My Children*.

First nominated in 1978, Lucci still had not won the coveted Emmy by the mid-1990s. By then, I believe many of us would have been upset and embarrassed because of the losses. Feeling humiliated, we may have stopped attending the events. Maybe we would have stopped working as hard as we had in the past. However, we always have a choice. Lucci made the decision to take her losses in good spirits, appearing on *Saturday Night Live* in a skit about her trying to win a game show and constantly losing. She was even in a TV commercial which made fun of all her losses. Upon her 19th nomination, Lucci finally won! Her persistence, commitment to doing great work and positive attitude finally paid off.

> *It's not that I'm so smart, it's just that I stay with problems longer.*
>
> Albert Einstein
> Physicist

Need even more encouragement? If overcoming 18 losses is not enough to convince you, consider what some top authors have endured. Their stories of continuing despite the losses are endless.

- Stephen King received 30 rejections of his book, *Carrie*, before finding a publisher. It became a best-seller and was made into a hit movie.

- J. K. Rowling's *Harry Potter and the Sorcerer's Stone* was rejected by, at least, eight publishers before being accepted by Bloomsbury in London. This novel launched one of the most successful series of books and movies.

- Jack Canfield and Mark Victor Hansen received over 140 rejection letters before finding a publisher for their first *Chicken Soup for the Soul*, which became one of the most successful book series ever.

- Alex Haley's *Roots, the Saga of an American Family* was rejected over 200 times. It was eventually published by Dell and became a best-seller and 12-hour television special.

- William Saroyan, playwright and author, received thousands of rejection letters for his various works before his first story was published. His best-known work is *The Time of Your Life,* a play that received a Pulitzer Prize and was made into a movie.

All these authors and thousands of others decided to reject the rejections again and again.

Still need encouragement?

I suggest you find your own favorite comeback story and focus on it for inspiration. There are literally thousands of them. You can look in the field of what interests you most. Use the Internet to find the stories and get all the details. Or maybe you have friends, family members, business or workplace colleagues whose comebacks inspire and motivate you. If so, talk to them so you can get direct encouragement to continue your pursuit despite your loss.

One of my favorite stories is about Tyler Perry. Before the success of his movies, like *The Diary of a Mad Black Woman* and *Madea's Family Reunion*, Perry was a homeless man living on the streets of New Orleans. Having been abused as a child, he had many painful memories. As a healing catharsis, he wrote letters to himself about daily activities and past experiences. He turned the writings into a play, *I Know I've Been Changed.*

In 1992, Perry moved to Atlanta and used his entire life's savings to finance the play. Only a handful of people came out to see it. Again, he found himself homeless, sleeping in his car or sleazy motels. Still, he held on to his dream. He revised the script and continued seeking performance opportunities. His perseverance paid off when, in 1998, *I Know I've Been Changed* had a short run at a local theatre. This time, the play was a big success and it was moved to Atlanta's prominent Fox Theatre. This was the beginning of Tyler's rise to super stardom as a writer, producer, and actor. Tyler was #25 on Forbes Magazine's list of the Top 100 Celebrities for 2010. On that list are six directors/producers.

> *If at first you don't succeed, get a bigger hammer.*
>
> Al Lewis
> Actor

Perry ranks number three, following James Cameron and Steven Spielberg. Now you can see why he is my favorite comeback story!

Do you have the serious persistence of Susan Lucci, Tyler Perry, the individual in your favorite comeback story, the hundreds of authors who received rejection letters and the thousands of other individuals who decided that losing would not define them or stop them? If you do, then keep at it until you get what you want.

> *You're obligated to keep trying to do the best you can every day.*
>
> Marian Wright Edelman
> Children's Advocate

If you decide you don't have that type of determination, or life issues are truly preventing you from continuing onward as planned, either adjust your goal or replace it. Find a new one that you can be passionate about and pursue it with all the commitment and enthusiasm you can muster. Your utmost success depends on your doing so.

Just Get Serious® About Success

Chapter 9 Exercise

MAKING SERIOUS PROGRESS

First, put a check next to the area(s) you plan to focus in order to make serious progress.

___ Moving beyond your C-Zone

   ___ Mental

   ___ Functional

   ___ Relational

___ Becoming inversely paranoid

___ Getting help

___ Celebrating your progress

___ Overcoming loses

Second, write below what you will do in the area(s) checked.

_____

_____

_____

_____

_____

_____

Third, get started and document your progress in your personal or Just Get Serious® Journal.

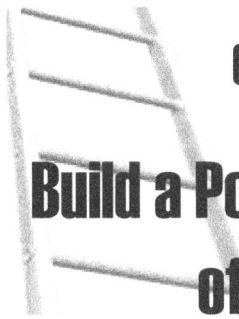

Chapter 10

Build a Positive Network of Support

In order to meet the challenge,
you have to have that support.

Jackie Joyner-Kersee
Olympic Athlete

Surround yourself with people
who take their work seriously

Colin Powell
Former Secretary of State

Personal relationships are the fertile soil
from which all advancement, all success,
all achievement in real life grows.

Ben Stein
Writer & Lawyer

One of my biggest lessons in life was learning I cannot achieve success by my efforts alone. I heard the author of *Click: the Ten Truths to Building Extraordinary Relationships*, George Fraser say, "All of life is about working with and through other people. There is no success you can obtain, sustain, or maintain on your own, by yourself or in a vacuum."

FORMAL SUPPORT

It is important to be aware of the formal support systems we can seek out or be invited to participate in. Some are paid services, while others are not. Some feature a one-on-one relationship while others are group-based. There are five main types of formal support: mentors, mastermind groups, coaches, advisors, and accountability partners. All of them are applicable to professional, entrepreneurial, and personal endeavors. Let's look at each one.

> *Mentoring is a brain to pick, an ear to listen, and a push in the right direction.*
>
> John C. Crosby
> Politician

Mentors are individuals who help you achieve your goals. Most of the time, they are more experienced than you are in your field. Both parties have their responsibilities in this relationship. The mentors bring a willingness to share their expertise, ideas, and direction. The mentees bring their openness, commitment, and willingness to do what is required. The timeframe can be open-ended or defined for a set period.

The Harvard Mentoring Project promotes the value of mentoring. See their website www.WhoMentoredYou.org for stories about people who attribute their success to mentors who helped them. Among the individuals are:

- Michael Lee-Chin, Chairman of National Commercial Bank in Jamaica, philanthropist, and businessman, mentored by Warren Buffett, investor and philanthropist.

- Marian Wright Edelman, founder and president of the Children's Defense Fund mentored by Howard Zinn, her history professor at Spelman College.

- Maya Angelou, writer, historian, actress, and civil rights activist, mentored by Mrs. Bertha Flowers, a family friend and teacher

(She is the subject of Angelou's book, *Mrs. Flowers: A Moment of Friendship*.)

- Kenneth Cole, footwear and clothing designer, mentored by his father.

- Kathie Lee Gifford, TV show host, actor, and singer, mentored by Barbara Walters, journalist, TV reporter and show host.

From this list, you can see mentors come in many different forms, including parents, teachers, industry experts, business people, and financial investors. Their assistance can be invaluable. During his acceptance speech for Artist of the Year at the American Music Awards in 2010, Justin Bieber thanked Usher for being his mentor and creating opportunities that led to him receiving the coveted award. That's the impact mentors can have.

> *Mentor: Someone whose hindsight can become your foresight.*
>
> Anonymous

Three of my mentors are Les Brown, Rene Godefroy, and Keith L. Brown. All are dynamic motivational speakers. Each of them taught me about the various aspects of the speaking and training profession, including marketing, negotiating, and using technology.

If you are a speaker, business owner, entrepreneur, or solopreneur (one-person business), consider getting a mentor. You can check with those who are most experienced in your field. Visit business-oriented websites like www.FastCompany.com for details on mentoring. Also, see if any corporations in your area are sponsoring mentoring programs. In the past, AT&T supported a mentoring initiative by pairing new women business owners with experienced AT&T women suppliers who shared their knowledge with their protégés (also known as mentees). Other companies have also sponsored similar programs.

Many professional and trade organizations provide mentoring for their members. The Georgia chapter of the National Speakers Association (NSA), for example, offers a program each year, running anywhere from 4 months to 12 months, depending on the format and the coordinator. I participated in several and found them extremely helpful. Check with your organizations to see what may be available to you.

A majority of major employers have mentoring groups where an employee is paired with a more experienced employee who offers expertise, advice and direction. See if your workplace offers such a program and consider participating.

Mastermind Groups are two or more individuals at a similar level in their careers or businesses who meet in person, via the Internet, or by phone to support each other's efforts. They share their knowledge, suggestions, and advice. The concept is described in the 1937 classic, *Think and Grow Rich* by Napoleon Hill. He explained it was "the coordination of knowledge and effort, in a spirit of harmony, between two or more people for the attainment of a definite purpose." Hill felt strongly that "no two minds ever come together without creating a third, invisible intangible force, which may be likened to a third mind." In other words, two fully functioning and contributing minds are better than one.

Early in my business, my involvement with a speakers mastermind group was beneficial for me. I have maintained contact with several of the members. If you are not in a group, plan to find one that is a good fit for you. If there isn't one available for you to join, then consider starting a group with one or more colleagues. You can find "how to" specifics at www.TheSuccessAlliance.com or use Google to find other resources.

Coaches are experts at getting people to make progress on their goals and dreams.

■ General Coaches may work one-on-one or the process can be group-based. Most paid coaches offer a complimentary initial session to familiarize you with their approach. You can ask friends and colleagues for referrals or check the Internet. You can also visit www.JustGetSerious.com for details about my program.

- Skill Specific Coaches are people with the necessary expertise in a specific field. Most of their services are provided for a fee. I am a member of the Les Brown coaching program. His direction has been invaluable to me in my development as a speaker and trainer. There are coaches for every field including acting, writing, sports, and music. All of them help individuals sharpen a specific skill set. As with general coaches, check

I absolutely believe that people, unless coached, never reach their maximum capabilities.

Bob Nardelli
Corporate Executive

the Internet and ask colleagues for recommendations.

Advisors are experts who provide direction and guidance. For entrepreneurs, I always recommend the Small Business Development Center (SBDC). They, along with other organizations, provide free advice on starting and growing a business. My current and past consultants have been extremely helpful to me in providing great ideas and direction. I also suggest the Small Business Administration (SBA) or the Service Core of Retired Executives (SCORE). You can check the Internet to see what is available in your specific area.

I've learned that the easiest way for me to grow as a person is to surround myself with people smarter than I am.

Andy Rooney
Commentator on 60 Minutes

Accountability Partners are two or more people in an arrangement in which they agree to support each other in pursuing their dreams by holding each other responsible for advancing on their plans. Many times, people fail to make significant progress because they do not have to report to anyone about what they have done.

The following example demonstrates how having someone to be

accountable to can result in extraordinary success. In the 1980s, three teenage boys, Sampson Davis, Rameck Hunt, and George Jenkins, made a promise to help each other fulfill their dreams to become doctors. They faced many obstacles because they were raised by single mothers and lived with the daily challenges of drugs and gangs on the streets of Newark, New Jersey. They overcame their challenges by holding each other responsible for

> *Count on having someone to be accountable to.*
>
> Donna Satchell

moving forward on their goals and giving each other support and encouragement. Today, Davis is an Emergency Medicine Physician at St. Michael's Medical Center in Newark; Hunt is a board certified internist at University Medical Center at Princeton; and Jenkins is an Assistant Professor of the Clinical Dentistry at Columbia University. You can read about their difficult, but successful, journey to become doctors in *The Pact: Three Young Men Make a Promise and Fulfill a Dream* or visit www.ThreeDoctorsFoundation.org.

You can use the same strategy that Davis, Hunt, and Jenkins used to reach your dreams. Find individuals who have similar goals and are serious about reaching them. Develop a plan to hold each other accountable for making progress and provide the emotional support needed to stay in the game.

INFORMAL SUPPORT

Beyond the formal support systems, let's look at the various roles positive people can play when it comes to our plans and desires.

> *80% of life's satisfaction comes from meaningful relationships.*
>
> Brian Tracey
> Author

In a formal support relationship, you ask someone to assist you in a specific way. You may even tell a friend or colleague, "Philip is my mentor" or "Joan has agreed to be my coach" or "Bob is my business advisor." People would understand the role and relationship. With informal support, people undertake the roles of Dream Maker, Loyal Supporter, or Cheerleader on their own and fulfill them through their words and actions. There are no set arrangements or specific time frames. The relationships are much more dynamic. Let's look at the three types.

Dream Makers are people who will have the greatest direct impact on your goals and dreams because they can open doors of opportunity for you. They can even break down some doors. What makes them so valuable is they are willing to help without your asking them and they may not be colleagues, friends or individuals you know very well. They see your talent, believe in your goals, and decide to make things happen for you. They could be hiring you, loaning you money, giving you a promotion, or helping with your business idea. We should plan to spend as much time as possible with these people sharing our plans and progress. We need to value and nurture these rare relationships.

As I said earlier, I attended college while working full-time as an administrative assistant at Clairol. During that time, I met Gerald Beddall, president of the company's U.S. operations, at a company luncheon. For the short time we were together, I talked about attending college in the evenings, my excellent grades, extra-curricular activities, and my desire to work in the marketing area. I wanted to leave a lasting impression

> *No matter what accomplishments you make, somebody helped you.*
>
> Althea Gibson
> Tennis Player

in his mind. When I graduated two years later, he offered me a position as an Assistant Product Manager in the Marketing Division. I was the first administrative support person to be presented with such an opportunity.

I still remember being in his office when he extended the offer. It was on a Friday afternoon. He briefly described the job and asked me to think about it over the weekend and give him an answer the following week. At that moment, I wanted to shout, "Yes, Yes, Yes … I will take it." For the previous six years, I had been going to college in the hopes of getting just such a position. Over the weekend, I kept nervously thinking he might change his mind. So I got to work extra early on Monday morning to call him and excitedly accept the job.

That promotion had a tremendous impact on my salary, my career, and my life. Now that I have told you what Mr. Beddall did for me, let me tell you what I did for him. I sent him a thank you note. I am embarrassed to say, "That's all!"

Two years later Mr. Beddall left Clairol to pursue other endeavors. On his last day at the company, I made an appointment to meet briefly with him. I thanked him again for the promotion and wished him well on his future plans. No gift, no good luck card and, even worse, no suggestion we stay in touch by exchanging addresses or phone numbers. What was I thinking? The problem was I was not thinking! How could I have such a valuable person in

Stay in touch with those that matter.

Anonymous

my life, who was also a president of a major company, and not plan to stay in contact with him? Today, I am still amazed at my ignorance at the time. Now, I know better so I would do better.

Here's another example of a Dream Maker. During an interview, the comedian Chris Rock explained how meeting Eddie Murphy led to his first movie role. The manager of the Comedy Strip introduced him to Murphy. Although Rock was not scheduled to perform that evening, Murphy asked the manager to give him a slot. Once on stage, he had the audience, including Murphy, laughing hysterically. Afterwards, Murphy told Rock he was flying to Los Angeles the following day to shoot a movie and asked if he would like to go. The next day, Rock was on a flight to L.A. It was his first time on a plane, first time in a hotel, and his first time in a movie. (He made a brief appearance as a parking valet in *Beverly Hills Cops II*). All those firsts happened because Murphy decided to give Rock an incredible opportunity. That is what Dream Makers do.

You may be asking yourself "How can I get someone to take such an interest in my goals and dreams?" Here are seven tips on how to make that happen.

1. Make your aspirations known to everyone because you never know who can help you. When I was at Clairol, everyone understood I wanted to work in the Marketing Department.

2. Find interesting ways to talk about what you are doing now that relates to what you want to do in the future. However, do not monopolize the conversation while discussing it. While talking with others at work about what they were doing, I made sure to bring up how great everything was going at college. If you are not comfortable talking about yourself, I suggest you read *Brag! The Art of Tooting Your Own Horn Without Blowing It*, by Peggy Klaus.

3. Know in advance what you would say or do if you had the opportunity to meet someone who can give you "that big break" or introduce you to someone who could.

4. As much as possible, be appropriately attired (for your profession or field) because you never know when you may meet your future Dream Maker. Understand you could run into the person in a non-business setting, so "appropriately attired" refers to the setting, not just the profession or field.

5. Because you do not know when you might bump into your Dream Maker or someone who knows him or her, it is always best to be respectful to everyone you meet. (See Chapter 13 – Respect People to Create a Foundation for Success.)

6. Be on top of your game (Remember, when given the chance, Chris Rock gave a great performance with Eddie Murphy in the audience).

7. Ask friends and colleagues to introduce you to individuals you believe could assist you. When meeting them, ask their advice or guidance, as appropriate. Also, offer to be of value to them. And remember to say "thank you" through a phone call or, better yet, with a hand-written note.

Once people have shown an interest in you or have helped in some way, stay in touch. Don't do what I did and lose contact with these valuable individuals. Instead, call, email, write or visit (whatever is most appropriate). Let them know about the progress you are making. If they have already assisted you, tell them what you are doing now and remind them that you are grateful for what they did for you.

Loyal Supporters are people who are constantly singing your praises and looking for ways to help you. Like Dream Makers, they are willing to help you by providing great ideas, advice, or assistance.

When I was as an administrative assistant at Clairol and received my Associate's Degree, one of the assistants, Roseann Paliotta, arranged a surprise luncheon for me. Everyone in my department was assembled in the conference room, including the assistants, the managers, directors, and the Vice President of our department. Even the President of the company's U.S. operations, Gerald Beddall was there. He knew about it because of Pat Alston, who worked for him. As she was leaving for the luncheon, she purposely told him where she was going in the hope he would attend,

> *It is amazingly empowering to have the support of a strong, motivated and inspirational group of people.*
>
> Susan Jeffers – Author

and he did. When I entered the conference room to give a document to my manager, I was completely stunned by the shouts of "Surprise! Surprise! Surprise!"

After recovering from the shock of it all, I spent time talking to everyone, including the company's president. This conversation led to the promotion I mentioned in the previous section.

Roseann and Pat were Loyal Supporters whose generosity and actions had a great impact on my life. But they were not the only ones who assisted me in my endeavors at college and work. There was Darrell, who had a journalism background, and volunteered to do the research for my theme papers. And there was Judi and Jerri, who I could always depend on to be there for me when I felt completely overwhelmed because of so many

Stay with friends who support you. Talk with them about how you are doing, how they are doing, and keep your practices together.

Mevlana Rumi – Philosopher

school and work projects. These individuals showed me how people, without important titles and large salaries, can help us achieve our goals. What they did for me defines how I treat people and reminds me to be a Loyal Supporter for others.

Consider the people in your life. Do you have Loyal Supporters? If you do, then value those relationships and find ways to assist them in their endeavors. If you do not, see the tips on the next few pages about how to develop supportive relationships.

Although Loyal Supporters are always on the lookout for ways to be of value to us, let's not fall into the trap of waiting for them to do something and never ask for help. If that is something you are not comfortable doing, see the Get Help section of Chapter 9.

Cheerleaders are individuals who have a sincere interest in your dreams. They want to help you; however, they may be too busy with their own responsibilities. Or they may not fully understand your goals so they don't always know how to assist you. But they are always there to cheer you on. Their encouragement can be a great boost to you.

My friend, Patricia, was a great Cheerleader for me. After my promotion into marketing, I often found myself upset and stressed-out because of the volume of work, the long hours, the constant changes, and never-ending learning. One afternoon I was in my office thinking, "What did I get myself into with this job? I wish I could just quit." Have you ever felt that way? If you have, you know what a miserable feeling it is. In my frustrated state, I opened a large envelope to find the current copy of Essence Magazine

Sometimes our light goes out but is blown into flame by another human being. Each of us owes deepest thanks to those who have rekindled this light.

Albert Schweitzer
Philosopher & Physician

with a note saying, "See page 76." I turned to the page and found an article about the top women in marketing with another note from Patricia saying, "One day you will be among these women." That message lifted my spirits, got me re-energized, and I never forgot it. The acts of kindness Cheerleaders provide can go a long way in encouraging us.

Actor and director Morgan Freeman has talked about the impact Cheerleaders had on his life during the early days of his career when things were not going well. "There were times I just said 'it is not going to work. I gotta eat. I gotta pay rent. I gotta do something else. This is not happening' and someone would always come along and give me something to eat or say 'You can't quit' … I was ready to start driving a cab, go work in somebody's office, anything … I would have quit many times, (but) there was always someone who (would say) 'you can do it.'" Because of these people, Freeman persevered and today he is a Golden Globe and Academy Award-winning actor. That's what Cheerleaders can do for us.

A word of encouragement during a failure is worth more than an hour of praise after a success.

William Saroyan
Writer

A Hand to Guide Me by Denzel Washington has 74 stories about people whose lives were greatly influenced by supportive individuals who helped them. They include well-known people like former President Jimmy Carter; comedian and actor, Whoopi Goldberg; former Secretary of State Colin Powell; and women's activist, Gloria Steinem. There are also lesser-known individuals like Dennis Smith, retired New York City firefighter; Martin Wong, neckwear designer; and David Boies, a trial attorney. I highly recommend this inspiring book. It helps us understand that no one achieves success on his or her own. Everyone needs supportive people to assist them. So plan to have them in your life and plan to be there for others.

Consider the people you are with most often, and ask yourself if you have any or enough Loyal Supporters and Cheerleaders. If not, think about ways to deepen the relationships with those you already know by:

- Spending more time with them (by phone or in person)

- Finding things to do together

- Doing the things I already mentioned like being of value, letting them know the progress you are making, and asking for help (Sometimes we don't have supportive people in our lives because we never asked for support).

Also, develop relationships with new people who could take an interest in your goals and dreams. Here are some ways to do that:

- First, meet new people.

  - Introduce yourself to individuals you do not know at the places you frequent on a regular basis (work, church, various meetings).

  - Join organizations focused on your field of endeavor. Also, consider recreation, faith-based, social, political, health, and personal development groups. For the last group, I suggest Toastmasters International. Although their focus is helping individuals improve their public speaking and leadership skills, you meet interesting and supportive people at chapter meetings. For information visit www.Toastmasters.org.

- o Take on a more active role in the organizations where you currently have membership.

- o Purposely sit next to and socialize with new people when attending networking events with friends and colleagues. Separate from those you know to spend time with those you don't know.

- o Volunteer at a hospital, homeless center, or nursing home.

- o Go to social gatherings where you are normally invited and usually do not attend.

- o Find places to go where you can meet people and where small talk would be acceptable (sporting events, art receptions, etc.)

- ■ When you meet new people, be genuinely interested in who they are and what they do. Find things you have in common, and tell them about yourself without dominating the conversation.

- ■ If there is mutual interest in getting to know each other better, make plans to get together in person, over the phone, or via email.

- ■ If you need to brush-up on your people skills to put your best foot forward or to understand how to engage others, I suggest *Breakthrough Networking – Building Relationships That Last* by Lillian D. Bjorseth and *Little Black Book of Connections 6.5: Assets for Networking Your Way to Rich Relationships* by Jeffrey Gitomer.

Next is a great exercise to help you understand the value of the relationships in your life.

Just Get Serious® About Success
Chapter 10 Exercise

THEIR VALUE – YOUR VALUE

In the past, people who completed this exercise have told me it was very insightful and caused them to look at their relationships from a different perspective. It has three separate parts, and I suggest you take your time considering the questions, your answers, and the implications of each one. Please feel free to share your thoughts about the exercise by emailing me at Donna@JustGetSerious.com.

	A	B	C	D	E	Total	Final Score
1-A _____							
1-B _____							
2-A _____							
2-B _____							
3-A _____							
3-B _____							
4-A _____							
4-B _____							
5-A _____							
5-B _____							

Part One

On all the rows ending with A (1-A, 2-A, 3-A, 4-A, 5-A), write the names of people you interact with most often – at work, in business, or personally. Place one name on each row. For now, leave blank the rows ending with B (i.e. 1-B, 2-B). We will handle the B lines in part two.

Next, for each person, answer the following questions using a scale of 1-10, with 1 being "rarely" and 10 being "always" and put the number in the column with the matching letter.

A. Do they encourage, motivate, and/or inspire you?

B. Do they offer to help you and then actually do so?

C. Do they have goals and dreams they are pursuing?
    (I have found that sometimes people without goals and dreams have a hard time understanding and being supportive of those who have them.)

D. Do they ask you specific questions about your goals, projects, or various endeavors you have told them about?
    (Are they paying attention to what you are saying? Are they really interested? Do they really care?)

E. Do they treat other people well (polite, kind, and helpful)?
    (Here, the range of "other people" is broad. It includes co-workers, friends, restaurant servers, and anyone else they have interacted with. Also, consider what you have observed them doing or saying first-hand. My experiences have taught me that how people treat others is a good indication of how they can eventually treat us.)

Once you have answered all five questions for each person, add up the numbers and put the sum in the column labeled "Total." Next, multiply the number by 2 and put the answer in the column labeled "Final Score." That number on each line will be between 10 and 100.

Part Two

On all the rows ending with B (1-B, 2-B, 3-B, 4-B, 5-B), write your name. For each row with your name, imagine you are the person whose name is immediately above yours and ask yourself how he or she would answer the same five questions (A – E) about you and put the number in the column with the matching letter. (This segment is known as "Now the shoe is on the other foot.")

Again, once you have answered the five questions, add up the numbers and put the sum in the column labeled "Total." Next, multiply the number by 2 and put the answer in the column labeled "Final Score." The number on each line will be between 10 and 100.

Part Three

Ask yourself, "What do these scores indicate about my relationships with other people and their relationships with me?" Here are some questions to consider:

- Do the scores surprise you?

- Are you satisfied with the scores?

- Do your friends and colleagues have higher or lower scores than you have? What does that indicate about your relationships?

- Are there changes you need to make to be a more valuable person to the individuals you have listed?

- Do you need to expand your network of friends and colleagues to have more supportive people in your life?

Depending on your answers, decide on what actions you want to take and then get started. Then write about your progress with people in your personal or Just Get Serious® journal.

You may be asking, "How about the negative people?" Don't worry, I have not forgotten about them. The next chapter is about the passive and pessimistic people in our lives.

Chapter 11

Reduce the Impact of Passive and Pessimistic People

*Not everyone is healthy enough to
have a front row seat in our lives.*
Susan Taylor – Writer & Editor

*No person is your friend (or kin) who demands
your silence, or denies your right to grow.*
Alice Walker – Writer

*We must not allow other people's limited
perceptions to define us.*
Virginia Satir – Psychotherapist

People are … kind, mean, friendly, reserved, helpful, uncooperative, generous, selfish, hateful, loving, concerned, disinterested, passionate, indifferent, rational, and illogical. The extremes people can go to help is inspiring. The extremes people can go to hurt is enraging. We feel we can't live with some people. For others, we can't live without them. My friend, Lynda, always says, "It takes all kinds of people to make a world," and she is right.

In the previous chapter, I showed the various types of positive people we need in our lives to be successful in reaching our goals. Now let's look at the types of passive and pessimistic people we may unfortunately encounter.

Passive People

Others have written much about the constructive impact of positive people in our lives and the damaging impact of negative people. But there is another group we often overlook – passive people. They are not negative, but being with them or expecting support from them can end up being a disappointment and a waste of time. Like positive people, there are three categories.

Disinterested

These individuals don't say negative things *or* positive things. They simply don't say anything. They don't ask about your goals or show any interest when you talk about what you are doing. They rarely ask questions beyond polite inquiries. I have had such people in my life. It took me a while to realize time spent with them was unproductive and left me feeling discouraged.

Do not try to make disinterested people interested in your plans and activities. I remember being upset when friends did not react to my "good news" with the enthusiasm I expected. I used to get frustrated when telling them about something challenging in my life, only to have them cut me off by talking about things they were doing.

I remember wanting to share with a friend the latest news about a board game I had created. As I excitedly talked about how a co-worker gave me the name of someone to contact at a major game manufacturer, the friend interrupted me to say how upset she was that, the night before, her boyfriend had not phoned her. I let her talk on and on until she was finished. Then she said something about calling me later to give me the rest of the story and walked away.

At that point, I realized not everyone we talk to is truly interested in our goals. Sometimes they are only politely listening. So when a thought pops into their minds, it is easy for them to interrupt us because they are not paying attention to what we are saying. That's why it is necessary to have Cheerleaders and Loyal Supporters eager to hear about our progress. It is also important to join organizations of people with similar goals who can have a mutual interest in what we are doing.

Non-Believers

These people do not believe you can achieve your goals, even if there is evidence to the contrary. There could be signs your plans just may work or things may turn in your favor, but they can't see it.

Award-winning comedian and actor Steve Martin had a Non-Believer in his life. An interviewer once asked one of Martin's close friends what his family was like. The friend said Martin's father was reserved and aloof when it came to his son's desire to be a comedian. He talked about being with the father at one of Martin's shows right before he made it big. The friend said the audience was in awe. They laughed uncontrollably at all of his jokes and applauded wildly at his zany antics. Steve received a standing ovation that seemed to last forever. Upon leaving the show, the

> *Convert the non-believers to believers by continuing to believe and proceed until you achieve.*
>
> Donna Satchell

father turned to Steve's friend and asked, "Do you think Steve's really got a chance in this business?" The friend was stunned. He probably wanted to reply with a one-word answer, "Obviously!"

Martin's father wrote a terrible review about Steve's first appearance on *Saturday Night Live*. It was for the newsletter of a professional association where he was the President. At a dinner celebration after the premiere of Martin's first movie, "The Jerk", a colleague commented to his father that he must be very proud of his son. He replied, "Well, he's no Charlie Chaplin."

Do you have similar people in your life who never see the progress you are making and don't believe you can achieve your goals? If so, do not allow their non-belief to undermine your belief in yourself. Limit your time, your contact, and your conversations with them. When it comes to family members, remember you did not choose them. But you can choose whether to let them affect your feelings about your chances for success.

You have to believe in yourself when no one does – that makes you a winner right there.

Venus Williams
Tennis Player

Quick Change Artists

These individuals are laughing with you today and tomorrow they are laughing at you. They cannot make up their minds about how they feel about your plans and progress. One day they are supportive about what you are doing and a few days (or even hours) later, they couldn't care less.

I witnessed such a person in action. Beverly, Julie, and I were having coffee at a Starbucks. Julie was excitedly telling us about her idea of forming a non-profit organization to help disadvantaged teenage boys get their lives back on track. Beverly and I agreed it sounded like a good idea and offered suggestions for her to consider. Beverly even told Julie she could put her in contact with a friend who had undertaken a similar project in California.

After an hour, Julie left. Beverly and I decided to stay and have more coffee. As we talked, Beverly said, "You know, Julie will never get that organization off the ground. She does not have the experience or the money needed. And what does she really know about kids? She is not a teacher or even a mother." When I started to disagree with her, Beverly cut me off and said, "I have known Julie for years, she always has outlandish dreams and none of them ever work."

That is the typical behavior of Quick Change Artists. Their lack of support and interest can also show up when they promise to help you in some way, but things always come up at the last minute to prevent them from assisting you. Many of their reasons are highly questionable. Don't count on them for any real support. Instead, limit the time you spend with them. And don't go out of your way to tell them anything because, within a short time, they will probably be talking disparagingly about you to others.

PESSIMISTIC PEOPLE

These people can have a harmful impact on your efforts in moving forward. Like the other two categories, they fall into three distinctive groups. How you interact with them depends on which one they are in.

Naysayers

These individuals will tell you all the external reasons why you cannot be a success. By external, I mean things that have nothing to do with you, per se. They talk about what the company, the organization, or various people have done or not done to prevent individuals who are your age, gender, nationality, race, or religion from getting a promotion, a raise, an award, or a loan. They will talk about how much education or experience you do not have. They will mention how those who are successful know the right people, have the right look, lots of talent or plenty of money. They like to cite example after example of others, like you, who have tried and have been unsuccessful. In bad or slow economic times, they will constantly talk about how it is not a good time to start a business, make a job move, expect a promotion or plan to buy a house.

> *Remember that no talent, no brains, no character, are required to set up in the fault-finding business.*
>
> Og Mandino – Author

When it comes to the remarks these people make, notice it is never about you. It is about the forces that will not allow you to achieve your desires. Their focus is usually on the past or current conditions. And while many times, they are telling the truth (even if it is *their* version of it), their remarks can be discouraging at best and demobilizing at worst if you listen.

Movie creator and director George Lucas said in an interview, "I decided to go to film school because I loved the idea of making movies. Everybody said it was a crazy thing to do because, in those days, nobody made it into the film business ... unless you were related to somebody. So everybody was thinking I was silly – 'You're never going to get a job.' But I wasn't moved by that. I set the goal of getting through film school." Initially, Lucas wanted to make documentaries; however, he changed his direction to entertainment films. That led to him eventually creating *Star Wars*, all of the Indiana Jones movies, and other successful films.

I believe every dream comes with at least one Naysayer attached to it as a way to test our belief in ourselves.

When I was going to college, I remember a co-worker named Emily saying, "The company will never promote you." She went on to tell me they have never promoted an administrative assistant into a management position in the Marketing Department (the area where I wanted to work). She talked about how others in positions similar to mine had gotten masters degrees and were never promoted. Because she had worked at the company longer than I had, Emily probably felt she was being helpful and telling me things I did not know. Notice she did not say anything about me personally. That's because everything was always about "them."

> *Never let what somebody else says distract you from your goals.*
>
> Michelle Obama
> First Lady of
> the United States

When I tell this story to a live audience I will often say, "If Emily was in the audience, sitting right here (pointing to a nearby seat), I doubt if she would think I am referring to her because I am not using her real name." I have found people love to express their opinions about any number of things, including our chances for success. Don't let their ideas influence you. Instead, turn a deaf ear to their remarks and continue moving forward.

In *Managing Workplace Negativity*, author Gary Topchik explains how many people do not realize they are being negative. He found when employees are confronted about their poor attitudes, about 80% do not see themselves that way at all. Sometimes, people do not understand how low-spirited and gloomy they are.

During one of my programs, I suggested that alerting negative people to their attitudes can sometimes lead to their changing. Months later, I was back at the same company and ran into Mary, who attended my previous class. She said after hearing me speak, she approached her aunt Carol about her negative outlook. Mary told Carol she could no longer spend time with her 10-year daughter unless she changed her attitude. Carol initially got upset and protested, saying she was not a negative person. But after that time whenever Mary saw Carol, she was less gossipy and mean-spirited. Mary could tell she was trying to be more pleasant.

> *Most negative people don't think they are.*
>
> Anonymous

You can consider letting the Naysayers in your life know how you feel. You may or may not have the same results as Mary did. But depending on the importance of the relationship and the individuals, it could be worth a try.

Criticizers

These people will ridicule you for pursuing your goals. After speaking with them, you feel like you were in a boxing match with Muhammad Ali. They have nothing good to say about what you are trying to do. They are famous for making fun of your efforts while you are in the presence of other people. They love to talk about your personal shortcomings as reasons why you cannot succeed. You don't have enough money or education or know the right people. You are too old or too young to pursue *that* dream.

> *Don't let anyone rob you of your curiosity, your creativity or your imagination*
>
> Mae Jemison
> Astronaut

You are not smart enough or don't have the talents or abilities.

Why would they say these unsupportive things? Many times, these people are unhappy with their own lives or feel insecure. Often, their disapproving remarks or "I was just joking" comments help them feel better about themselves at your expense.

Do not talk to these people about your dreams because you will probably end up feeling like a fool. It is best to discontinue a relationship with them or avoid them whenever possible. Sometimes they "come with the territory," being other people we enjoy being around or employees we have to work with. They can even be family members we live with or see at functions, like weddings, funerals, and holiday gatherings. In those cases, you cannot escape their presence. Therefore, limit your conversation, ignore their petty remarks, and, if necessary, take steps to build or maintain your level of belief (see Chapter 2) after being with them.

A while ago, I was having lunch with a group of colleagues. Alisa, who is always outspoken, asked me loudly, "So, how are you coming with that book?" I said everything was moving along well, it was just taking longer than I had anticipated. When she asked why, I started explaining I was interviewing several people and was planning to include their stories in the book. Before I could finish, she interrupted me and remarked in a sarcastic tone, "What you are writing – the great

American novel?" A couple of colleagues chuckled. I just smiled. The next time I saw Alisa and she asked about my book, I simply replied, "I am still working on it. So what have you been up to?" and she started talking about herself.

I mentioned Barrington Irving in Chapter 5. He is the youngest person and the first person of African descent (Jamaican) to fly solo around the world. After completing his historic event, he said to a CNN interviewer, "They told me I was too young. They told me I did not have enough money. They told me I don't have the experience. They told me I don't have the strength. I don't have the knowledge. Everyone told me what I could not do. They told me I would never come back home. But guess what?" He smiled broadly to indicate 'but I did.' See his interview at JGSBook.com (Videos).

> *Criticism is something we can avoid easily by saying nothing, doing nothing, and being nothing.*
>
> Aristotle
> Philosopher

Irving's remarks remind me of what was written about Fred Astaire, the award-winning dancer, actor and choreographer. Notes taken about his initial screen test included that he could not act, and could dance "a little." Those disappointing comments did not begin to reflect his talent and the impact he would have on the entertainment field. Because of his achievements, he is number five on the American Film Institute's list of the 50 greatest American screen legends.

Astaire's "low grades" are quite similar to what Fred Smith received for an assignment he did as a student at Yale University. His paper was about the idea of providing overnight delivery service. His professor found the concept interesting, but only gave it a C because he did not think it was feasible. Smith used his idea as the foundation

> *Any fool can criticize, condemn, and complain – and most fools do.*
>
> Dale Carnegie
> Writer & Lecturer

for FedEx, which he founded in 1971.

Irving, Astaire, and Smith are clearly not the only people to hear critical comments about their goals and ideas. The literary industry is notorious for its disapprovals and, sometimes, cruel opinions. The comments below were written by publishers to some authors about their submissions. Their works were later published by others and received national, and in some cases, international acclaim.

- James Baldwin's *Giovanni's Room* – "Hopelessly bad." Once his book was released, it was hailed by many as a masterpiece and is still read and studied today.

- *Lord of the Flies* by William Golding – "An uninteresting and absurd fantasy which was rubbish and dull." It was selected by *Time Magazine* as one of the 100 best English Language novels ever published.

- *Lolita* by Vladimir Nabokov – "... overwhelmingly nauseating ...the whole thing is an unsure cross between hideous reality and improbable fantasy. I recommend that it be buried under a stone for a thousand years." Although many felt *Lolita* should be censored, it is on *Time Magazine*'s list of the 100 Best English Language Novels.

- *Feel the Fear and Do It Anyhow* by Susan Jeffers, Ph.D. – "Lady Di could be bicycling nude down the street giving this book away and nobody would read it." Millions of copies of Jeffers' book were sold in over a hundred countries. It has been translated into 35 languages.

Getting written criticism is one thing, but what about verbal negative remarks? On *American Idol*, many contestants faced Simon Cowell's often blunt and cruel comments. So what does one do in such cases? We must be strong enough in our resolve and have enough confidence in our abilities to withstand the negative remarks thrown at us. This is not easy, particularly if you have your own doubts. Make sure you have overcome many of them before pursuing your dreams. If necessary, re-read Chapters 2 and 3 on strengthening self-belief.

Consider Jennifer Hudson. After one of her performances on *American Idol*, Cowell said to her and the audience, "*I think* you are out of your depth in this competition. *I think* there are better singers ... *I don't think* you are capable of doing anything better to have any chance of winning this competition."

What would you do if you heard similar words about you and your chances of success? Think carefully before saying, "It wouldn't bother me." We must have the determination to ignore the emotions that come with hearing such opinions. One thing I noticed in Simon's comments was he used the phrase "I think" three times. Upon hearing the comments from Criticizers, remember they are only saying what they "think." Remember how very wrong Cowell was.

> *Someone's opinion of you does not have to become your reality.*
>
> Les Brown
> Motivational Expert

Two years after losing to Fantasia Barrino on *Idol*, Hudson won numerous awards, including a Golden Globe and an Oscar for her role in her first movie, *Dream Girls*. During her appearance on *The Oprah Winfrey Show*, Cowell called in to say he was eating "massive doses of humble pie" and described her performance in the movie as "extraordinary."

Don't let Criticizers stop you or cause you to lose your enthusiasm. When necessary, make changes and do things differently. But continue moving forward as long as you believe in your dreams.

Dream Saboteurs

Of the three types of Pessimistic People, this one is the most dangerous to your goals, your dreams, and in some cases, even your life. Why?

Because they are purposely creating obstacles for you. They come in the form of mean-spirited co-workers, jealous friends, insecure managers, and others. Their intent is for you to fail. They spend hours plotting how to make that happen.

Why would they do such things? Your success threatens them. Maybe they think if you become successful, they will lose your friendship. Maybe they feel your success will reflect poorly on them because, in comparison, they appear to have done little or nothing. Maybe they feel your being successful shows they are not smart or talented. The list of reasons could go on and on and you may never know for sure. Do not talk to these people about yourself or your goals. The important thing is to get them out

> *A successful person is one who can lay a firm foundation with the bricks that others throw at him or her.*
>
> David Brinkley
> TV News Anchor

of your life now if possible before they wreak the havoc they are plotting. If for some reason you cannot, then at least avoid them as much as possible.

Early in my career, I worked for someone who turned out to be a Dream Saboteur. Robin had been my manager for about two years. There was nothing I could do to satisfy her during that time. There was always something wrong with everything I did, be it a major project or simple letter. When she resigned, I was glad to have the opportunity to work for someone else. On her last day at the company, her last task was to give me my performance review, which should have taken place weeks before. But she kept delaying it for various reasons.

At our final meeting, she said my performance over the past 12 months had gotten better in some areas and if I kept improving, I would be a good assistant. Despite my taking on additional responsibilities and projects, she still felt I was just average. Everyone I had ever worked for always thought my work was excellent, except her. At the end of our meeting, Robin told me to talk with human resources manager about the increase I would receive because she was too busy packing up her belongings to figure it out.

Imagine my shock when the HR manager said Robin had privately told her I was a terrible assistant and I did not deserve a raise. Since she was no longer at the company, I could not confront her and personally challenge her allegations. Robin claimed I was uncooperative, not willing to learn the new systems, and did not work as hard as everyone else. I was in tears. The question of "why" haunted me for a long time. The meeting with the HR manager ended with the decision to put me on probation and review my performance in six months!

What did I do? After much deliberation, I quit! Now, if you are in a similar situation, I am not saying you need do to that. I was prepared to quit. As I always advise people, put yourself in a financial situation where you are not forced to endure unfairness. Because of that philosophy, I had limited credit card debt; hence, resigning was an option and I took it. Plan to keep your financial house in order; so if you are ever in a similar situation, you can make the decisions that are best for you instead of your creditors.

Although there are Dream Saboteurs out there, most of us will never have to face what Carl Brashear dealt with. He threatened the Navy's status quo by being African-American and wanting to be a U.S. Navy Master Diver. What he endured because of those who plotted to sabotage his dream is enraging. There were evil threatening notes written to frighten him; physical confrontations to intimidate him; vile words spoken to humiliate him; test scores changed to dishearten him; despicable deeds committed to stop his progress; and hostile actions to endanger his life. Despite all these efforts to stop him, Brashear persevered and, in 1954, became America's first African-American U.S. Navy diver.

Then the unthinkable happened. In 1966, one of his legs was severely injured in an on-ship accident. Suffering unbelievable pain from persistent infections and gangrene, Brashear made the difficult decision to have his leg amputated so he could return to diving as soon as possible. In an interview, Brashear recalls the doctors laughing and saying "The fool's crazy! He doesn't have a snowball's chance in hell of staying in the Navy. And a diver? No way! Impossible!"

Brashear faced incredible opposition to becoming the Navy's first amputee diver. He went through months of excruciating physical therapy to strengthen his body to meet the reinstatement requirements. In April 1968, Brashear passed the harsh physical test, making him the first amputee restored to full service as a U.S. Navy diver. The movie *Men of Honor*, starring Cuba Gooding Jr. and Robert DeNiro, is about his determination, perseverance, and courage.

> *I ain't going to let nobody steal my dream.*
>
> Carl Brashear
> U.S. Navy Master Diver

Other people have faced Dream Saboteurs in their quest to achieve their dreams. The list is long, and includes individuals like Dr. Elizabeth Blackwell, the first woman doctor in the U.S; Jackie Robinson, first African-American Major League baseball player; Dolores Fernandez Huetra, founder of the United Farm Workers; of course, Martin Luther King Jr., and hundreds of others who decided they would not be stopped despite all the efforts of those who maliciously opposed them.

Do not let the pessimists deter you. For Naysayers and Criticizers, take one or more of the following actions:

1. Alert them to their negative attitudes. Remember the story about Mary and her family member.

2. Avoid them completely.

3. Ignore what they say.

4. Limit what you tell them

5. Continue to believe in yourself and your dream, and, if necessary, take steps to solidify your belief (see Chapter 3).

In the case of Dream Saboteurs:

1. Call upon an inner resolution that you will not be stopped.

2. Call upon your faith, beliefs and practices (prayer, meditation) to see you through.

3. If necessary, call upon the legal entities and other appropriate groups or individuals who can help you.

Two Last Thoughts about Passive and Pessimistic Individuals

First, remember that in Chapter 2 I mentioned Cheryl Richardson's concept about the hardware store. It applies here as well. Talking to passive and pessimistic people about our plans is "like going to the hardware store for milk." Think about it: How many times have you gone to the wrong people for something you wanted? If you are like me, the answer is "far too often." That brings me to a second thought: "Would we expect to find milk in a hardware store?" No. My third thought: If we go to the hardware store and don't find milk, is it the store's fault? No, of course it isn't. Yet, we get upset when people who are usually unsupportive make negative comments to us. Why continue going to them? Is it because we want them to change into encouraging and helpful people? That is not going to happen. Instead of spending time with them, it would be better to develop friendships with new people who can be supportive of us. See Chapter 10 for seven ways to do that.

Second point: As a child, I once told my grandmother about a new girl at school who was my new best friend. She smiled and asked me "How do you know that? You just met her." I was confused by the question, which seemed more like a statement, so I never answered her. Later, I understood what she meant when I was trying to avoid some of my new, so-called friends who had turned into fiends who lied, and intentionally hurt others' feelings.

Sometimes we bring people into the inner circle of our lives much too early. We start spending huge amounts of time with people we just met, sharing with them our innermost thoughts and dreams. But do we really know them yet? The answer is "probably not." It would be far better to take the time to find out about people before declaring them our friends. Also, observe the way they treat and talk about people. It can be a good indication of how they will eventually act with you.

> *Like plants, relationships take time to germinate and grow into the fullest they can be.*
>
> Cleopatra Bell
> Author

To conclude this chapter (and the previous one), there is an exercise on the following page that I have given participants attending my achievement programs over the years. They have found it to be an eye-opening exercise that was both valuable and insightful. If you have thoughts about the exercise that you would like to share with me, feel free to email me at Donna@JustGetSerious.com.

Just Get Serious® About Success

Chapter 11 Exercise

THEIR ROLE – YOUR ROLE

Please re-create the form below on a sheet of paper with about 10 rows. You can also download it from www.JGSBook.com.

First, think of the people you interact with most often at work, business, and personally. Write their names in column #1.

Question #1 Their Name?	Question #2 Their Role?	Question #3 Your Role?
1.		
2.		
3.		
4.		
5.		
6.		
7.		
8.		
9.		
10.		

Second, under column #2 write the role you see them playing in your life relative to your goals and dreams. The roles were described in this chapter and the previous one. They are:

- Positive
  - Dream Maker
  - Loyal Supporter
  - Cheerleader

- Passive
  - Disinterested
  - Non-Believer
  - Quick Change Artist

- Pessimistic
  - Naysayer
  - Criticizer
  - Dream Saboteur

Third, under column #3, write the role you play in their lives. Question #3 is very important, because many times we want lots of positive people in our lives, doing all kinds of great things to support us. Consider this: Are you willing to be that type of person for others? Based on the roles you listed on the chart, are there changes you need to make with people in your life?

In order to be successful, value and strengthen the relationships you have with Dream Makers, Loyal Supporters and Cheerleaders. Equally important, we should fulfill those roles for others. When was the last time you assisted individuals you know in meaningful ways – helping them get a job or promotion, sharing your experience, introducing them to people they need to meet, speaking highly of them to others, giving them well-intended advice, or simply offering words of encouragement?

Limit or discontinue your interaction with those who are Disinterested, Non-Believers, and Quick-Change Artists. We should also ask ourselves, when have we intentionally or unintentionally played such a role with others by being unconcerned about their endeavors, not thinking they could achieve their goals or been inconsistent in how we supported them?

When possible, totally avoid Naysayers and Criticizers or limit our contact with them. At the same time, stop disapproving of others' ideas and/or telling them all the reasons why their ideas will not work.

Plan to sever ties with those who are or have the potential to be Dream Saboteurs. Likewise, we must vow to never stand in the way of others or deliberately ruin their chances of success.

Reflect on the changes you will make in your relationships and then act upon your decisions so you can have more support and be more supportive.

Chapter 12

Drop the Drama ... Be a Positive Person

Dreams and drama don't mix well.

Donna Satchell

A bad attitude is like a flat tire. If you don't change it, you'll never go anywhere.

Anonymous

Your attitude determines whether you're living life or life's living you. Attitude determines whether you're on the way or in the way.

Keith Harrell – Speaker & Author

In the previous chapter, we explored how positive, passive, and pessimistic people can impact our goals and dreams. Now, let's look at ourselves. Are we always as positive as we can be? Or do we live in such a way that we could beat TNT's slogan of "We Know Drama" because we not only know it but also know how to create it? Some people create it with so much regularity they get bored and restless when there is no drama in their lives.

I am very concerned that "drama" is becoming fashionable. We have numerous reality shows where it is served to us on an ongoing basis. I see women wearing T-shirts with the slogan "I'm a drama queen." I have even seen them on young girls. A few years ago, my niece Imani and I were talking about her school life and she said, "Aunt Donna, there's just too much drama going on." At the time, she was only 14 years old! "Too much drama" at 14!

> *Your time is too precious to be sacrificed in wasted days combating the menial forces of hate, jealously, and envy.*
>
> Og Mandino – Author

When we have drama in our lives, we cannot fully work on our goals and dreams, because drama is distracting, draining, and destructive. People ask me, "What is the difference between being disappointed, upset, or angry, and drama?" I see the first three resulting from our reaction to a situation. I see drama as our deliberately creating the situation. How do we do that?

Regardless of the type of drama (men drama, work drama, family drama, etc.), we use three main ingredients in the recipe to create it.

1. "The Base." This is the event or situation triggering the drama. It is caused by our doing one or more of the following:

   - Having unrealistic expectations of people

   - Having realistic, but unstated expectations of others

   - Talking before thinking

   - Believing there's only one way

   - Playing the victim long after the "crime"

- Talking about things that are of no concern of ours

- Purposely disrespecting or embarrassing anyone

- Taking things personally – thinking everyone is out to hurt, embarrass, or deliberately offend us

- Making a mountain out of a mole hill or blowing things out of proportion

A little rudeness and disrespect can elevate a meaningless interaction to a battle of wills and add drama to an otherwise dull day.

Bill Watterson – Author

2. Next, we add the "seasoning or spices." This adds the flavor. Seasoning, or spices, is our reaction to the situation we have created.

   - If we want "hot" drama, we add high negative emotions (crying, shouting, screaming, slamming doors or the phone, throwing objects, storming out of the room or house, breaking things, punching walls, hitting, slapping, or other physical confrontations)

   - If we want "mild" drama, we add low negative emotions (sulking, not talking at all, withdrawing, lamenting)

3. The final and most important ingredient is "the preservative." This extends the shelf-life of the drama. You may have heard the expression, "Here today, gone tomorrow." With drama, it becomes "Here today, here tomorrow, here next week, next month, next year. It seems like it is always here." After all, we want to make sure it is around for a long time. So we do one or more of the following:

   - Always thinking about the situation

   - Constantly talking to everyone about what happened

   - Refusing to forgive the person

   - Not accepting responsibility for our role in the situation

When we are living in drama, we are stressed and drained. We are unfocused and uncommitted. If that sounds like you, then de-dramatize your life so you can have more time and energy to work on your dreams and goals. Like most recipes, without the right ingredients, you cannot create the item. Therefore, to remove drama, drop the "main ingredient(s)" by:

> *To see your drama clearly is to be liberated from it.*
>
> Ken Keyes
> Writer

- Having realistic expectations of others. Know what people are capable of doing, willing to do, or interested in doing. It is self-serving to want more from people than they can actually give.

- Telling others what you want them to do. Don't expect people to sit around being mind readers, trying to figure out what you are thinking or what you want.

- Understanding your way is not the only way to do something. Be open to others' creativity, knowledge and insights.

- Discussing only those things that actually concern you. Be truthful and avoid gossip and hearsay.

- Looking for ways to uplift others and make them feel comfortable in your presence.

- Thinking through what you are going to say, why you are planning to say it, and what the consequences may be.

- Relinquishing the victim role. Unfortunately, we have all been hurt, treated poorly, or injured. Learn from the experience so it does not happen again.

- Realizing it is not always about you. My colleague, Sarita Maybin often says, "If you knew how seldom it is about you, you would get depressed!" Life happens … things happen … many times people are not focused on you but on themselves. So decide to QTIP (Quit Taking It Personally).

- Seeing situations from a balanced perspective. Make sure your reactions are appropriate to the magnitude of the situation.

Maybe you are not creating the drama; maybe it is other people. I call them "dramatists." They always have something negative going on. They are either in trouble, heading for trouble, or just coming out of trouble. They are always criticizing, blaming, or just telling their side of the story. Dramatists constantly need us to help them out. Remember the famous quote from the movie *Jerry Maguire* – "You complete me." Well, when it comes to these people, that quote becomes "You deplete me." They are energy-drainers, time-robbers, and money-scavengers. With them in our lives, we cannot fully work on our plans and dreams because we are worn out after a meeting, phone conversation, email, or text message involving them.

> *People talk worse about people than they talk good about people because a lot of people like drama.*
>
> Hillary Duff
> Actress

Stop their negative influence by stopping, or at least drastically reducing, your contact with them. If they ask why you are being distant, tell them you are focusing on your plans and goals. If that's not possible because you work or live with them, then:

- Consciously limit your physical contact with them (avoid one-on-one social interactions).

- Talk with them as little as possible.

- Point out how they need to take personal responsibility for the situation they are describing to you (when you cannot avoid hearing about it).

- No longer loan them money, offer advice, or help them out of their self-created mess.

- Always have someplace to go or something to do when they call or stop by to visit.

If you are serious about your success, I suggest you focus on being positive instead of being drama-driven. Optimism is one of the greatest traits to have in life. While drama is draining, positivity is empowering. Research shows there are many health benefits to positivity, including living longer, having less illness, and being able to more quickly recover from sickness. Individuals in positive work environments accomplish more than those in negative ones. Also, optimistic people are less likely to be laid-off or fired. Positive people are better at solving problems and getting others to assist them. Being optimistic means others will enjoy talking to you, helping you, and being around you.

> *Attitudes are contagious. Are yours worth catching?*
>
> Dennis Mannering
> Speaker

In *How Full is Your Bucket?*, Tom Rath and Donald Clifton, Ph.D. cite numerous studies indicating the benefits of having a positive attitude. Here are some of their key findings:

- By increasing our positive emotions, we can add 10 years to our lives.

- On the average, positive people go to the doctor about once a year, while negative people go about 3.5 times a year.

- A study of Harvard graduates found that how they viewed negative situations in their lives today was a strong indication of their physical health years later. A positive mental attitude in early life leads to positive physical health in later life.

- The impact a positive attitude can have on others is enormous. In one study, nine out of ten people reported being more productive when they were working with positive people.

One could easily say, "It pays to be positive." However, it is one thing to say you are optimistic and another to be that way on a consistent basis. Below are my 15 ways to K.I.P. – Keep It Positive.

1. See the good in a given situation, or at least believe in the possibility of good eventually occurring.

When things do not go the way we would like, we often focus only on the present moment. For example, when being laid off from a job, people may only think about what they have lost (possibly benefits, great people to work with, a location close to home, prestigious title). Or they focus on the things they dislike about looking for another job (writing a resume, searching the Internet and applying for positions, being interviewed). However, the eventual outcome could be a job paying more money or doing more enjoyable or fulfilling work. If they only think about what they have lost or do not like, they will not be able to understand the good opportunities that could result. This lack of positive foresight can keep them stuck on being negative and not taking the actions they need to be productive in their job search.

> *No matter how dark things seem to be or actually are, raise your sights and see possibilities – always see them, for they're always there.*
>
> Norman Vincent Peale
> Minister & Author

2. Choose your words carefully before your speak.

Whenever possible, speak words of encouragement, support, and helpfulness. If you must say something that is less than positive about someone or a situation, think about the best words to use.

Many times, we are on automatic when it comes to how we talk. We all have natural tendencies. Some of us are very direct while others are indirect or even vague. Some of us naturally phrase what we say in a positive manner while others can be more negative. What we say affects the people whom we are talking to. It also affects how people will view us. For example, saying "She is stupid" creates a different impression about the person speaking than does saying, "She made a big mistake." Being conscious of what we are about to say can help us express things differently.

3. Think constructively about yourself.

What words do you use when talking to yourself about what you have done or are planning to do? Are they words like exciting, interesting, smart, attractive, or funny? Are they words more like boring, dumb, ugly, or slow? What we think affects how we function in life. Keep it positive on the inside so you have experiences that are more positive on the outside. This is true about how we think of others as well.

4. Limit how much time you think about or talk about an upsetting situation.

Unfortunately, unpleasant things do happen and may have to be dealt with. Thinking about how to address or solve a matter is time well spent. Thinking, "poor me," or "that's unfair" is not.

We probably all know someone like Carol. Two years ago, she was unjustly fired from her job. Even though she has gotten another job, she still finds a way to talk about the unfair situation that led to her firing. In a similar way, Gregory is always talking about his ex-girlfriend who treated him poorly three years ago. A professional colleague of mine, Millicent St. Claire, has a slogan that Carolyn, Gregory and others could benefit from practicing LIGMO: "Let It Go & Move On".

> *Wise men speak because they have something to say; fools because they have to say something.*
>
> Plato — Philosopher

5. Have a "solution approach" to an issue instead of a "problem approach."

When faced with a challenge, think of all the options you have to correct the situation. Many people do the opposite. They focus on the problems first in meetings, during lunchtime conversations, in emails, and phone calls. This is the opposite of what I was taught early in my working career.

I had a manager who insisted that if you wanted to talk to him about a problem, you also had to have a solution. It did not have to be the final solution, a good solution, or even a workable solution, but you had to have some type of solution or he didn't want to hear about the problem. That changed the way I thought and what I talked about to him. Eventually, I found myself thinking in a more-solution oriented way, even about personal issues. So understand the problem and focus on the solutions and see the difference it makes for you.

> *Impossible only means that you haven't found the solution yet.*
>
> Anonymous

6. Choose carefully to whom you talk about an upsetting situation.

When unpleasant things happen, we may need to talk to someone. Who we choose can make all the difference. Do not talk to people who can only point out the unfairness of the situation or how others are to blame. Talk to people who can help you brainstorm about corrective measures, encourage you to take appropriate actions or who can help you in some way, even if it is only to put things in their proper perspective or know that everything will work out in time.

7. Practice patience.

When we want something, we usually think about getting it within a short time. In our fast-paced world, we feel everything should happen immediately, which is not always the case. Impatience can easily lead us to become pessimistic because we are more concerned with what we do not have. Instead, let's believe we will eventually get what we desire through hard work and persistence.

> *Don't ever say it'll never happen or it'll never happen.*
>
> Mary J. Blige
> Performer

8.   Realize "the grass is not always greener."

This age-old sentiment still has real value today. Thinking other people have things which would make us happy can be the fast track to negativity. It is important to understand all of us have both a "foreground" as well as a "background" to our lives. The foreground is what everyone sees. The foreground is also the impression people have of what they think your life is like.

The background is what your life is really like. It is what people usually do not fully see or understand. This can be in line with what people think or very different from it. I believe most of the time our impressions about others are far from true. Our time would be better spent in the positive pursuit of creating what we want in our lives rather than comparing our lives with those of others.

I was watching a show about Julia Roberts, the award-winning actress. Regarding a specific period in her life, one of the individuals interviewed said, "It was not a good time to be Julia Roberts." That comment stayed in my mind as a reminder that even those we idolize or respect have times when things are not working well. Their determination to remain positive and persevere leads them to success.

9.   Have a learning approach to life.

When unpleasant things happen, we can become upset or

sad. However, if we concentrate on "What did I learn?" we can find value in many disappointments. Let's look at the previous example of being laid off. If the event came as a huge shock to us, maybe the lesson is to be more aware of what is happening in the company or industry so we are not taken aback in the future. Maybe we need to build a better network of business colleagues who can keep us apprised about what is going on. Maybe we need to ask ourselves if our attitudes and behavior caused us to be viewed as liabilities instead of assets so we were among those let go. Answers to these questions can help us do things differently in our next job.

10. Associate with positive people.

People's attitudes influence us. If you are around negative people, you become more like them. Whenever possible, be around optimistic individuals, and limit the time you spend with pessimistic people always seeing "doom and gloom." If you cannot completely avoid them (such as co-workers, managers, and family members), at least limit your interactions with them as much as possible.

It is not just attitudes that rub-off on us. It is also behaviors and ways of speaking. When I worked for an international consulting firm, my manager, Les Ware, lived in England. He came to New York only once a month, so we talked on the phone several times a day. After a few months of working with him, I found people I did not know would immediately ask me, "Where are you from?" Puzzled, I replied, "New York." They would then ask, "Did you ever live in Boston?" When I answered "No, never," they remarked, "You certainly sound like you did." After hearing this comment several times,

Tell me with whom you travel, and I'll tell you who you are.

Anonymous

I realized I had unintentionally picked up Ware's accent. (A Boston accent is similar to an English accent). The way I did that is the same way we pick up other behaviors and ways of thinking.

In Sidney Poitier's book, *A Measure of a Man*, he writes, "If you walk down the street and someone is with you, he'll adjust to your pace or you to his and you'll never be aware of it. There is no effort. It simply happens. And the same thing can happen with the rhythm of your life." So be aware of the people you associate with and ask yourself, "Am I becoming like them or are they becoming like me?" If you need to make changes in how often you interact with them, then do so.

11. Have an attitude of gratitude.

I have read countless personal development books. In all of them, the authors stress the importance of gratitude in being positive and becoming successful. Below are three ways to develop and maintain that all important attitude.

- Take time to write in a journal all the things you are grateful for in your life. Documenting them can help you see your life differently. Make it an activity you do on a regular basis. This practice serves two purposes: First, it can put you a more thankful frame of mind. Second, it gives you a diary of your thoughts to read when you are finding it difficult to feel positive and appreciative.

> *The hardest arithmetic to master is that which enables us to count our blessings.*
>
> Eric Hoffer
> Writer & Philosopher

- Create a gratitude box where you frequently add items which remind you of joy-filled times in your life. The objects you place in it can be cards, photos, letters, small souvenirs, and keepsakes. As with the journal, you can go through this box when you are facing life challenges and feeling unhappy. I created such a box. Whenever I look through the objects in it, I can easily remember times that were special to me and experiences for which I am immensely thankful.

- Practice "relative to what" thinking. I read about this concept in *Looking Out For #1* by Robert J. Ringer. He called it his "theory of relativity" (not to be confused with Dr. Albert Einstein's theory). Ringer felt we view many situations as being unfortunate until we think of them relative to circumstances that are more tragic. Once we see things from a different perspective, we are able to view the same events with a sense of gratitude. For example, let's consider breaking up with someone you loved or not getting a well-deserved promotion at work. Both of these are awful situations. Yet, when compared to finding out you or a loved one has a terminal illness, both of them seem minor. Such thinking is best expressed in the quote, "I once was distraught because I had no shoes, until I met a man who had no feet" (author unknown).

  "Relative to what" thinking was expressed during the aftermath of the 2010 Haiti earthquake. One of the survivors told a reporter, "There are things that were important yesterday that are not important today."

  For more ways to increase your gratefulness, I recommend the book *Attitudes of Gratitude* by M.J. Ryan. The author describes over 25 activities to achieve grateful thinking.

  Decide on a way to practice gratitude that works best for you. Do it on a continual basis and then watch your sense of thankfulness and appreciation increase immensely.

12. Don't let others rain on your parade.

We have already looked at ways to deal with the naysayers, criticizers and dream saboteurs in Chapter 11. However, there is another group of discouraging people - the rainmakers. You are feeling great because you got a promotion, a new job, or exciting news to share and here they come to "rain on your parade," "burst your bubble," or "steal your thrills." It is not overt, instead rather subtle but quite deliberate. It can be in the way they look at you or their attitude, words, or actions. Their objective is to make you feel uncomfortable or undeserving. We need to be alert to how they influence our positive thoughts and behaviors.

> *People only rain on your parade because they don't have their own.*
>
> Anonymous

We can find ourselves taking extreme measure to appease these people. I have heard stories from program participants like Ruth. She decided to become less vocal during meetings so people who opposed her promotion would not feel threatened by her.

Then there was Dana. He was hired for a position which staff members thought should have gone to their favorite co-worker. He decided to gain their acceptance by always staying out late with them during his employer's quarterly conferences, though he really wanted to be in his hotel room relaxing after the long day of meetings. Dana said many of their conversations over drinks made him uncomfortable, but he was attempting "get on their good side."

I have my own story. After my promotion to Assistant Product Manager, one of the managers took me out to lunch. While we were eating, he said, "Donna, you are a nice person." (Words following that type of opening are usually not good and it was true with what came next.) "But you will never really be accepted in this department because you used to be a secretary. It is not about who you are but who you used to be." He went on to say if I left the company and got marketing experience elsewhere and then came back, things would probably be different.

Shortly after that, one of my colleagues suggested I talk to a writer for the company's quarterly newsletter about how I graduated from college and then got promoted. After much hesitation on my part and much persuading on her part, I called the communications department and talked with Alex, one of the newsletter writers. He thought the story was a great idea. Remembering what the manager told me, I decided it might not be the best time for it. Alex asked me to call back whenever I was ready to do the interview.

Never dull your shine for somebody else.

Tyra Banks
Supermodel &
Media Mogul

Weeks later, the newsletter came out. As I read the articles, I thought, "My story deserves to be in this paper." The following day I called Alex. I was shocked when the person answering the phone told me he was no longer working there. I explained to her the reason for my call and that I was ready to schedule the interview. I was taken aback when she said, "Sounds interesting, but we already have our plans laid out for the year. I will think about it and get back to you." She never called or responded to my phone messages. Suffice it to say, the article was never published.

I was disappointed my story never appeared in the newsletter, but I gained a valuable life lesson – trying to appease people can cost you opportunities you may never get again.

If you have rainmakers in your life, I suggest stopping their meddlesome influence by maintaining your good disposition; knowing you deserve what you have received; being confident, yet approachable; continuing to work diligently; and becoming pleasant. Remember, their

I don't know the key to success, but the key to failure is trying to please everyone.

Bill Cosby
Comedian & Actor

objective is to make you feel uncomfortable or undeserving. When they realize they cannot ruffle your feathers, they eventually go away.

13. Listen to, read, or watch something inspiring and motivational every day.

There are endless books, e-newsletters, online radio shows, articles, audio programs, and seminars that can get you thinking more constructively. Decide which is best for you and make it one of your daily activities.

14. Don't keep all your eggs in one basket.

My grandmother often used the above phrase. In researching its origin, I found it is, for the most part, used to support the concept of diversity in financial investments. I had always thought it meant having several sources contributing to your sense of well-being and joy. I clearly recall a time when that was true of my life.

At the time, I was 1) getting outstanding performance reviews at work; 2) on the dean's list at college; 3) working on a board game and imagining it would be a big success like Trivial Pursuit; 4) dating a great guy who loved me; and 5) in excellent physical health. I clearly remember thinking I was living out what my grandmother meant. I had five baskets and if one of them broke, meaning something negative was happening (i.e. failed a test; got a poor review at work; my boyfriend and I had a disagreement) other things were going great and I could still be positive and happy.

I suggest you have various sources for your happiness so you can always feel good about something.

15. If you need to, please seek professional help.

If you find that you are always in a bad mood and cannot get over feeling miserable, then consider seeing a professional. If your employer has an Employee Assistance Plan (EAP), look into taking advantage of it. Consider talking with an advisor at your faith-based organization, or seeking the services of a professional counselor.

There will always be situations or people who give you reasons to be drama-driven or negative. Do not take the bait. Instead, stay positive. You will be happier and healthier for it.

Just Get Serious® About Success

Chapter 12 Exercise

DROP THE DRAMA – BE POSITIVE

1. Complete the chart below (if necessary re-read the chapter).

What suggestions from this chapter can I use to get or stay drama-free and positive?	How will I benefit from following these suggestions?*

2. *Now that you know the benefits, get started by taking action on what you have written today.

Chapter 13

Respect People to Create the Foundation for Success

A good deed here, a good deed there, a good thought here, a good comment there, all added up to my career in one way or another.
Sidney Poitier – Actor

Handle every interaction with every person as if you will have to spend the rest of your life with that person in a very small room.
Anonymous

Every human being, of whatever origin, of whatever station, deserves respect.
Ralph Waldo Emerson – Author

Whatever goals and dreams we are working to achieve, other people will play a role in our progress. Therefore, respecting individuals in our everyday lives is a key to our success. It makes no difference whether we interact with them often, seldom, or only once.

Despite its importance, research indicates respect is on the decline in the U.S. *The Status Report on Rudeness in America,* a nationwide study, found Americans feel "disrespect, lack of consideration, and rudeness are serious, pervasive problems affecting them on a personal, gut level." Key findings include:

- 79% believe the lack of respect and courtesy should be regarded as a serious national problem.

- 69% feel "I am less likely to be nice when I have to deal with someone who is very rude and impolite."

- 62% said witnessing rude and disrespectful behavior bothers them a lot.

- 52% feel the residue from disrespect lingers with them.

- 49% believe people will give better treatment to someone who is especially respectful and kind.

These results indicate our ability to respect other people is important for several reasons:

- People do their best work when they are respected. I know when I feel slighted, my initial reaction is to retaliate by becoming unhelpful and declining to contribute my ideas and opinions. However, because I know in the long run I will only be hurting myself, I temper my reaction. But not everyone is like me, so disrespect can easily lead to those important to our success doing less than their best.

> *Respect a man; he will do the more.*
>
> James Howell
> Writer

- Positive ramifications are always possible when we respect and value others. Have you ever been pleasant to someone and he or she did something extra for you because of your attitude?

214

Remember, nearly 50% of the people surveyed believe someone who is especially respectful and kind will be better treated by other people.

A friend of mine used to work for one of the major airlines. Since I always viewed him as somewhat aloof, I was shocked when he told me he would often upgrade to first class those passengers who were friendly and pleasant to him. Imagine having the unexpected opportunity to fly in spacious first class (at no additional cost) to an important appointment. Arriving relaxed and well rested could increase the likelihood of having a productive and successful meeting.

■ There can be negative consequences when people feel disrespected. This often happens when the disrespected person is in a subordinate position.

Remember, 69% of those surveyed felt "I am less likely to be nice when I have to deal with someone who is very rude and impolite."

The facilitator of a seminar I attended told an interesting story I will never forget. He was in New York's LaGuardia airport when his flight, along with most others, was cancelled because of a snowstorm. He was in line to be re-booked, and the man in front of him stepped forward for his turn to be served. When told he would be rescheduled for a flight leaving the following day, this passenger became irate. He screamed that this was unacceptable and stated he was a platinum level frequent flyer for the airline. (Note: this happened prior to 9/11. Today such behavior would not be tolerated.)

The passenger rudely demanded to speak to a supervisor. He continued

> *It matters not how much you know or can do if you cannot connect effectively with others with respect.*
>
> Jahi Muhammad
> Author & Lecturer

215

his ranting and raving. Finally, they put him on a flight leaving that evening. When the ticket agent handed him his ticket, he snatched it from her and angrily stormed away. As the bewildered and disrespected agent placed the irate passenger's luggage on the conveyor belt, the facilitator said he heard her say in a whisper to the employee next to her, "He might make it to Chicago tonight,

If you respect others, others will respect you.

Anonymous

but his bags won't." Certainly two wrongs don't make a right; but rudeness can make people do things they wouldn't ordinarily do in order to retaliate for the way they were treated.

Imagine arriving at your destination only to find that your luggage with important documents was still in the city you left. Something like that can happen when we disrespect people.

Additional thoughts on why respecting others is important:

- We may have to rely on or interact with someone we recently disrespected.

- Many people, including me, view those who disrespect others with low regard and are hesitant to hire, promote, or do business with them.

- For those of us with spiritual or religious beliefs, respecting others allows us to practice one of the main principles of many faiths and "to walk our talk."

- If we want to be valued, we need to value others. Through the Law of Karma and the Law of Reciprocity, what we give out comes back to us in various ways. In other words, much of what happens to us comes from what we do to and for others.

During my career, Karen, one of my managers, respected my abilities and helped me secure a position in the company's Atlanta office. After I relocated, we met when I was in New York City on a business trip. Karen told me she had given birth the year before and stayed home for a couple of months. Then the company offered her a part-time position similar to her last assignment as a senior product manager. This was something they usually did not do. Karen was very pleased with the job because it allowed her to do work she enjoyed and still spend time with her daughter.

Later that night, I realized that reciprocity was at work. Karen had helped me get a job in Atlanta, a place where I wanted to live. In return, she got a position that allowed her get what she wanted – more time at home with her family.

In *Choosing Civility*, the author P.M. Forni explains how being inattentive, speaking ill of others, not being inclusive, and other inconsiderate behaviors are commonly practiced by a majority of people. He feels, "The quality of our lives is about treating each other well in every situation. We are all the trustees of one another's happiness and well-being in life." I could not agree more. I use the phrases STOP and START to remind me how to treat others.

> *Treat others as you want them to treat you because what goes around comes around.*
>
> Anonymous

When my niece, Imani, was about 10 years old, I created a word game that we played often. It was making up acronyms (only a motivational speaker, like me, would create something like that and think it was fun!). We thought of several good ones, but one was especially worth remembering – STOP = Stop Treating Others Poorly. Poorly meaning being inconsiderate, selfish, and unhelpful.

STOP TREATING OTHERS POORLY

Donna Satchell & Imani Gay

To respect others, stop:

1. Forgetting to say "please" and "thank you" and other common courtesies.

2. Gossiping.

3. Being unkind.

4. Being unhelpful.

5. Acting superior.

6. Belittling others' ideas.

7. Disliking someone simply because others do.

8. Making fun of people different from you.

9. Withholding useful or valuable information from others.

10. Making "newcomers" feel like "outsiders."

11. Devaluing others' opinions and suggestions by not listening to them.

12. Refusing to share the credit with those who have helped or assisted you.

13. Withholding congratulatory comments or compliments from those who deserve them.

14. Monopolizing conversations by talking only about you and being uninterested in others.

15. Thinking and acting as if the "important people" (celebrities, wealthy individuals, or people in prominent positions) are the only ones who really matter.

16. Using the ideas of others and not giving them credit.

17. Being late and thinking it's OK for people to have to wait for you.

18. Refusing to say, "I'm sorry" or "I apologize" when you know you should.

19. Talking about things that were shared with you in confidence.

20. Telling jokes that may embarrass others.

21. Using words, tones, or gestures with anyone that would have gotten you reprimanded as a child.

To value people, do the opposite of these statements. For example, number 20 is "stop telling jokes that may embarrass others." So only use humor everyone would enjoy. Number 6 is "stop belittling others' ideas." Therefore, be interested in hearing everyone's thoughts.

You can also use the acronym START as a reminder of what to do.

START THINKING, APPRECIATING, RESPECTING, THANKING

Start – Begin now. You cannot afford to hold off on this concept.

Thinking – Most of us have heard the expression, "Think before you speak and act." Do we do it as much as possible?

How often do you think through what you are going to say? For important conversations, this is critical. Do you always express yourself in the most positive way possible? Could there be repercussions (positive or negative) because of what you are getting ready to say? Have you thought about them? These are some of the questions to ask so you don't end up with "your foot in your mouth." It also includes emails and texts.

The same approach applies to actions. Before doing something, ask yourself, "Why am I acting or reacting in this way? Am I behaving only in my own self-interest?" Are you thinking about both short-term and long-term consequences? Have you considered all your options? Have you chosen the best one, or are you operating on impulse?

Thinking through our words and our actions can prevent us from disrespecting others and short-circuiting our progress to success.

Appreciating – Value everyone, including people who are different than you in background, age, race, gender, or other traits. You can do this through words and actions which makes others feel included, listened to, and thought of as important members of your team, company, or organization. Also, enrich your life by being open to hearing peoples' experiences and understanding things from their point of view. Increase your knowledge and ways of thinking by being willing to listen to ideas and opinions that are unlike yours. The adage "If we always agree, one of us is not necessary," points to the importance of those with varying outlooks.

> *Respect is appreciation of the separateness of the other person, of the ways in which he or she is unique.*
>
> Annie Gottlieb
> Writer

In his book, *The Seven Habits for Highly Effective People*, Dr. Stephen Covey explains that many differences between people are based on their life experiences. He feels "the person who is truly effective has the humility and reverence to recognize his own perceptual limitations and to appreciate the rich resources available through interaction with the hearts and minds of other human beings. That person values the differences because those differences add to his knowledge, to his understanding of reality."

Respecting – Use the good manners most of us were taught as children. It is amazing how many people have forgotten the importance of etiquette. I gave a presentation to a group of 200 employees at a major company and talked of the importance of saying "please" and using "time of day" courtesies (like "good morning", "good evening"). People applauded loudly to show their agreement, and shouted comments like, "You're so right" … "Now that's the truth." … "I wish my manager was here to hear this" … "Please come to my office and tell that to my co-workers." I felt as if I were a minister making a profound statement in front of the congregation. The employees' reactions confirmed how much courteous behavior is missing in many places and just how important it is to people.

Thanking – Expressing gratitude shows people we appreciate their efforts. I was at a conference where a panel of women executives gave their insights on achieving success. Among them was Carol Tome, the Chief Financial Officer for Home Depot. She said the first thing she does when she arrives at her office is to write a thank you note to someone. She has been doing this for years. This struck me as a great way to let people know how much I appreciate them, so I started doing it. Along with cards, I also use emails and phone calls. I do whatever works best depending on the situation.

> *I learned that every day you should reach out and touch someone.*
>
> Maya Angelou
> Poet & Writer

Several months later, I decided to share Tome's idea with attendees in my programs and wanted to give her credit for it. However, by then I was not completely certain whether the advice came from her or another panelist. So I called Tome's office to verify she was the person. Her assistant confirmed I was right. She then added if the thank you note was for an employee who worked in one of the Home Depot corporate buildings, she (the assistant) would personally deliver it. Her assistant also said a couple of years ago Tome was responsible for a major project involving several hundred employees. When the project was completed, she wrote a thank you note to each of them. Yes, hundreds of employees received a personal handwritten note! That is how important Tome believes it is to say thank you.

> *Silent gratitude isn't much use to anyone.*
>
> Gladys B. Stern
> Author

Think about it. Do you say thank you enough? Do you say it to each person who has helped or assisted you in some way, both small and large? Make expressing thank you (via written note, email, text, or phone) a daily practice and watch how it changes your relationship with people you work with and live with.

Now, let's look in detail at five of the many ways to make people feel respected and valued.

1. Act in courteous ways.

As busy adults preoccupied with life's issues and concerns, we tend to forget to hold the door for others, talk to everyone in a courteous manner, and offer our seat to someone elderly, disabled, or pregnant. Such deeds can make a difference in our success.

I was on my way to an interview for a job I really wanted. As I walked into the reception area, I held door for the woman behind me. It is something I always do because I dislike letting the door slam in someone's face, even if he or she is a few feet away. While I was waiting for the interviewer, I decided to freshen my makeup in the

> *It's the image that lingers after you leave the room with which people do business. That's what people remember.*
>
> Susan Wranik
> Speech Pathologist

ladies room, where I saw the woman for whom I held the door. I complimented her on the hat she was wearing. She smiled and said thank you. As you have probably figured out already, that woman ended up being the interviewer. I wish you could have seen how her face lit up when she approached me in the reception area. Our short, but pleasant encounters meant our meeting started on very cordial note. And yes, I got the job!

I am not the only one who has had such an experience. Wanting to present a benefits program, Jackie Boards, owner of Hands-on Business, called a company asking the name of the best person to talk with. Brenda Johnson answered the phone and Boards assumed she was the receptionist. Boards, as always, was pleasant and upbeat and Johnson suggested he drop off the information. Upon visiting the office, he found out Johnson was actually the HR Coordinator and had direct contact with the Vice President of Benefits. Johnson took the initiative to set up Boards' initial meeting with the benefits department. She became a strong advocate for his program. Because of her efforts on his behalf, he won a contract involving over 200 employees.

You never know who can help you. Also, you never know who is answering phones so be engaging and talk professionally with everyone. This is particularly true today with so many companies downsizing and reorganizing. Many employees have dual roles and many managers do not have assistants to answer phones and respond to emails. Therefore, being pleasant, positive, and appreciative can make all the difference in the world.

In *The Power of Nice*, authors Linda Kaplan Thaler and Robin Koval reveal how they built The Kaplan-Thaler Group into a successful advertising firm by being nice. They write about how making everyone they encountered feel important and doing small acts of kindness was the foundation of their business. It paid off for them in securing contracts, achieving close to $1 billion in billings, and receiving CLIO Awards (international annual honors for advertising excellence).

Kaplan and Koval suggest we get into the habit of doing nice things for others so it becomes second nature and I agree with them.

2. Be helpful and of value.

Years ago, at a company social event, I struck up a conversation with Ed Rodriquez. As Manager of Fleet Administration, he coordinated everything connected with the company cars used by the sales force. At the time, I was an Administrative Assistant going to college in the evenings. During our initial conversation, Ed mentioned he had two daughters. Whenever I saw Ed, I would inquire about them. He would tell me stories about how well they were doing. As they were getting ready to graduate from high school, he inquired about the college I was attending. I brought in brochures and offered to talk with them about my experiences to help them make decisions about college.

In the meantime, I had accepted a sales analyst job in Atlanta. That meant I was going to be part of the sales force and would receive a company car. Ed was excited about helping me. When we met, Ed explained the car he selected for me had been driven for less than one year and was in excellent condition. He then reviewed all the rules about having the vehicle, and I gladly signed the required paperwork.

A few hours later, Ed called me and requested another meeting. I thought he could not get the car we discussed earlier. Since my current car was in need of major repairs, whatever he secured for me would be fine. Imagine my surprise when Ed proudly announced that since I have been so kind and helpful, he had arranged for me to get a new car! He had already spoken with my new manager and got everything approved. I only had to make my choice from several models and colors. I was thrilled. It had been years since I had a new car! And I got one because of my genuine desire to help.

3. Be interested instead of interesting.

In the time-tested classic, *How to Win Friends & Influence People*,

Dale Carnegie advises, "Talk in terms of the other person's interests. You can make more friends in two months by becoming more interested in other people than you can in two years by trying to get people interested in you."

Some people understand the value of making people feel important and do it well. My friend Veronica told me about meeting former President Clinton when he was honored with the Freedom Award in Memphis, Tennessee. After they were introduced, he asked her "And what do you do?" She mentioned being an interior designer. Veronica was impressed by the number of questions he asked about her business and how he was genuinely interested in what she

I never learned a thing while I was talking.

Larry King
TV & Radio Show Host

was saying. Although other people were trying to get his attention, he continued to look directly at her. Veronica said of that meeting, "You rarely meet individuals who can 'pull off' giving you their undivided attention. It is truly a gift to be able to do that."

During their conversation, one of the secret service agents started to interrupt them so the former president could move on to another group of people. Clinton made a slight gesture indicating he was not finished talking yet. Veronica felt she had never experienced such genuine interest by someone who was a complete stranger. She felt the encounter taught her how to better connect with people.

Never fail to know that if you are doing all the talking, you are boring somebody.

Helen Gurley Brown
Founder, Cosmopolitan

A Hand to Guide Me, by Denzel Washington, includes a story about Clinton describing growing up in Arkansas and learning "to appreciate all kinds of people and pay attention to everybody." Clinton said the editor of his own book could not believe that he remembered the names of everyone he had met. Clinton went on to say his great-uncle taught him, "everyone has a story and the more of others you understand, the better your grasp on human nature." He wrote one of the main reasons he became President of the United States was that he learned to keep his "eyes and ears open, to soak everything in before judging a person, a situation or a complex issue."

If Clinton feels paying attention to others was a reason for his election to the presidency, think about how it can benefit you at work, in your business, or with your home life. We can become more "interested" by actually being so and thinking the person you are talking with has a great story to tell you or valuable insights or information to share. If we felt that way, we would listen more – ask questions – pay attention. In other words, we would be "interested."

4. Talk positively about people. Do not gossip.

What exactly is gossip? I describe it as talking about another person or persons with the intent to belittle, ridicule, or insult. In *The Four Agreements*, Don Miquel Ruiz compares gossip to a computer virus, stating, "(It is) computer language written in the same language all the other codes are written in, but has a harmful intent."

Have I ever gossiped about someone? I am embarrassed to say, "Yes." I believe most of us have gossiped at one time or another. The saying, "When you know better, you do better" applies to gossip. And now I know better.

A gossip is one who talks to you about others; a bore is one who talks to you about himself; and a brilliant conversationalist is one who talks to you about yourself.

Lisa Kirk – Actress, Singer

Why do we gossip in the first place? Years ago, I remember a noted psychologist saying that at the root of all gossip is the need to feel superior to the person you are talking about. That was a WOW moment for me. I had never thought about it like that. After that, whenever I heard people gossiping, I could hear the suggestion of superiority in the unspoken words of "I would never do anything that stupid," "I am smarter, or prettier," or "I would have made a better decision."

Without going into all the messy details, I have seen how gossip got someone fired from a job she loved, turned friends into enemies, and caused an individual to go into a rage that could have easily resulted in a brutal confrontation if I was not present to calm down the person because she felt so hurt and betrayed.

Have I ever been the victim of gossip? Yes, and believe me, it is painful.

At best, gossip is the idle conversation at the water cooler and a waste of time and energy. At worst, it can lead to people being disrespected, feeling devalued, and/or mentally withdrawing from a company team, business partnership, friendship, or family. It can be the cause of people being unjustly fired or wrongly being reprimanded. At the extreme, gossip can result in individuals getting angry, vengeful, or violent. So when it comes to gossip, I cannot stress enough – "Don't start it. Don't spread it. Don't listen to it."

> *Great minds discuss ideas. Average minds discuss events. Small minds discuss people.*
>
> Eleanor Roosevelt
> First Lady, United States
> (1933 - 1945)

5. Treat others as equals.

Arrogance starts with thinking we are superior in some way to others. It shows up as condescending words, disparaging tones and/or dismissive gestures or facial expressions. Even if you hold a higher level job, make more money, or have more degrees, don't think that acting superior does not come with a price.

When I worked as an administrative assistant in various human resources and sales departments, decision-makers (vice presidents, directors and mangers) would often ask me and fellow employees how individuals treated us before deciding on the next steps in the interview or sales process. I have seen how being rude to the receptionist, security guard, and similar staff members caused people to not be hired, not receive a substantial order, or not be considered as a suitable business partner. So if you want to be successful at work or in your business or personal life, avoid flippant remarks and pretentious behaviors.

Some time ago, I had a meeting at a restaurant with a potential client, I will call her Sheila Williams. Williams, who was always pleasant during our phone calls, was behaving very rudely towards our server. She was snappy with her order and spoke in a condescending way when she realized that English was not the waiter's native language. Even her gestures for more water reeked of being snobbish. I remained pleasant with the waiter and tried to communicate that I was pleased with all he was doing to satisfy us.

> *The best index to a person's character is how he treats people who can't fight back.*
>
> Abigail Van Buren
> Columnist

At the end of the meal, Williams decided we should get our desserts "to go." She loved the restaurant's chocolate mint cake but had to get back to the office for a meeting. When I got home, I opened the box with the delicious-looking dessert. Then I suddenly remembered what a friend had told me years ago. She worked in restaurants when in college and said if rude customers knew what goes on behind the kitchen doors, they would act differently. Her words made me throw the cake away without taking a bite. Later that week, Williams called to tell me she decided to go with another speaker. I was somewhat relieved because the rude behaviors she exhibited with the server would probably surface in some way while working with me. I know many people who have similar feelings and are hesitant or refuse to hire, or enter into business endeavors with people like Williams.

*   *   *   *   *

After hearing Carol Tome talk about writing a "thank you" note every day, I decided to adopt a similar practice. I felt connecting with people in such a manner would be a great way to start the day. One morning, though, I simply had no one to thank. But I sent a note of congratulations to a colleague. From that point on, I gave myself the option of either thanking or applauding, at least one person daily. Then on a day I had no one to thank or congratulate, I called a friend and offered to help with a project he was working on. I added, assisting others to my options, creating three ways for me to respect and value people everyday.

To make sure I do not forget, I created the following reminder which I keep by my computer.

> As my first act of the day,
> who can I ...
>
> **A**ssist with information,
> encouragement or help
>
> **C**ongratulate or compliment
>
> **T**hank for what they have done
> for me or others

If you are interested in having my A.C.T. sign, you can download it from www.JGSBook.com (JGS Club).

Just Get Serious® About Success
Chapter 13 Exercise

RESPECT AND VALUE OTHERS

1. For this activity, review the ideas in the chapter and complete the following chart.

In order to respect and value others ...

Three things I should start doing	Two things I will stop doing.	One thing I will pass along to others for them to consider doing.*

*Helps make our world a more respectful place for everyone.

2. Every day, act on what you have written.

Chapter 14

Work Well With Others – Use the Power of Teamwork to Succeed

Effective teamwork is all about making a good, well-balanced salad not whipping individuals into a single batch of V8.

Sandra Richardson – OD Consultant

You will never succeed in life playing on a team of one.

Donna Satchell

Teamwork is so important that it is virtually impossible for you to reach the heights of your capabilities or make the money that you want without becoming very good at it.

Brian Tracy – Author

"Teamwork makes the dream work" is not just a catchy phrase; it is one of the truths about success. Whatever our goals are, we need to work with others to achieve them.

There were many places and undertakings where we will be part of a team, including the workplace, business endeavors, professional and social groups, advocacy projects, and faith-based organizations. You can even think of a family as a team. On an evaluation form, one of my program participants wrote, "This is all very profound. I plan to use the techniques you presented about teamwork with my wife and children."

> *A major reason capable people fail to advance is that they don't work well with their colleagues.*
>
> Lee Iacocca
> Corporate Executive

Teams can consist of two people or more than a hundred. You can have a formal team or an informal one. It could be a team with a long-term future together or one with a short-term goal.

Here's an example of an informal team with a short-term goal. When I worked in New York City, I made a daily trip on the Metro-North commuter trains. People would sit next to each other engaged in their individual activities – reading, working, sleeping, or talking. Suddenly, the train would come to a screeching halt. Then we would hear the dreaded announcement: "The train has derailed and we will not be moving for several hours. We suggest you find other ways to get to your destination."

Immediately, people would start shouting questions to each other. "Anyone headed to Wall Street?" "Who wants to share a cab to the Upper East Side?" "Anyone going to Park Avenue in midtown?" Small teams would emerge with one common purpose – getting to work on time. Some would share taxis, while others agreed to walk together to a bus or subway line. Although these individuals were now in small groups for a short time, several of the guidelines for teamwork helped them accomplish their goal:

- Have a clear mission or objective.

- Listen to everyone's ideas.

- Select a leader (in this case, an informal leader always seemed to emerge).

- Make a decision everyone can agree to support.

- Create a plan.

- Take action.

- Keep the negative comments to a minimum by focusing on the solution. One or two individuals would always start griping with remarks like, "These trains are always breaking down," "We pay too much for such poor service," and "Can't they ever get their act together?" Suddenly someone would step in and say, "We can't do anything about that right now. Let's make a decision and get moving."

These groups would achieve their mission with people eventually arriving at work. Similar types of informal and short-term teams emerge during emergencies including fires, auto accidents, and plane disasters and result in successful evacuations and rescues.

With a longer-term focus, solid teamwork has resulted in success in all fields. There are famous songwriting teams like Jimmy Jam and Terry Lewis, Mick Jagger and Keith Richards, Richard Rodgers and Oscar Hammerstein (Rogers & Hammerstein), and the husband and wife team of Nick Ashford and Valerie Simpson (Ashford & Simpson). With all of these, each brought their unique talents, skills, and abilities to the creation of their songs. The music produced by these teams and thousands of others could not have been made by each person working independently.

The list of famous (and not-so-famous) singing teams is literally endless. As you read this chapter, somewhere in America, young people (and not-so-young adults) are getting together to plan, practice, and form singing duos, trios, or larger groups to create music and songs unlike anything each person could create by himself or herself. Some of these teams will be tomorrow's singing sensations.

Team efforts are behind today's companies, both large and small, theatrical productions, business conventions, local events held by civic, faith-based, professional, and social organizations in your community, and even traditional family gatherings, such as reunions and weddings.

Award-winning performer Queen Latifah shared some interesting insights about teamwork and her career while on *The Larry King Show*. She said, "I loved playing organized sports ... It taught me how to be a team player. It taught me how to sacrifice, how to share, how to celebrate, how to compete, how to be composed ... So, all these things I was able to take into this career. You cannot shoot a movie without 150 people ... We all make it happen together. So, that teaches you how to be a team player.

> *Alone we can do so little; together we can do so much.*
>
> Helen Keller
> Writer & Activist

I need to work with costume, wardrobe, hair, lighting, grips – everyone has to work together." Teamwork makes the movies happen, and it can make your dreams and goals happen, as well.

Remember Jordan Dean, the girl with a dog-sitting business I wrote about in Chapter 9? At 12 years old, she and three of her friends want to start a non-profit animal rescue organization and are working together to solicit funds from retail businesses and individuals. These 12-year old girls realize the value of teamwork. How about you?

As you move forward on your goals and dreams, think about the individuals you interact with most often as members of your informal or formal team. This is particularly important if they provide expertise and have a high level of involvement with you. For this book, I consider those on my team to be my editor, accountability partner, mastermind partner, Small Business Development Center consultant, and several business colleagues.

If you are employed, you may already be working in a team-structured environment. If you are not, consider your team to be those you work with to get things done. If you have personal goals, think about who

234

you get together with most often to achieve them. Regarding individuals as team members changes how you see them. They become valued partners in your journey to success. Then the power of teamwork can work for you.

Teamwork is not just about you thinking of others as team players, but also about how they think of you. I remember talking with visual artist Brenda Singletary about a program she was planning. We were brainstorming names of other artists she would invite to participate. I mentioned a name and Brenda immediately said, "Oh, no – not her. She doesn't play well with others." I laughed to myself as I heard the phrase, feeling Brenda was probably right. Each time I had been with that person, she seemed aloof, self-absorbed, and very critical of others.

Now, I have a question for you. What would people say if your name was mentioned to be on a special project for work, your professional association, your faith-based organization, or any other group? Would the response be:

1. "Yes, let's include her. She always has good ideas."

2. "I'm not sure. Let's come back to his name later on."

3. "No, not her. She spends too much time talking about people."

4. "Definitely, he's great during last-minute crises."

5. "No, you can't depend on him. There are always excuses why things aren't done."

6. "Yes, he is great to work with and can be depended on to do what he commits to."

7. "No! No! Too much drama."

8. "Yes, she's the best! She is always so positive and pleasant."

9. "I'm not sure. I don't know a lot about her."

10. "I say 'no.' He seems to prefer working alone."

Your success at work, in business and with personal endeavors depends, in part, on people being interested in working with you. You have probably already figured out that you think people have such an interest if you answered "yes" or "that's me" to responses of 1, 4, 6, or 8. If you did, give yourself a pat on the back. This chapter will provide you with ways to hone your skills of working with others so you can get even better. If those were not your choices, do not worry. You can develop the necessary traits for people to view you as a team player. Read on to find out how.

When it comes to working with others, sometimes we are team leaders, other times we are the team members. Here are nine strategies and tips to keep in mind regardless of your role.

1. Be aware of the why, what, and how of the team.

You would be surprised at the number of times I have done teamwork programs and the members did not know or were uncertain of the team's purpose, mission, and short-term or long-term goals.

The members of the best corporate and organizational teams I have worked on always knew this information. It is essential in order for members to take appropriate actions and make knowledgeable suggestions.

Ellen Crooke, Vice President and News Director for WXIA 11 Alive, told me she made sure all her staff members fully understood the new mission before her station publicly announced the new focus for their news programs. She went on to say, "The most successful newsrooms and the most successful organizations have a unified mission that everyone knows. Not everyone needs to agree with the mission. But everyone needs

> *Teamwork is the ability to work together toward a common vision.*
>
> Dale Carnegie
> Industrialist

to understand it and be committed to it. They all must be working toward the same goals." That attitude and approach led to WXIA winning ten regional Emmy Awards and eight regional Edward R. Murrow awards (coveted honors in the news field).

> *No one can whistle a symphony. It takes an orchestra to play it.*
>
> H.E. Luccock
> Professor,
> Yale Divinity School

Even if it is a small group involved in a business or personal endeavor, understanding the mission is fundamental. Everyone on my book publishing team knows why I am writing this book, what my goals are, how I plan to market it, as well as the target audience, and how I plan to reach them. These details are important for them to give me valuable ideas and to help me move forward.

Suggestions:

- Team Members – Know the mission, vision, and goals. Make them the foundation of your suggestions, decisions, and actions.

- Team Leaders – If possible, have the team members create the mission/vision statement and the goals or revise them based on their input. If that's not possible, make sure everyone knows what they are and is committed to achieving them.

2. Be committed to what you say you are going to do. Embody the quote: "The buck stops here."

One of my teams has only two people. Lynda Shorter and I founded Women Aspiring Together To Succeed (WATTS) in June 2000 and since then we have coordinated and facilitated over 95 meetings. We have help from members at all the sessions; however, Lynda and I are "the chief, cook, and bottle-washers." Everything starts and stops with us.

Some time ago, Lynda went to Florida the week before our December meeting. She planned to return on Saturday evening and be at the meeting on Sunday. It was essential for her to be there because over 50 women would be attending. As usual, there was a lot to do, including distributing handouts, encouraging women to participate in pre-program activities, setting up the food, opening the meeting, coordinating introductions, and facilitating the discussion. For this particular meeting, her presence was even more crucial. I was slated to be the photographer at another important event that evening, so I had to leave when the meeting officially ended at 5:30 p.m. I would not be able to stay for an hour cleaning up. Also, Lynda was going to present the program and bring the decorations.

> *Individual commitment to a group effort - that is what makes a team work, a company work, a society work, a civilization work.*
>
> Vince Lombardi
> Football Coach

Lynda planned to drive to Atlanta on Saturday. I called her several times that evening and when I could not contact her at midnight, I started to panic. I finally reached Lynda on Sunday morning and she was still in Florida! She had encountered a family emergency and could not leave. Before I was able to say anything, she quickly explained that she had already gotten in touch with Marsha, who would present the program; Janet would bring the decorations and set up everything; Michelle and Carolyn would help with the food preparation. I could still leave at 5:30 p.m. as planned because she had arranged for three other members to clean-up. Despite having a personal crisis, she had taken care of everything by getting individuals to help me. That's a perfect example of being committed and personally responsible.

Suggestions:

- Team Members – Do what you say you are going to do and if you cannot, take it upon yourself to find others to replace you. (Note: having good relationships with people will make this easier to do.)

- Team Leaders – Set an example of personal responsibility that everyone sees and can follow.

3. Be courteous and polite with all the members.

Remember the figures I cited earlier: 79% percent of Americans felt rudeness was a serious national problem and 99% percent of those same people felt they were not rude. Those figures also apply to people in teams. Discourteous behavior can result in members feeling disrespected, and the results can be disastrous. This is especially true when team members are volunteers.

Debbie, the president of an organization I was a member of, asked me to recommend someone to serve as Vice President of Communications. She was having a difficult time finding a person to fill this important role, which involved creating the newsletter and redesigning the website. I suggested Debbie ask Terri, one of the newer members. She was a technology guru and a freelance writer for several national magazines.

When Debbie approached her about the position, Terri declined, saying it would be too much work. After contacting other people, Debbie was still unable to find someone and called me for additional suggestions. Still thinking Terri was the best person, I volunteered to call her myself. I explained to Terri how valuable her contributions would be and how others, including me, could help her. After a bit of serious arm-twisting, she finally agreed.

People will forget what you said, people will forget what you did, but people will never forget how you made them feel.

Maya Angelou
Author & Poet

Several weeks later, I heard Terri had resigned. I was shocked! She did not seem like the type of person who would accept a position and then suddenly quit. I called her to see what happened and Terri told me the following story.

"Debbie phoned me around 7:00 in the morning and immediately asked when I would be submitting my plans for the redesign of the website. Since I was not fully awake, it took me a minute to recognize her voice.

I chuckled slightly, wondering why Debbie would call someone's home so early and demand something without first saying, 'Good morning.' Debbie continued in a brassy tone, 'Sounds like you don't take your responsibilities seriously.' I mentioned something about it being 7:00 in the morning, but she ignored my remark and repeated her question. I said I would get back to her. Later that day, I called Debbie and resigned." Terri went on to say, "Donna, I am not willing to be on a team with someone who is so rude and demanding, particularly the leader, especially when I'm not getting paid for all I would be doing."

A year later, the organization is still without a Vice President of Communications. The website is a mess, and no one is writing a newsletter. Why? Because a team member (in this case, the leader) failed to use good manners with another member.

Suggestions:

- Team Members – Use common courtesies (please, thank you) and good manners with members.

- Team Leaders – Consistently model the above behaviors.

- Both team members and leaders – Review the tips in Chapter 13, "Respect People to Create the Foundation for Success."

4. Focus on what people can do and not what they cannot do.

During my teens, teamwork for me was playing on junior high and high school basketball, volleyball, and softball teams. It was a mandatory part of physical education, so I had to participate. Athletics was definitely not my strong suit. My serves never seemed to go over the net in volleyball; my bat never seemed to connect with the ball in softball; and I never seemed to get down the court fast enough in basketball. I was among the girls others made fun of and

> *Win together,*
> *lose together,*
> *play together,*
> *stay together.*
>
> Debra Mancuso
> Athlete

secretly talked about. I dreaded playing. Because I was young and did not know better, I let my classmates' gossip make me become disinterested in winning. So I rarely did my best. The same thing can happen on your teams when members focus on what other members cannot do rather than what they are doing well.

Suggestions:

- Team Members – Do not spend time talking disparagingly about what other members cannot do well. Instead, help them or provide suggestions on how they can improve and do things better. When doing so, avoid condescending words and tones. Everyone wants to be treated as respected adults.

- Team Leaders – Make it known that you value what members can contribute and you will not tolerate disparaging conversations. Also, if necessary, plan to provide assistance to those who need it.

5. Contribute your opinions and ideas.

My first full-time job was as a file clerk at an insurance company. I was part of a three-person team working with Susan and Valerie, assistants for the directors in the Human Resources Department. They immediately took on the task of teaching me everything I needed to know.

Their biggest job was getting me to speak up at staff meetings. Since I was new, I preferred to keep my opinions to myself. But, they would not let me do that. They were constantly saying, "Donna, what do you think?" When I gave a limited answer, like "Sounds good to me," they asked, "Well, what makes it sound good?" "What are ways you think it could be done better?" and "How would you do it differently?" They made me feel I had a responsibility to have an opinion or idea and state it.

> *In teamwork, silence isn't golden, it's deadly.*
>
> Mark Sanborn
> Leadership Consultant

241

At one staff meeting, I bashfully suggested we purchase monogrammed cups for everyone who had helped us on a major project. In the past, the department held a luncheon for them but never gave gifts. Susan and Valerie loved my idea and decided to go with it. The attendees were thrilled when, at the end of the meal, coffee was served in initialed, gold trimmed cups they could take home. They were a hit! My idea of giving individual gifts became a budgeted line item for that particular project.

Suggestions:

- Team Members – Speak up. Make your ideas and opinions known. Do not let your newness on the team, your age, or your limited experiences keep you from offering suggestions and opinions.

- Team Leaders – Demonstrate that you are sincerely interested in everyone's thoughts and you expect everyone to feel the same way. Emphasize that both new and experienced members have valuable ideas.

6. Consider members' ideas before negatively reacting to them.

When members offer their suggestions, they are showing how they can be of value to the group. I have witnessed people trying to convey what they thought was a good idea, only to have it shot down before they had finished talking. Not only have I seen it happen, but I have also been the person shot down and sometimes, the person doing the shooting.

> *An idea is a fragile thing. Turning it off is much easier than keeping it lit. Ideas shine because somebody had them and nobody turned them off.*
>
> Tom Peters – Business Management Consultant

Being the idea person, I know how it feels to have others quickly dismiss my thoughts as "not workable," "off strategy," "too expensive," "too difficult," or the too-common "we tried that already." When ideas are promptly written off, it is easy for people to feel undervalued as members of a team. They can end up withdrawing mentally by no longer contributing what is on their minds.

> *We have two ears and only one tongue in order that we may hear more and speak less.*
>
> Diogenes Laertius
> Writer

Conversely, I have been the person who shot down an idea before giving it my full consideration. So I know how easy that is to do. And I have seen people shut down because of my unreceptive reaction.

I think most of us can improve in this area by being better listeners, taking the time to consider what others have to say, and realizing that even within a seemingly unworkable suggestion could be the seed of a brilliant idea.

Suggestions:

- Team Members – Listen to everyone's thoughts without interrupting or passing judgment (avoid remarks or visual reactions indicating dislike or disinterest while individuals are talking). Whenever possible, take time to discuss and brainstorm ideas to see how they could work.

- Team Leaders – Set a good example of respecting everyone's contributions and privately express your disapproval to those who do not.

7. Appreciate members and share the credit.

In *How Full is Your Bucket?*, the authors cite a national survey that found 65% of American employees reported receiving no acknowledgement of their good work. From my experience and stories I have heard, a similar figure applies for non-workplace teams as well. Think about the teams where you are a member. Are you contributing to the 35% who are receiving praise or the 65% who are not? It is easy to point to team leaders and complain they are not giving enough recognition. However, we can all improve the situation by acknowledging each other's efforts, both publicly and privately. Don't think, "It doesn't really make a difference." Research indicates it does.

A study by the U.S. Department of Labor found that not feeling appreciated is the #1 reason people leave their jobs. You may be thinking, "No, they leave for more money." They may end up with a job paying more, but the main reason many start looking was because they felt unvalued. I know this was definitely true of every job change I made. The same reason applies to non-workplace teams. Feeling burned-out and unappreciated has resulted in many people (including myself) withdrawing from leadership roles and various positions in organizations.

> *If you think a complimentary thought about someone, don't just think it. Dare to compliment people and pass on compliments to them from others.*
>
> Catherine Ponder – Author

Behind all successes there are supporting cast members. It is important for those who are recognized to share the credit with them. Doing so:

- Increases the likelihood their efforts will continue.

- Results in individuals having pride in their work.

- Makes contributing members want to do more.

- Encourages non-contributing members to work harder.

- Fosters a spirit of team collaboration.

During the interview segment of one of her specials, Beyonce talks about how hard she and her team work to put on her spectacular performances. "When I work … I'm like a machine and I think my team is just as crazy as I am because they are right there with me pushing it and pushing themselves. It is overwhelming. It's hard. In the end, it is a team effort." Then you see Beyonce thanking her dancers, band members, the crew and everyone involved for their hard work, saying how much she appreciates them. That's sharing the credit.

I learned the value of sharing the credit from many people. But Greg Jones was a master at it. He was a Trade Marketing Manager I worked with when I was a Category Manager. In planning for a major campaign, Jones held a meeting with several staff members and me to brainstorm ways to promote one of the brands. We talked about holding a sweepstakes, offering a buy-one-get-one-free, including a small gift in the carton, and other strategies.

Then Greg mentioned bundling the hair color product with a bar of Keri soap. That was clearly his idea. After kicking it around for a while, I suggested we use Keri bath oil instead. I explained shoppers would view it as having a higher value. Everyone agreed and we moved on to talk about how to make it happen.

After that initial meeting, Greg told everyone how brilliant my idea was. The first time he did, I reminded him it was actually his idea; I had simply added to it. Greg just shrugged his shoulders and said how great the promotion was going to be. He was right. Both the client and the shoppers loved it. As a result of Greg's sharing the credit, everyone involved received a lot of praise for the successful program, and I got special recognition.

> *The deepest principle of human nature is the craving to be appreciated.*
>
> William James
> Psychologist

Over the years, I watched Jones act in similar ways in many situations. He was the first to praise personally, to acknowledge publicly, and to make sure people were treated fairly. I learned a lot about how to treat people from him.

During a dinner with a former co-worker, we talked about past employees and both of us felt Jones was the type of person who would achieve tremendous success because everyone wanted to work with him. Do people feel that way about you?

Suggestions:

- Team Members – First, pay attention to people, their work and their contributions so you can see their valuable contributions. Second, do not just think about it – acknowledge it. Let them know how you feel by saying something, sending an email, card or handwritten note (whichever is most appropriate).

- Team Leaders – Set an example by publicly and/or privately acknowledging people's contributions (whichever you think they would prefer) and make sure to include all those who were involved, regardless of the size of their contribution.

  Make recognizing people a major priority. Remember the story in Chapter 13 about how Carol Tome of The Home Depot writes daily thank you letters and sent several hundred notes to employees who worked on a project under her leadership. Think about how you can follow her example.

8. Use empathy and respect when giving feedback or disagreeing with other members.

Recently, I explained this chapter to a colleague, Jennifer, who immediately said she wanted to give it to her new assistant, Rob to read. Jennifer sarcastically described situations showing Rob's poor manners and lack of commitment. I knew Jennifer's demeanor would make it hard for him to receive her direction favorably. I suggested she use two essential elements when giving constructive feedback or advice: empathy and respect.

Empathy involves seeing the situation or issue from the other individual's point of view. Yes, maybe he or she should know something or have done better. But be empathetic; remember when you were a beginner. Also reflect on times now when you are new to situations and may not do what is expected or correct.

Respect means communicating in a way that conveys the other person has value. Shouting, pointing fingers, patronizing expressions, dictatorial tones, or an arrogant attitude can easily drown out well-intended words. Research shows that vocal tone, facial expressions, and gestures can have a greater impact during a conversation than the words alone. Keep that in mind when you are planning to discuss anything. When using emails, texts, and other written communication, be careful of the words and phrases you use. If you are unsure how others will perceive your message, get someone's opinion before sending it. You can also follow the adage "When in doubt, leave it out" or better yet, pick up the phone and call the person.

> *Deal with the faults of others as gently as with your own.*
>
> Anonymous

Suggestions:

- Team Members – Remember to be respectful and compassionate in your communications, especially the critical ones

- Team Leaders – Consider and act on the words of Daniel Goleman, author of *Primal Leadership*: "Leaders who lack empathy will unwittingly be off-key and act in ways that set off negative reactions."

9. Use your own experience of what works and what does not work as you interact with others as a team member or team leader.

Hopefully, when working with others, you have always had good experiences. However, in all likelihood, they were sometimes less than ideal or possibly even downright terrible. Use your personal knowledge in deciding how you will treat those you are working with. It never ceases to amaze me how many times people do not do that.

If you dislike managers speaking to you in demanding tones, then why do that with members of a committee you are chairing? If you get upset when business colleagues talk about you behind your back, why do the same thing when working on a fundraiser for the PTA? If you become infuriated when people don't keep their commitments at work, why be one of those people when you're on a project for the church committee. On the other hand, if you like being recognized for your contributions, be sure to make others feel valued for theirs. If you feel good when managers and co-workers say, "Good morning," as they pass your desk, use similar greetings when approaching others.

Team work is not "hard work;" it is "heart work." It is making members the focus of heartfelt thoughts and behaviors. It is achieving team objectives and goals through consideration, respect, sincere caring, and genuine commitment.

Recently, I was asked to join a group of speakers who were considering holding a joint event. Sitting through their first meeting, I realized I could not be on their team. There was too much disagreeing, interrupting, and correcting of each other at what should have been an easy-going, getting-to-know-you type of meeting. I declined their invitation to participate. Months later, I found out the event never took place and the group had disbanded because of so much in-fighting.

A team is more than a collection of people. It is a process of give and take.

Barbara Glacel
Teamwork Consultant

Early in my business as a speaker, I was fortunate to be part of a solid team effort. It involved five speakers based in Atlanta and Alabama. Our objective was to create an incredible evening of inspiration and empowerment. We met regularly for weeks to plan out everything. Our meetings were filled with enthusiasm as everyone brought their most creative ideas. We treated each other the way Quincy Jones told all the performers to act at the recording of *We are the World*: "Leave your egos at the door." Regardless of experience or years in the business, we considered each other as equals and everyone's opinions mattered. We selected the best suggestions and moved in to action, securing the venue, planning the program, and promoting the event. We ended up with over 500 people attending. A local radio personality kicked off the festivities and Les Brown was our MC. We videotaped the event and created both a DVD and CD titled "Motivational Monday – Live from Atlanta!" Awesome teamwork resulted in an awesome program. You can have similar results from your team efforts by using the nine tips described in this chapter.

> *I rely on the team. I defer to it and sacrifice for it, because the team, not the individual, is the ultimate champion.*
>
> Mia Hamm
> Soccer Player

Lastly, never underestimate the value of being a team player and the doors of opportunity it can open for you. During an interview, Sally Ride was asked why NASA chose her to be the first American woman in space. Her response included "understanding of the importance of teamwork" and having the "ability to recognize (my) role as a member of a team." If being a team player helped Ride travel into space, imagine how it can help you achieve your goals. With that thought in mind, complete the end-of-chapter activity on the following page.

Just Get Serious® About Success
Chapter 14 Exercise

TEAMWORK

Consider all the opportunities you have to work with others. List the name(s) of the business and personal teams you belong to in the first column of the chart on the next page.

Ask yourself: Are you being the best team member or team leader you can be with each group? I believe the slogan, "There is always room for improvement," applies to teamwork.

Imagine your name is mentioned during a conversation about a new role, position, or special project with each group. Read through the following three questions and fill out the areas in the chart below each one.

1. What do you think people on each team would say about having you fill a position or be on a special project with them?

2. What do you want people to think and say about you? List the specific words you would like them to use in talking to you.

3. What new ways of working with your team members can create the impression you described in question #2? Your answers could be the same across all the teams or different.

After you complete the chart, consider your answers to question #3 and decide how you can use them when working with members of each group so you can become the best possible team player or leader.

Group Name	Question #1	Question #2	Question #3
Write group name vertically			
Write group name vertically			
Write group name vertically			

You can also download the form from www.JGSBook.com (click on JGS Club).

Chapter 15

Be Open-Minded to Find New Pathways to Your Success

People are very open-minded about new things as long as they're exactly like the old ones.

Charles F. Kettering – Inventor

Minds are like parachutes. They only function when they are open.

James Dewar – Chemist & Physicist

Without an open-minded mind, you can never be a great success.

Martha Stewart – Business Magnate

Having an open mind is like having a key to many doors leading towards success. Other people have ideas, insights, and suggestions that can be of value to us. Why reinvent the wheel? If something is working for others, we might want to try using it as long as we are not breaking any laws, rules, or confidentialities.

While I was not a rigid, close-minded individual in the past, I would not have listed openness as one of my strengths. I certainly did not value it as I do today. There are five areas where being open-minded can positively impact our success. They are:

- Getting feedback and advice

- Asking others their opinions

- Hearing new ideas or suggestions

- Having and seeking opportunities to learn

- Considering your career and business options

GETTING FEEDBACK AND ADVICE

My ability to receive feedback today is the result of being a member of Toastmasters International®, an organization dedicated to helping people overcome their public speaking fears and develop leadership skills. Most chapters follow standard rules established by the national office. When a member gives a speech, another member provides a verbal evaluation of it, explaining what the speaker did well and how he or she could improve the presentation. The speakers cannot interrupt their evaluators. They cannot challenge them by explaining or justifying anything.

The first time I received an evaluation as a Toastmasters speaker, I clearly remember choking back the impulse to say, "You're wrong! It was funny." I wanted to explain how the evaluator's suggestions would not work for me and how I had worked on the speech for weeks. But, as difficult as it was, I followed the rules and remained silent.

After the meeting, I asked a member why we were not allowed to voice our objections or opinions. She said most people are not comfortable telling others what they do not like or could do better. So interrupting the evaluators would, most likely, cause them to stop talking before they finished what they wanted to say. She explained, "You don't have to agree with the person. You just have to listen to what is being said." This made a lot of sense to me, not just about hearing comments regarding my speeches but also how to deal with feedback and advice in all areas of my life. Think about it; doesn't that make sense to you?

An open mind requires a closed mouth.

Donna Satchell

The Johari Window™ can also help us understand the value of feedback. It was developed by psychologists Joseph Luft and Harry Ingham. The concept divides our personal awareness in four areas:

1. Arena is what we know about ourselves and what others know about us.

2. Hidden is what we know about ourselves but we keep from others.

3. Unknown is what we do not know about ourselves and others do not know about us.

4. Blind Spot is what we do not know about ourselves but others know about us. Of the four areas, this one that relates most to open-mindedness. For our purposes, it is what we do not know that is required to be successful but others do know.

What does the Blind Spot have to do with openness? Let's think about the following scenarios.

■   A colleague sees you have a particular shortcoming (e.g. delegating, speaking up, and adhering to deadlines). If you improved, you could achieve more of your goals. Wouldn't you want to know what he observed or felt?

■   A friend sees you have a particular strength you are not aware of (e.g. writing, organizing, or analyzing). If you developed it, you might be more successful at work or in business. Wouldn't you want to know what the strength is?

■ A manager is aware of the traits or behaviors you need to be successful and you don't know about them. Wouldn't you want to find out what she knows?

Although valuable, we often don't want to hear about areas where we can improve. In the past, I would think such comments reflected poorly on me. I felt I needed to know how to do everything well or I was not as smart as others.

Do you ever have similar thoughts?

Such thinking can cause us to be closed-minded to what others are telling us. So what should we do when hearing feedback and advice? We can take it professionally, not personally. Too often, we take it personally and react in one (or more) of five ways:

1. Justify our behavior
   We defend what we did through lengthy explanations meant to show we were right in our thinking or actions.

2. Dismiss the comment or opinion
   We decide not to pay any attention to what the person said because we feel he or she does not like us, support us, understand us, or is out to get us.

3. Minimize the comment
   We reason the information has little or limited value because of the person's age, gender, inexperience, lack of education, or knowledge.

4. Blame others
   We think and talk about how someone else is responsible for what happened.

5. Mentally attack
   We "mentally criticize" the person for the things we perceive he or she has done wrong regarding the situation.

From personal experience, I know not taking it personally is easier said than done.

Early in my marketing/sales career, I was an Assistant Product Manager, working on the Miss Clairol hair color brand. The Senior Product Manager, Terri, and I were making plans for shooting a TV infomercial in Los Angeles. After going over all the intricate details, she gave me basic information about flights, hotel, and rental cars. She also mentioned the attire would be casual. Over the weekend, I spent hours shopping and purchased a very expensive pair of designer jeans, a sharp red blazer, white shirt, a pair of red loafers, and a matching belt. They were all for the upcoming trip to L.A.

On the shooting location, I felt like a true professional. I knew exactly what to do, and I looked great. Everything went well. We returned to New York and the following day had a debrief meeting. The first thing Terri sharply asked me was, "What made you think you could wear jeans to the shooting? You should never wear jeans on a business trip!" I immediately shouted back, "You did! You said casual dress." She fired back, "I said causal, not jeans." I went into major mental attack mode. I felt like slapping her! I wanted to say, "I looked better in my well-pressed Calvin Klein's™, red shoes, and matching jacket than you did in your wrinkled white linen pants that did not match your wrinkled, white linen jacket!" but I thought better of it. Instead, I furiously stormed out of her office.

At lunchtime, I told my friends how outlandish Terri's remarks were. I reasoned she said them because she did not like me. One friend inquired whether anyone else was wearing jeans. I curtly replied "No" and asked, "What does that have to do with anything?" He said, "Well maybe Terri was just telling you the protocol for a commercial shoot." I quickly replied, "So you are taking her side," in an accusatory tone. You can see I had a lot to learn.

When you find yourself receiving feedback or advice, avoid taking it personally and instead take it professionally (ATIP – ITIP). You can do that by resisting the urge to interrupt the person, listening to the comment, and then asking yourself:

1. Is what they said true or partially true? If yes, then consider question #2. If not, then ask yourself why you think they made the remark. Maybe check with others about the validity of what they said to determine if you need to consider it further.

2. Is it possible others have the same or similar thought? This question helps you see beyond one person's opinion.

3. Is what they said hindering you in some way from achieving your goals or being more successful? If yes, see question #4. If no, consider pocketing it for now. However, you may want to reconsider it later, especially if you hear a similar remark from someone else.

4. How can you use what they said?

5. When will you use what they said?

ASKING OTHERS THEIR OPINIONS

Have you ever found yourself in the following situation? Someone asks your opinion about something and when you respond with an unfavorable remark, the person immediately starts to disagree with you or justify his or her behavior or plans. When that happens to me, I think, "Why did you bother to ask me?"

For many years, I was guilty of similar questioning until I had an attitude-changing experience. I asked Les Brown, the world-renowned motivational speaker, to listen to a presentation I was preparing to give the following day. He started telling me what he thought I needed to change. I immediately interrupted him and began explaining why I felt my approach was correct. As I think back to the conversation, I see how absurd and rude I was being. Les Brown is a speaking expert with over 20 years experience presenting to major corporations and audiences of thousands. He makes over $20,000 per speech. At the time, I was very new to the speaking profession and was barely making a hundred dollars a speech. Yet, I felt I could question his reasoning! Now that makes no sense at all!

After debating with Brown for several minutes, he finally said, "I can't believe you are asking what I think and you are not listening to me." He said something about me being hardheaded and asked if I was always like that. Brown then said he was not going to give me any more ideas and he stopped talking. I was shocked. I hold Les Brown in very high esteem and certainly value his opinion. I did not mean to offend or annoy him.

An open mind leaves a chance for someone to drop a worthwhile thought in it.

Anonymous

Over the next several weeks, I made a conscious effort to listen to my thoughts and reactions when I asked people what they thought. I realized I was not really open to hearing a conflicting point of view. I simply wanted people to verify what I was thinking or doing was correct. I knew I had to get a lot better.

Do you feel that way at times?

If so, below are five steps I found beneficial:

1. Before asking people what they think, ask yourself: "Do I really want their opinion?" "Do I want validation or information?" "What will I do with what they say?"

2. Shift your thinking from the need to be right to the need to know.

3. Listen to what they are saying without interrupting, except to get more information or if something is unclear. Resist the urge to defend your point of view so you can fully hear and understand theirs.

4. Thank the individuals for sharing their opinion or thoughts.

5. Take time to consider what was told to you; then, decide what to do.

If you use their idea or a portion of it, thank them again with a phone call or hand-written note so they know it was of value to you.

HEARING NEW IDEAS OR SUGGESTIONS

In the early 1990s, I was dating someone who worked as a manager at one of the fast-food chains. I will call him Jimmy. He was always telling me how frustrated he was with his job (the long hours, low pay, unreliable employees, not meeting sales quota, etc). I would often come up with ideas about how he could improve things.

One day I suggested what I thought was a great idea – he could recommend to upper management that they start taking credit cards. At the time, no fast-food chains in Atlanta were accepting them (early 1990's). I clearly recall Jimmy's reaction. He looked at me like I was crazy and asked, "Have you ever worked in a fast-food restaurant?" When I replied, "You know I haven't," he began telling me my suggestion was ridiculous, "We are too busy. We can't stop to handle credit cards. That takes time. We got long lines of people to serve."

> *Where there is an open mind, there will always be a frontier.*
>
> Dorothea Brande
> Writer & Editor

Unimpressed with his argument, I said they could do a test in a couple of stores and see what happens. He again said the idea was not worth considering. "You have never worked in a restaurant. You don't know what it's like. We don't have time to check people's IDs and get them to sign receipts. We have got to get moving." From his tone, I could tell the only place I was heading with my idea was into an argument, so I decided to drop it.

About two years later, I walked through the security area and headed for Concourse T at Hartsfield-Jackson Atlanta International Airport. Right in front of me was validation for my idea – a Burger King with a huge sign announcing "Now Accepting Credit Cards."

I know Jimmy did not mention my idea to anyone because he thought it was ludicrous. I now realize at the time of my suggestion, Burger King and other fast-food restaurants were already working on systems to accept credit cards without impeding on timing. When I saw the sign, Jimmy and I were no longer dating so I did not contact him. What's important about this story is he would not even consider my suggestion because I never worked in a fast-food restaurant and he felt I couldn't possibly propose a feasible idea.

Have you ever had a similar thought or reaction? Have you ever dismissed what people were saying because they did not work in your industry or have the experience or knowledge to validate their thinking? Be open to suggestions from others, even if they never had your particular job or business, had the type of manager you are working with, or have the education you value. Do not let their being young or old influence whether or not you listen to them.

Also, we must avoid shortsighted thinking because it can prevent us from being open-minded. We would not be alone in doing that. Many industry experts, presidents of companies and those with PhDs are known to have had limited vision. Below are five ways of thinking (similar to Jimmy's) which have proven to be shortsighted:

■ "It is an idle dream to imagine that automobiles will take the place of railways in the long distance movement of passengers."
American Railroad Congress, 1913

■ "Who the hell wants to hear actors talk?"
Harry M. Warner,
President of Warner Brothers Pictures, 1927
(Responding to a suggestion for the company to make
movies where audiences can hear the actors' voices)

- "There is no hope for the fanciful idea of reaching the Moon because of insurmountable barriers to escaping the Earth's gravity."
  Dr. Forest Ray Moulton
  Astronomer, University of Chicago, 1932

- "Television won't be able to hold on to any market it captures after the first six months. People will soon get tired of staring at a plywood box every night."
  Darryl F. Zanuck, Head of 20th Century-Fox, 1946

- "There is no reason for any individual to have a computer in their home."
  Ken Olson, President of Digital Corporation, 1977

In the past, people actually believed these statements to be true. Think of the opposition individuals received when they proposed ideas challenging any of them. For example, imagine the reaction when someone first presented the idea of people using their computers in their homes for non-business use. No doubt, they encountered lots of skepticism and odd looks!

How can we avoid being closed-minded to new ideas?

1. Listen to what the person is saying without interrupting. You never know when the idea or a portion of the idea has value.

2. Silence your internal critic (voice) that is saying, "Bad idea, it will never work." "He doesn't know what he is talking about." "We tried that before and it failed." "She never worked here." "My industry is different than theirs."

3. Realize the way the world is today is not the way it will be tomorrow. What people need and want today is not necessarily what they will need and want tomorrow. What your field or occupation looks like today may not be how it will look tomorrow.

4. Do research to understand fully the trends and what the future is projected to be like.

5. Decide if the suggestion is worth considering. If it is, then consider it.

Here are my final thoughts on what you have read thus far about getting feedback, asking others their opinions, and hearing new ideas:

- If you use meditation, intuition, or prayer to make decisions, then use them in considering what to do with what you have been told. Also, utilize what you know about yourself (your strengths, goals, and dreams) in deciding your next steps.

- There is a difference between listening and acting. We can listen without acting. We cannot act, however, on what we have not fully listened to. So listening is key.

HAVING AND SEEKING OPPORTUNITIES TO LEARN

One of my biggest regrets is not being open minded enough to learn to play golf. I had many chances to do so. As an analyst and manager at Clairol, I would attend the company's national and regional sales meeting several times a year. It was a 2- or 3-day event with numerous business sessions. These full days of learning started early in the morning and ended early evening. To provide time for enjoyment, there was always an afternoon set aside for company-paid recreational activities, including golf and golf lessons. Did I ever consider signing up? No. I always selected the spa, the city tour, or the other choices I thought would be fun. Always! In seven years, I never once considered registering for beginners golf classes. That is being closed-minded!

Learn everything you can. There will always come a time when you will be grateful you did.

Sarah Caldwell
Opera Conductor

I am embarrassed to say when my manager planned our first regional meeting, I looked at the agenda and was the first to complain about not having any options other than playing golf. Clearly, I was not going to consider learning to play! After several of us loudly voiced our disapproval, my manager added other activities. If I had the same opportunity today, I would at least try playing golf. I might have even liked it. Nowadays many deals are made on the golf course. So I miss opportunities to grow my business because I was close-minded in the past. Do not be like I was. Instead, embrace or at least consider opportunities to learn all sorts of things that come your way.

When computers came into the workplace in the early 90s, some of the employees continued doing things as they had in the past. Others learned how to use them, but complained the entire time. The result? Many were left behind and were ill equipped for the drastic shift to a technological workplace. But others succeeded, adapting and even excelling, in this new environment. One of them was Mike Hartley. He had been a salesperson

The beautiful thing about learning is nobody can take it away from you.

B.B. King
Singer

his entire career and was in his late 50s. Although he was close to retirement, he did not hesitate to attend the training classes. He not only learned, but he also mastered the material presented. Because of his willingness to change, he was promoted to a position involving maintaining and upgrading computers. He became a well-respected and highly sought-after resource for employees at the company.

What is changing at your workplace or in your line of business? What new procedures and technologies are being introduced? Are you eagerly learning, constantly complaining, or relentlessly resisting? The latter two lead to frustration, misery, and a lack of progress and success. Changes in technology and other areas are here to stay; therefore, be open to learning to have the success you desire.

A relative once said to me "Donna, you can't teach an old dog new tricks." I wanted to say, "I thought we were talking about people, not animals!" However, I decided not to respond. I did not want to prolong what was becoming – in my mind – a ridiculous conversation about the limits of human potential. People are learning all sorts of things late in life.

■ The award-winning actor, Morgan Freeman, learned to fly at age 64. At 70, he regularly flies himself to work, traveling between his homes in Mississippi and Hollywood.

■ Nola Ochs, became the oldest person to graduate with a masters degree at age 98 after earning her bachelor's degree at age 95.

■ George Dawson learned to read at 98 years of age. At age 101, he appeared on "The Oprah Winfrey Show", "Good Morning America", and other television programs where he talked about reading his favorite book, *The Bible*.

I hope these three people inspire you to learn and keep learning.

CONSIDERING YOUR CAREER AND BUSINESS OPTIONS

Today, the workplace and the economy are forcing people to reconsider how they will earn a living as their jobs drastically change or they find themselves laid off.

For many people, along with the question of "Where do I find another job?" is the question, "If I was not happy with what I was doing in the past, do I want to get a new job doing similar work or should I explore new areas?" Some people are going for the latter, including individuals such as:

> *You've got to keep an open mind.*
>
> Chris Wallace
> Journalist

■ Cory Chacon, who left her career as an international marketing executive for a major record label to become a concierge with the Muse Hotel in New York City.

■ Matthew West, who decided to become a personal chef after giving up a 10+-year career as a software salesperson. He competed in the 2010 National Sears Chef Challenge.

- Jon Cunningham, who became a lifestyle photographer after being a business consultant for several years.

- Debra Chin, a software marketer who became the owner of a Bella Bridesmaid franchise. She used her financial and marketing skills to pursue her passion for fashion and entrepreneurship.

In the early chapters, I shared details about making a major career change from the analytical field to being a speaker, trainer, and life coach.

Among the people I interviewed for this book is Brad Crose. He made a major change by leaving a ten-year career as an I.T. professional to attend law school and become a patent and trademark attorney. You can read his story in Chapter 20 – Be Inspired.

A unique opportunity is available for people who want to explore new directions. VocationVacations® offers two- or and three-day trips where you "test-drive" a career or business with a person actually engaged in the profession you are considering. The company offers over 125 business and career experiences through over 300 experts. Founder Brian Kurth's vision is providing individuals with an experience of what their dream job or business is like before they decide to leave their current job. Visit VocationVacations.com for details. There are many other websites and businesses focused on helping people change jobs as well as investigate and start businesses. Use the Internet to find them.

Some people are finding two careers are better than one. One job meets their financial needs and the other career addresses their emotional needs. One such person is Natalie Dunbar. She works as an engineer for a major company and writes romance novels. Describing herself as a "Calgon Take Me Away" kind of girl, several of Dunbar's books have been nominated for industry awards.

In a similar way, Selita Victoria has a full-time job; however her passions are hospitality and entertaining. She pursues them as proprietor of the

Omni House, a unique banquet facility catering to individuals who want an elegant, exciting, and eclectic setting for their social or business events. Despite having a demanding 9-to-5 job as a Property Manager, Selita started a business which requires lots of care and concern for all her clients and guests. Read about how she got started with this wonderful endeavor in Chapter 20 – Be Inspired.

In today's world of work and business, it is best to be open-minded about how you will make a living. Sometimes our career and business paths takes us where we want to be; other times, they don't. Recently, I was talking with a graphic designer who was working in a bakery because he could not find a job in his field after he was laid off. If that happens to you, I suggest being open-minded to the new experience by approaching it with a positive attitude, being ready to learn new skills and excited about meeting new people.

*   *   *   *   *

E.B. White was an essayist, author of the award-winning children's book, *Charlotte's Web*, and a long-time contributor to the *New Yorker* magazine. He made an insightful observation when he wrote:

"The world is full of people who have never, since childhood, met an open doorway with an open mind."

Don't be one of those people. Instead, be open-minded.

Just Get Serious® About Success
Chapter 15 Exercise

BE OPEN-MINDED

1. Complete the chart below.

From the information in this chapter, what are some ways I can be more open-minded?	How can I benefit from doing what I have listed?

2. Now that you know the benefits, get started today putting what you wrote into practice.

Chapter 16

Move Beyond the Past to Focus on the Present and Future

To carry a grudge is like being
stung to death by one bee.

Anonymous

Mistakes are a fact of life. It is the response
to the error that counts.

Nikki Giovanni – Poet

It is very important for every human
being to forgive herself or himself because
if you live, you will make mistakes – it is
inevitable. But once you do and you see
the mistake, then forgive yourself and say, well,
if I'd known better, I'd have done better.'

Maya Angelou – Author & Poet

It was a life-changing moment for me. I was in my late twenties and was reading a personal development book that I borrowed from a friend. I do not remember its title, but I definitely remember the story the author shared to introduce the topic of forgiveness. He boarded a plane in New York. Sitting next to him was a young lady. I will refer to her as Renee and him as Brian. Once they were airborne, he struck up a conversation with her. Brian asked Renee the usual flying-partner questions: her name, why was she flying to New York, was it for business, pleasure, or both, and what type of work did she do? After a few minutes of polite conversation, she turned to the window as if she did not want to talk with him any further. Brian decided to stop bothering her and read his book instead.

After being in the air for some time, Brian noticed Renee was silently crying. He asked if there was anything he could do. Although hesitant at first, she eventually opened up and told Brian she was very upset because she and her husband were in the middle of getting a divorce. He had left her for another woman. She said at that very moment, her husband was in the Caribbean vacationing with his new girlfriend. Renee was extremely upset about the situation. Brian tried to calm her by saying she would eventually meet someone special, and she should focus on the good things going on in her life.

While she had previously mentioned liking her job and being involved in an exciting project, she was not comforted at all by his advice. After talking with her further, he knew she and her husband had been separated for almost three years. When he gently suggested she forgive her husband and move on with her life, Renee replied she would never forgive him for what he had done.

In the book, Brian explained that whether or not Renee's husband had valid reasons to leave her, he was sure Renee's emotional state was not affecting him at all. It was only affecting her. Brian told her forgiving him would free her from being stuck in the mental trap of constantly thinking about the situation with all its "if-only scenarios." She was unconvinced, and continued to talk about how happy they used to be, how he was a terrible person for

> *Getting over a painful experience is much like crossing monkey bars. You have to let go at some point in order to move forward.*
>
> Anonymous

cheating on her, and how she wished things could be different.

This was an eye-opening story for me. Like Renee, I was stuck in a similar thought pattern about the past. My ex-husband and I had divorced about two years earlier, yet I was still thinking about how we would still be together if only he had been different. I don't believe I was actually in a state of unforgiveness (although I may have been), but I was very much focused on the past rather than the present. After reading about Renee, I realized I could continue to be like I was for months or even years. I vowed not to let that happen. Instead of sitting around thinking "if only," I started going out more and making exciting plans for myself. Eventually, I went to college.

INHIBITORS TO MOVING FORWARD

In life, there will be disappointment, hurts, or mistakes (intentional and unintentional). Many times, they come from friends, family members, loved ones, co-workers, managers, strangers, or even our own misguided behavior. Constantly looking back to them does little to help us achieve our goals and dreams. Instead of making progress, we can find ourselves unable to move forward for several reasons:

Decide to release others from the many ways they have failed you, disappointed you, and misunderstood you. Make a vow to live in the now.

Dr. Torri Griffin
Relationship Counselor

- What we think determines what we do. When we are thinking about a past disappointment, hurt or mistake, we are not fully focused (or engaged in) what we need to do to make headway on our goals.

- Focusing on negative situations can become physically draining. At best, it can cause minor ailments, like headaches which can temporarily prevent us from moving forward. At worst, it can cause us to have major illnesses that incapacitate us for long periods. In her book, *You Can Heal Your Life*, Louise Hay writes that diseases are a result of the body not being at ease due to negative emotions.

- We can lose our base of supportive colleagues, friends, advisors, and others as they become tired of hearing our stories over and over again. They lose interest in helping us achieve our goals and dreams because we are stuck in the past.

- We find it difficult to participate fully in the happiness of others because we are preoccupied with our own thoughts of anger and disappointment.

- Our continued thinking about small disappointments, hurts and mistakes can cause us to "blow things out of portion" relative to their real impact.

- We start to make small and large mistakes because we are so preoccupied.

- We cannot sleep or cannot eat well. The result is that we do not have the energy to do the things we need to do.

It can be beneficial to venture temporarily into the past to decide what action to take or to determine what lessons we have learned. Also, there are times we need to hold conversations about a previous incident to get advice and suggestions. But we don't want to be permanently stuck there. Here are some signs you are focusing too much on the past. You are:

- Continually thinking about what happened.

- Constantly talking about it.

- Unwilling to forgive the other person(s).

- Unwilling to forgive yourself.

- Unable to see the situation from a learning perspective.

- Forgetting conversations with friends because you are so engrossed in the painful past.

- Physically or mentally drained.

By focusing on the past, we cannot fully enjoy the present ...

As I mentioned in Chapter 9, I volunteered to represent my college's Alpha Chi chapter and give a speech at the national convention in New Orleans. It was the worst speech of my life! I was extremely nervous, so I hurried through the material, talking so fast people could barely understand what I was saying. I was completely preoccupied with the thought that I should have practiced more. I dropped my note cards, and after picking them up, had a hard time reordering them and refocusing. At the end of my presentation, instead of asking, "Are there any questions" I just ran from the lectern. I twisted my ankle as I stumbled down the stairs leaving the stage. I felt like a complete failure.

To make the situation even worse, I could not stop thinking and talking about that speech for the remainder of the trip (three full days). It occupied my every thought and every conversation. My poor performance robbed me of the chance to enjoy fully the incredible New Orleans cuisine, the great jazz clubs, the wonderful art galleries, the great weather, and the fabulous people I met. Instead of putting the speech behind me, I kept telling everyone how terrible I was. Responses like, "You weren't that bad," "It really was OK," did not console me. The rest of my trip was ruined by a 20-minute speech. I wish I had decided to "get over it" sooner so I could have enjoyed my time in New Orleans.

> *I decided I can't pay a person to rewind time, so I may as well get over it.*
>
> Serena Williams
> Tennis Player

That trip is a metaphor for many of our life experiences. Since that time, I have decided to recover from life's embarrassing moments, disappointments, misunderstandings, and poor decisions as quickly as possible. I don't want a repeat of my trip in New Orleans. I do not want to miss out on what is going well or even what is going great in my life at any moment.

Moving Forward

Focusing on the past can lead to making mistakes in the present ...

For a while last year, I was completely preoccupied with the theft of my cell phone. Now you may be thinking, "Now, Donna, that's really small." Well it was a very expensive phone – a Blackberry Curve I purchased at the full retail price. It was stolen at a friend's birthday celebration where I had been invited to be the speaker.

Since I arrived at the venue early, I graciously volunteered to help with the setup. I put my phone down for a moment and in the sea of family and friends, someone picked up it up. The Master of Ceremonies made several announcements asking whoever had accidentally taken it to return it. Of course, no one came forward.

I was furious for days. I found myself constantly distracted; engrossed in internal conversation about what I should have done differently. I kept wondering, "How could people at a family gathering steal something from one of the guests?" and "Why didn't I buy the insurance for it?"

This incident was consuming my mind, focus, and time. One day I was walking through the mall, so distracted by the thought of what had happened that I dropped my keys and I did not realize it. Thankfully, a female bystander shouted to me, "Miss, your keys!" As I picked them up, I pictured what would have happened had she not brought it to my attention. I would have ended up standing at my car with no keys! At that point, I realized I was too focused on the past and needed to get over it. How did I do that? I used method #4 from the following list.

> *As long as you don't forgive, who and whatever it is will occupy rent-free space in your mind.*
>
> Isabelle Holland
> Author

In addition to being unable to enjoy the present and making costly mistakes, we can get stuck being angry, fearful of making decisions, distrustful of others without cause and revengeful by focusing on the past.

All of these lead to an inability to make progress on our goals and dreams. How can we prevent that from happening? Here are 10 ways we can move beyond the past. You may have to use a couple of them if one alone is not working for you.

1. Forgive Others.

At the root of most negative, past-focused thinking is an inability to forgive others for what they did. In *Bus 9 to Paradise*, Leo Buscaglia, Ph.D., wrote, "Grudges carried for a lifetime are a pretty heavy load. They create much bitterness and suspicion. No one is guiltless. If we hope to be forgiven for our actions or shortcomings, we might start by attempting to forgive others for theirs. In the act of forgiving, we release ourselves from bondage. It then becomes possible for us to move forward."

> *When you haven't forgiven those who've hurt you, you turn your back against your future. When you do forgive, you start walking forward.*
>
> Tyler Perry – Actor, Writer

You can forgive mentally by deciding to let go of the situation. You can also use writing as a healing catharsis to get rid of the negative emotions so you can feel better and get on with your life.

Forgiveness may also be expressed to the individual(s) in a face-to-face conversation or through a note or phone call. In cases of serious infringement, I suggest seeking professional advice before proceeding.

2. Forgive Yourself and Seek the Forgiveness of Others.

If you made the mistake, forgive yourself. Know that we all make poor decisions or err at various times in our lives. Hold yourself accountable for making progress instead of punishing yourself for not being perfect. If you have disappointed or hurt others, apologize with sincerity and ask their forgiveness. In both cases, decide what you will do differently in the future to avoid making the same mistake or upsetting or harming others.

3. Stop Talking Constantly About the Situation to Everyone.

You are wearing people out with your endless conversations about the past. If necessary, talk to one or two trusted individuals who can give you positive advice or direction to consider. Beyond that, become more interested in what is going on with those around you instead of always bringing up your past experiences. Ask questions, make suggestions, and think of ideas to help them.

4. Think of the Lesson You Can Garner from the Situation.

Consider this quote by an unknown author, "If you lose, don't lose the lesson." Make the lesson constructive instead of negative. For example, "In the future, I will be more careful of those I trust" vs. "In the future, I will distrust everyone."

> *LIFE =*
> *Lessons Intended*
> *For Everyone*
>
> Anonymous

Several years ago, I went through a very painful situation with a friend. She borrowed a huge sum of money from me and never repaid it. After the loan she simply disappeared by moving and changing jobs. Now, no doubt, she had all this planned before asking me to loan her the money. When her check bounced and I could not find her, I was furious at her and at myself. At the time, I thought about tracking her down and taking her to court. Because of how she had treated other people, I knew it would be a very messy affair with ugly lies and accusations. The question that kept coming to me was, "If I would not take her to court because of how she treated others, why was she my friend in the first place?" Instead of pursuing her, I decided to "lose the loot and learn the lesson (LTL, LTL)." For me, how people treat others is an indication of how they will eventually treat me. So I focus on only bringing into my inner circle people who respect and are helpful to others as well as me.

The only real mistake is the one from which we learn nothing.

John Powell
Author

In my situation, the "loot" was money, but it does not have to be. Loot is anything that is of value to you. It could be a good friend, a loved one, a prized possession, a great opportunity, an important client. Whatever it is, when you lose it, there will be feelings of sadness, frustration, anger, or regret. However, if you focus on the lesson you gained for yourself, it will not be a total loss.

5. Be of Help to Others.

Volunteer at a homeless center, hospital, senior citizen home, the Red Cross, or other organization. Help a friend, family member, neighbor or someone you know who needs assistance. Being of service to others can help shift your thinking from the past to how you are of value to others in the present. Books like, *The Healing Power of Doing Good* and *Why Good Things Happen to Good People*, cite research about the emotional rewards of volunteerism and helping others.

6. Put Your Principles into Practice.

Realize the incident allows you to put into practice your spiritual or faith-based principles of acceptance, understanding, and forgiveness.

7. Consider Approaching the Person Who Hurt You.

If appropriate, consider approaching the person who disappointed or hurt you to let them know how you feel about the situation. Possibly

277

getting their point of view about what happened or their apology will be beneficial for you. You may even find out their actions were not intentional or they did not know you were disappointed or hurt by their words or actions.

8. If Necessary, Join a Support Group.

There are situations that require the help of others in order to get past them. Do not be embarrassed if you decide that is what you need. Find out the details about the meetings, and do the research to make sure it is the right group for you, and then plan to attend.

9. Seek Legal and Professional Assistance.

Some incidents dealing with loss, injury, or damage may require you to obtain legal assistance or get law enforcement authorities involved. You may also need to seek individual professional counseling to work on your internal feelings and reactions. If that is necessary, do it.

10. Drop the Drama.

Read the ideas expressed in Chapter 8 – Drop the Drama and Be a Positive Person. Many of them are also useful in moving beyond the past, especially those on gratitude and changing our outlook through "relative-to-what" thinking.

*   *   *   *   *

To take a lighthearted look at moving beyond the past, I suggest you visit www.GetOverItDay.com. As of this writing, this website is a humorous and optimistic approach to looking at the disappointments and hurts we have experienced. It even has an amusing video you can watch. Get Over It Day™ is March 9. Its creator, Jeff Goldbatt, conceived the "holiday" in 2005, based on his thought that everyone has something to get over. I believe he is right about that.

My final thoughts on this subject: We can't move forward always looking back. Whatever the situation is, find a way to get past it. Your future success depends on that.

If you are having challenges in this area, re-read the ten strategies. Then work on the exercise on the next page.

Just Get Serious® About Success
Chapter 16 Exercise

MOVE BEYOND THE PAST

1. Complete the chart below.

What suggestions from this chapter can I use?	How will I benefit from following these suggestions?*

2. *Now that you know the benefits, get started today taking action on what you have written.

Chapter 17

When it's Time to Go

> *People come into your life for a reason,*
> *a season, or a lifetime. When you figure out*
> *which it is, you'll know exactly what to do.*
>
> Michelle Ventor
>
> *Some individuals leave trails of gloom;*
> *others, trails of joy.*
> *Some leave trails of bitterness;*
> *others, trails of harmony.*
> *Some leave trails of pessimism;*
> *others, trails of optimism.*
> *Some leave trails of criticism;*
> *others, trails of gratitude.*
> *What kind of trails do you leave?*
>
> (Quote Abridged)
>
> William Arthur Ward
> Scholar, Pastor and Teacher

Not all relationships are going to last forever.

By relationships, I mean work, professional, business, and personal associations with other people. They can end for many reasons.

Whatever they may be, I suggest people remember … *whenever possible, go with grace.*

By "grace," I mean respecting the other person and not creating an enemy, resentment or "hard feelings." You may be thinking, "What does this have to do with being successful?" The answer is everything. Let's look at the following main reasons:

> *When it is time to go, do go. But, whenever possible, go with grace.*
>
> Donna Satchell

- People resurfacing in your life

- It's a small world

- Needing future assistance

PEOPLE RESURFACING IN YOUR LIFE

You never know when someone will resurface in your life as a manager, interviewer, or potential business partner. So plan to leave work, business, and personal relationships on a positive note.

Years ago, I was working at a major consulting firm in New York City. One day, I glanced down the corridor to see if a co-worker was at her cubicle. I saw a woman talking with another employee; however, I could not see her face. I will never forget that moment. For the first time in my life, I thought I recognized someone by seeing the person from the back. It was a strange feeling. Her stance and body structure seemed very familiar. As I was trying to figure out who it was, the woman turned around and I saw her face. I was shocked! It was Sarah Willis (not her real name). I worked for Sarah at a previous job years ago. She was the main reason I had left. What was she doing here?

> *There will come a time when you believe everything is finished. That could be the beginning.*
>
> Louis L'Amour
> Writer

We recognized each other at the same time. She was the first to speak.

"Oh my goodness, Donna Satchell!" I was dumbfounded. It was like seeing a ghost. As we walked towards each other, my mind was still yelling, "What are you doing here?" Standing face-to-face, I smiled as I asked that question. Her response further shocked me.

"I was just hired as the Director of HR."

I was stunned. As my mouth said "Oh my goodness … Congratulations," I was thinking, "You are working HERE?"

I had worked for Sarah for three long, challenging years, and she did not make my experience an enjoyable one. There were always issues with her, including constantly changing directions and deadlines, miscommunications, and loads of rework. She was moody, hopelessly unorganized, and very critical of everything I did. Since there was no possibility of transferring to another department, I left the company on Wall Street and got a job on the upper east side of Manhattan. Despite our bumping heads on several occasions and my strong dislike for her, I always tried to be civil. My last day on the job was a pleasant one with Sarah wishing me well and my hoping never to work with her or anyone like her ever again.

> *If you want a happy ending, that depends, of course, on where you stop your story.*
>
> Orson Wells
> Actor, Director, Writer

Now she was in a major HR position at my current employer! I was thankful our parting had been on good terms. We had lunch on one or two occasions while she was there. Sarah left the company within two years to pursue an international opportunity.

A colleague of mine told me about finding himself in a similar situation, only it was a bit more complicated. Not only had he and Pam worked together, they had also dated for a while. Despite mutually deciding to stop seeing each other, Bobby said it was always awkward running into Pam in the cafeteria or at meetings. When he decided to accept a position at another company, he felt relieved knowing their accidental run-ins would not continue to happen. Guess what? Unbeknownst to either of them, she accepted a job two years later at the same company where he was working. Much to their mutual surprise, they ran into each other by the elevators during her first week on her new job.

> *The doors we open and close each day decide the lives we live.*
>
> Flora Whittemore
> Writer

Two stories and one important message: When ending a relationship, act as if you are going to see the individuals again because you probably will.

IT'S A SMALL WORLD

In today's world, it seems like everyone knows everyone else. So, plan to avoid hard feelings when ending relationships. Your new colleagues may know people from your past.

I believe the concept of six degrees of separation has collapsed to being only one or two degrees. It is possible to end up interviewing with someone who knows your former supervisor, end up wanting to do business with someone who knows your former client or business colleague, or end up calling on a potential client who is friends with someone you dated, was married to, or worked with. Or, in my case, having someone in your training class who knows one of your former colleagues.

> *A reputation for a thousand years may depend upon the conduct of a single moment.*
>
> Ernest Bramah
> Author

I was presenting a two-day program for a client in Atlanta. During the morning session, I mentioned having worked at Clairol. One participant immediately asked if I knew Mike Moore. I replied, "Yes, we had worked together." She said they were good friends and she was planning to see him that evening at church. She would mention meeting me. Imagine what her thoughts would have been if he said something unpleasant about me, particularly since on the following day, I was presenting part two of my program on *Teamwork – Working Well with Others*.

The above reasons and stories point to the importance of "going with grace". With that in mind, here are seven tips to consider before you resign or leave a job:

1. Give sufficient notice so the search for your replacement can begin. For most workplaces, it should be a two-week notice; however, do what is customary for your position and industry.

2. Choose the reason for resigning wisely. Avoid damaging the careers of others or speaking ill of them just because you are departing.

3. Make it known that you are willing to be of help and value until your last day of work.

4. Determine the individuals you would like to use as references in the future and talk to them about that possibility before you leave.

5. If you do not have them, collect personal email addresses and phone numbers from the people you plan on staying in touch with.

6. Clean up your area space, cubicle or office. Leave everything in good condition.

7. Thank the appropriate individuals for being of help to you during your employment.

Here are seven tips on what to avoid doing on your last days at work:

1. Do not tell someone all the negative things you thought about him, her, or the organization in general.

2. Do not use the exit interview or any conversations to speak badly of the company, co-workers, managers, or others.

3. Do not raid the break room or supply closet or take anything that does not belong to you.

4. Do not leave things in such a way that it would be difficult for your replacement to function.

5. Do not use social media (such as Facebook or Twitter) to bash the company or individuals you used to work with.

6. Do not send personal emails criticizing your former company, managers, or co-workers.

7. Do not act (or think) as if you will never see the people you worked with again.

Below are three tips to remember after you have left:

1. Stay in touch with those people who you had valuable relationships with.

2. Do not reveal any confidential information about the company, organization, or projects you worked on.

3. Resist the temptation to talk negatively about former co-workers and managers at your new place of employment or with anyone.

I also suggest keeping all these tips in mind when you end a business relationship or stop being a member of a social, professional, business or faith-based organization.

Recently, I attended a business-building event where everyone described a challenge they were having with their business in order to solicit ideas from those present. One woman, who I will call Sandy, explained she was an artist and needed to develop more contacts in

> *What matters isn't being applauded when you arrive, for that is common, but being missed when you leave.*
>
> Baltasar Gracian
> Philosopher

her field. Someone suggested she get in touch with a sculptor in the area. The person said the sculptor was always looking for new talent and those serious about their craft to collaborate with. Sandy immediately said something about working with him in the past and having left on less than positive terms. She then added, "I guess I could have handled things better." Avoiding ill will is not just for employees in the workplace, it applies to those in creative fields and entrepreneurs as well.

Let's further examine how to articulate the reason you give for leaving. It can make all the difference in the world in how you are perceived and what happens in the future. I speak from experience. In my career, I found myself promoted to a position with lots of responsibility, lots of perks, lots of company recognition, lots of business travel, lots of frustration, lots of demands, and lots of headaches. I was on assignment at the client's location for an annual project which lasted about six weeks the first year. Because of a new direction for the project and increased complexity, the following year I was away for ten weeks. Although I was home on the weekends, I found myself becoming more and more stressed-out and unhappy. By the third year, I was away for 14 weeks!

Along with the work demands of the assignment and the travel, the manager I was working with was becoming increasingly difficult. I was miserable. I hated not being able to relax at home in the evenings, talk to friends in Atlanta without ensuing a large phone bill, or walk around my favorite park after dinner.

What did I do? On the last day of the last 14-week assignment, I quit! I resigned without the benefit of having another job. Now, I am definitely not suggesting that if you have such feelings, you do the same thing. I was prepared to quit. I had saved sufficient money to do so. Plus, I had thought long and hard about my decision and the ramifications.

I could have given one of several reasons for resigning – a difficult client, a demanding manager, an impossible workload, ever-changing systems, too much travel, or the client's endless technology problems.

I chose to use too much travel. Upon hearing I had resigned, co-workers and managers kept questioning me about my decision and insinuating the manager was the cause. But I kept saying while he was not the easiest person to work with, he was not the reason.

> *It takes 20 years to build a reputation and five minutes to ruin it. If you think about that, you'll do things differently.*
>
> Warren Buffett
> Financier

Between when I resigned and officially left, I was offered another position at the same salary with less travel, a less demanding client, and a less challenging manager. I accepted the position and worked with the company for another four years. They made the offer because I did not point a finger at my manager or the top client and make them the reason for my decision to leave. If I had done that, the company would not have presented me with another opportunity.

Again, choose the reason for your departure carefully. Keep it as positive or, at least, as neutral as possible. It determines how you are viewed, what happens to others, and possibly, what happens to you.

The same sensitivity applies when getting a promotion or transfer to another department. You never know when you will find yourself working in the previous department again or when individuals from that department will be in your new area. Make a conscious effort to be positive in everything you say about the previous co-workers, managers, and anything connected with the work.

As I said earlier, we live in an amazingly small world. I had started working for a new company. After a few weeks, I asked Laura, one of the senior managers, if I could join her for lunch. We talked about how difficult it was for women to be recognized in corporate America. The Vice President of Human Resources at my previous company immediately came to my mind. Not using his name, I mentioned the challenges women had getting promoted because of him. As I said the name of the company, Laura immediately interrupted me with, "Oh my goodness, my uncle works there. Do you know him?" Then she said the name of the person I was getting ready to talk about! Laura went on to say, "My uncle is so fair and understanding. He was really sensitive to the issues of women and minorities and is always looking to help or promote them." Luckily, because people are usually only half-listening, Laura never realized I had not finished my story.

> *Don't assume people see the world as you do. We all see through different eyes.*
>
> Donna Satchell

Imagine what would have happened if she had not interrupted me and I had spoken her uncle's name and then said how awful he was! What an embarrassing situation that would have been. It would have also created a terrible impression with someone I had just met and with whom I was trying to build a business relationship. From that experience, I do not assume people see individuals the same way I do and I do assume they may personally know the person I am getting ready to talk about. Although this happened in the workplace, it could happen anywhere. Be cautious of those you talk about because other people may have a very different opinion of them or may know them personally.

NEEDING FUTURE ASSISTANCE

You do not know when you will need assistance from someone with whom you have severed a relationship. Therefore, attempt to end relationships on good terms.

I had been dating Gregory for several months and I thought we were the ideal couple. One day he called and said the words most of us would hate to hear, "I think we should date other people." After recovering from the shock of his announcement, I went ballistic, shouting "We? I don't want to date other people. You do!" He said something about continuing to be friends, at which point I screamed, "No way! Never! I want you to pick up everything you have here (in my apartment) right now! After that, I am not interested in seeing you and hearing from you again." I then started to accuse him of wanting to get back with his ex-girlfriend. It was like one of those dramatic break-up scenes you would see in the movies. I was so upset I decided to drop off his things at his house that evening. I left them at his door with a very ugly note.

Never succumb to the temptation of bitterness.

Dr. Martin Luther King, Jr.
Civil Rights Leader

You can see our parting was on very bad terms, mostly because of me. Even though I always thought he could have handled the situation better, I could have, as well. For weeks, I refused to return his phone calls or respond to any of his letters and cards.

A few months later, I decided to do something I had been talking about doing for years – attend college. I was working full-time and I planned to go in the evenings. Because the bus system stopped running before classes would be over, I needed to buy a car. I did extensive research to find the best buy. Eventually, I settled on my selection … a Toyota Tercel.

When I went to the dealership, I found out the basic model I wanted was only available with a manual transmission, which I did not know how to drive. I thought, "No problem. It can't be that hard. I will just take a couple of lessons." To my shock, all the driving schools in my area only used automatic transmission cars. Now I had a problem. I had ordered a car I did not know how to drive, and I could not find any schools offering lessons to help me. At the time, there was only one person I knew who owned a car with a manual transmission. Yes, you guessed it – Gregory!

When the dreams we have are bigger than the grudges we are holding, we will ask for help. However, the objective should be to have few grudges.

Donna Satchell

I found myself making one of the most embarrassing and difficult calls of my life. It went something like this:

Donna: Hi there (trying to sound very upbeat).

Gregory: Well – what a surprise. A very pleasant surprise!

Donna: So how have you been?

Gregory: Just fine. I got a promotion at work. And the new job is really kicking my behind.

Donna: Well, congratulations! That's great news. I know you really wanted a promotion.

Gregory: Thanks. So what's up with you? What's going on with your job?

Donna: Nothing much, the same old thing. Nothing has really changed.

Gregory: So to what do I owe the pleasure of this call?

Donna: Well (now I was starting to get nervous. I felt like my throat was closing up on me) … Well, I finally decided to go to college. I plan to take classes in the fall.

Gregory: WOW! That's great.

Donna: And I bought a car.

Gregory: WOW! Congratulations … What did you get?

Donna: I ordered a Toyota Tercel.

Gregory: Sounds good (from the tone of his voice, I could tell he was trying to figure out "what does this have to do with me?")

Donna: It's a stick shift.

Now there was a long pause before he responded with one word. Actually, it was a one-word question … "And?"

Donna: None of the driving schools offer lessons on a stick shift. So can you help me out?

Gregory: Well, sure. Once your car comes in, I will give you lessons. No problem.

Now there was a long pause on my part before I said, "Well, I really want to take lessons before the car comes in."

Again, he responded with one word "And?"

Donna: Can you give me lessons … on your car?

After me pleading "please" several times, he finally agreed. A few weeks later, I drove my new car out of the dealership, with Gregory proudly sitting in the passenger seat next to me. For those of you who are curious, yes, we started dating again … and that's another story for another book!

What a valuable lesson I learned from that experience. Since then, I have tried to end all my personal relationships on good terms. While that has not been possible in all cases, it is always my intention. I suggest you consider making it yours as well.

You may be thinking, "What does that have to do with being successful?" At times, there are things we will need help doing or acquiring in order to reach our goals. We don't want to find ourselves asking people for assistance after we treated them poorly in ending a relationship. We cannot always count on them being as understanding and generous as Gregory was to me.

I often say, "When the dreams we have are bigger than the grudge we are holding, we will ask for help." However, the objective should be to have very few grudges.

I am still trying to figure out the best way to leave personal relationships without there being hard feelings. Although I am definitely not an expert on this area, I have left and "been left" enough times to suggest five thoughts for you to consider. They are:

1. You just may see this person again some day. So I recommend, "Avoid acting like a fool in the present so you don't feel like a fool in the future."

2. Leave in a way that it is possible for you to ask for help at a later date.

3. Don't try to imitate the drama-driven break-ups we often see in the movies or on TV. Some of those scenes should have an accompanying caption or voiceover warning, "Don't try this at home."

4. Give yourself some solace by reflecting on the words of Theodor Seuss Geisel, (best known as Dr. Seuss, the famous writer of children's books) "Don't cry because it's over. Smile because it happened."

5. If you cannot move beyond the negative emotions of a break-up (sadness, angry, depression), seek professional counseling to assist you.

Just Get Serious® About Success
Chapter 17 Exercise

WHEN IT'S TIME TO GO

Plan to re-read this chapter when you anticipate leaving a job, an organization, or a personal relationship. Remember to keep your emotions under control, consider tomorrow as well as today, make rational decisions, and take the appropriate thought-through actions as you depart. Prior to that time, review the chapter and write below the ideas and tips you will use.

_____

_____

_____

_____

_____

_____

_____

_____

Chapter 18

Just Get Serious

Anyone can dabble, but once you've made that commitment, your blood has that particular thing in it, and it's very hard for people to stop you.

Bill Cosby – Comedian & Actor

There's a difference between interest and commitment. When you're interested in doing something, you do it only when it's convenient. When you're committed to something, you accept no excuses, only results.

Ken Blanchard – Author

Are you taking it seriously, or just trying it out?

Donna Satchell

In the quote above, "it" represents our dreams, goals, aspirations, and the things we say we want to achieve. "Trying it out" is what we do when we are not ready to get serious about a job, a personal or business venture, organization, friendship, relationship, or other endeavors.

"Trying it out" is not necessarily a bad thing, particularly when it is a new undertaking. In the beginning, it can be hard to be serious when we are not sure of what is involved and whether or not we enjoy, or are truly interested in something. However, we do not want to confuse "trying it out" with "being serious." The former has several drawbacks:

- Limited support from others. People are usually not willing to commit time, energy, or money to help someone who is "trying out" an endeavor, be it a business, professional, or personal undertaking.

- Limited success and rewards because we are not fully committed and are doing less than our best.

- Limited and slow results can easily discourage us to the point where we stop doing what is necessary.

For these reasons, the sooner we can move from trying it out to being serious, the better.

Like belief, there are levels of seriousness. This became clear to me several years ago. I was having dinner with a gentleman I had been dating for a couple of months. During the evening, he grabbed my hand, looked in my eyes and said, "Donna, I am serious about you." At that moment, my heart starting beating a little faster, my hands started to shake ever so slightly, and I was momentarily speechless. (Yes, me, a speaker was speechless!)

After a few seconds, I regained my composure and then started in with rapid-fire questions. "What are we doing for Thanksgiving?" "What are we doing for Christmas?" "What plans do you want to make for New Years?" "When can I meet your parents?" "When do you want to meet my family?" The questions just kept pouring out of me because he said he was "serious." Suddenly, I realized he was not answering any of them.

I looked in his eyes and his face. His expression was saying to me,

"Donna, I am serious … but I am not *that serious*!"

As I thought about our conversation the following day, I realized there are levels of seriousness. There has to be because he said he was serious … and I was serious. But what we were talking about was completely different. Over the next several months, I tried to characterize the levels of serious. Initially, I came up with three. I shared my thoughts about them in my speeches and they were very well received.

To improve my thinking about the levels, I listened intently as people explained why they were not making progress on their goals, observed people's actions and inactions, and considered ideas I read about in personal development books. I then realized three was not enough to cover what happens with people and their goals. So, I added two more levels and ended up with five:

1. Not Serious

2. Slightly Serious

3. Sometimes Serious

4. Solidly Serious

5. Seriously Serious

Let's take a look at each one.

LEVEL #1 – NOT SERIOUS

Two quotes describe people at this level: "All thought and no action" and "All talk and no action." You know you are at this level when you look around and realize you have not done anything at all towards your goals and dreams. There is no Evidence of Effort (EoE).

You say you want to lose weight. However, you have not changed your eating habits at all, are not exercising, and are not even forgoing the use of your car and walking a block to the supermarket. Or you say you want to have your own business, but you do not know what is required to start a business in your state, do not have a marketing plan, and do not understand how much your endeavor will cost. Or you want a new job in an exciting new field; however, you have not taken the first step in a job search or updated your five-year-old resume. Or you say you want to be in a monogamous committed relationship, but you are still dating several people. Why? Because you are Not Serious!

At age 27, I wanted to go to college, but I was Not Serious. At 29, I was still thinking about it and at 31, guess what? I still had not taken any action. There was no EoE (Evidence of Effort). I had not visited any colleges. I had not investigated which colleges would be best for me. I had not made any appointments to meet with college advisors. I had not looked into the tuition reimbursement plans offered at my job. I had done nothing.

At age 32, I finally got serious. In January of that year, I said to myself "I will be in someone's college" by the fall. Then I started doing the things people do when they are serious about continuing their education. I met with college advisers. I found out the details of my employer's tuition refund program. I saved money for books. I purchased a car so I would be able to get home from the evening classes. And in September, I took my first class. If you read the earlier chapters, you know that six years later, I graduated summa cum laude with a bachelor's degree in business administration.

> *Unless commitment is made, there are only promises and hopes; but no plans.*
>
> Peter F. Drucker
> Management Consultant

In some ways Not Serious is the easiest level to move from. It requires doing something on a consistent basis. It does not necessarily have to be a huge undertaking. If necessary, take "baby steps" (small, achievable actions). So, if you are at this level, decide what steps, even small ones, you can take in order to move forward to the next level – Slightly Serious.

If you want to write a book, for example, write something every day, even if it is only for a few minutes. If you want to lose weight, exercise daily for just 10 to 15 minutes. If you want to save money, put your loose change in a jar every day. If you want a new job, update your resume, start networking and research opportunities online. If you want to be in a committed monogamous relationship, decide who will be the "person of significance" in

> *Take the first step in faith. You don't have to see the whole staircase, just take the first step.*
>
> Dr. Martin Luther King Jr.
> Civil Rights Leader

your life and stop contacting people in your little black book.

To move to the next level and stop being Not Serious:

- Write your goals and a plan to achieve them (see the exercise at the end of Chapter 6). If necessary, get help from an experienced person in your field of endeavor.

- Create EoE by moving forward, even if it is in small steps.

- If necessary, re-read the following chapters: Believe In Yourself (2); Create Visual Goals (7); Be Positive (10) and any other chapters you feel would be helpful.

LEVEL #2 – SLIGHTLY SERIOUS (AKA "TRYING IT OUT")

An appropriate quote describing people at this level is: "After all was said and done – more was said than done." Here, individuals are taking action but need to amplify their intensity if they want to "stay in the game." Depending on their intended endeavors, they may want to make more sales calls, attend more meetings, become more focused, get more help, or in some way increase their efforts. They may consider watching less TV, spending less time with passive or negative people, going to the mall and the movies less often, or making other changes so they have more time, money, and energy for their goals.

For several years, I was talking about writing a book. After a year of thinking about it, I still had no book, no outline, and no plan to make it happen, not even a specific date to begin writing. I realized I was Not Serious. To move forward, I purchased and read books about writing, took several classes on the topic and even began to write and distribute a free motivational newsletter. Now I had some EoE (books on the topic, certificates and handouts from classes, a monthly newsletter). That was a good start, but after a while, I realized I still did not have a book.

What we think, or what we know, or what we believe is, in the end, of little consequence. The only consequence is what we do.

John Ruskin
Author & Social Commentator

During the last month of 2008, I was mentally chastising myself for my limited efforts. I decided to re-read *So You Want to Write* again for some tips on how to get started. As I turned to the first page, a coupon fell out. It was for a free coaching session with the author, valued at $125.00. I remember purchasing the book from her and promising I would call to set up an appointment. The coupon's expiration date was September 18, 2007 and it had been good for one year. To my dismay, I realized I had wanted to write a book for over two years!

Think about your goals and dreams. How long have you had some of them? Has time slipped away from you, like it did for me? That can happen so easily. The shock of how much time had passed stunned me into taking more action. I suggest you do the same thing.

On that date (December 1), I quickly wrote out an outline for my book (since I had been thinking about it for years, it wasn't too difficult). I then spent the next two hours looking through the many personal development books I had and made two key decisions: (1) I would write a book with approximately 125 pages. From creating my newsletters, I knew if I typed for two hours a day, I could have 95 pages done by the 31st of December. That knowledge motivated me. (2) I would type two hours every day for 45 days, starting the next day. By the end of that time, I would have more pages than I actually needed for my book.

I suggest you do a similar exercise to get started on your dreams and goals. Figure out the details you need to pursue and accomplish what you desire. If you need assistance in getting the information or making decisions, find knowledgeable, positive, and supportive people to help you. Once you have the specifics, then move forward.

By December 25, I had a draft manuscript of approximately 75 pages. I made good progress in less than a month - 60% of the book was done! I had moved beyond the level of being Slightly Serious.

After making such great progress, I decided to take a break for a few days – after all, it was Christmas. That was a big mistake! A few days off turned into a week of attending all the festive events taking place. Then it seemed to take a lot of energy for me to get started again. Without the consistent effort and excitement, it was easy for doubts to start growing in my mind. I thought, "There are thousands of self-development books already on the shelves. What would make my book so different that people would purchase it?"

No longer focused, I read what I had already typed and started finding fault with it. The more I read, the more doubts I had. My goal of typing every day turned to typing every couple of days and then typing once a week. Then I decided to change direction and I changed the title. But before moving forward again, I decided to take another break and completely clear my mind so I could restart with a clean slate.

> *Never grow a wishbone, daughter, where your backbone ought to be.*
>
> Clementine Paddleford
> Journalist

Before I knew it, I was taking no further action and had no additional EoE (beyond my initial writings). I had fallen back to being Not Serious. Don't let the same thing happen to you.

You can prevent going back to Level #1 (Not Serious) by:

- Continuing to believe in yourself. Do not let your doubts or negative opinions of others rob you of your initial enthusiasm and focus.

- Avoiding the use of unserious words and phrases like try, might, maybe, depends, and "I'll see."

- Sticking to your plan.

- Taking consistent action.

- Getting an advisor or mentor to help you map out a solid plan of action, as necessary.

- Getting a coach to keep you moving forward.

You can move beyond Level #2 by spending more time, energy and money on your endeavors.

LEVEL # 3 – SOMETIMES SERIOUS

The quote characterizing people at this level is, "When they're hot, they're hot. And when they're not, they're not." A graph of their activities would show peaks and valleys. Things they don't know how to do, are afraid to do, find hard to do, or are unwilling to get help to do create fluctuations in their actions.

> *It's not what you do once in a while, it's what you do day in and day out that makes the difference.*
>
> Jenny Craig
> Founder of Jenny Craig

Inconsistent behaviors result when people do not do what they say they are going to do. For instance, let's take the goal of healthy eating. They are doing great for months and then come the end-of-year holidays. Suddenly, they start to use Sometimes Serious words like but, just, only, and phrases like "after all, it's the holidays."

Several years ago, I was holding a training program for a client. During the lunch break, I noticed Tim, one of the attendees, was still in the room reading and drinking from a large water bottle. "No lunch today?" I asked. Tim replied, "No, I am fasting." I inquired, "How long have you been doing that?" Tim answered, "For about seven years, twice a week on Mondays and Thursdays." My enthusiastic reply was "That's great. Fasting takes a lot of discipline. Have you ever changed the days or missed one?" "No, never" was his very definite response.

A thought came to my mind and I asked him, "What do you do on Thanksgiving?" Tim explained, "That

Stay committed to your decisions, but stay flexible in your approach.

Tony Robbins
Author, Motivation Expert

holiday used to be a challenge, particularly the first year. You see, I decided to start fasting twice a week in about March or April. I thought Monday and Thursday would be the best days. I never thought of Thanksgiving being on Thursday. A week before that big day, my friends were taking bets about whether or not I would break down. You see, I love to eat, particularly back then. So, Thanksgiving was a challenging day. The food was very tempting, but I resisted and did not give in, despite comments from my friends."

You may be thinking that Tim is a bit fanatical. Still, I commend him for staying on course. I also realize "life happens" and sometimes flexibility is necessary. If Tim's objective was your goal, you could consider fasting on Friday and still accomplish your target of two days. Decide to stick to your plan and if changes are needed, then stick to making your planned progress.

Another way we can become Sometimes Serious is by having too many goals. As an example, an author once told me that one January he decided to write a book on communication skills by the end of that year, and he accomplished his goal. The following year, he decided to write three books. The result? By that December, he had not completed one of them. Why? He felt he had attempted to write too many books within a given period. When we have too many goals, we can have lots of highs and lows in activities, and usually nothing gets finished at all. If you start to see that happening, reduce your number of goals. Sometimes it is better to have a narrow focus instead of one that is too broad to handle. So control the number of items you put on your plate.

We can also end up being Sometimes Serious by allowing too many disruptions to interfere with our plans. These disruptions include invitations, requests, drama-driven friends with their need for immediate help, and other non-urgent and unimportant situations that impede our progress. The solution? Take time to consider fully the activities you get involved with before saying "yes." Whenever possible, limit your disruptions.

If you think the progress on your goals resembles a roller-coaster ride, then you are in the Sometimes Serious zone. Re-read the scenarios I described above and take the appropriate action.

- If you have too many disruptions, apply the D&D strategies (delay and details). Learn to say, "No" (with limited info), "next time," "maybe later," and "let's make a deal" described in the Disruptions section of Chapter 8.

- If you have too many goals, determine which ones are most important for you to pursue right now and focus your time and energy on them.

- If you must change your plans, focus on making progress as you decide on the adjustments needed.

If none of the above is the cause, then take time to reflect on what is creating your ebb and flow. Consider:

- Is it your belief in yourself? Read Fluctuating Beliefs in Chapter 3.

- Is it drama-driven friends and their non-urgent emergencies? Read about dropping the main ingredient of drama in Chapter 12.

- Is it past mistakes and failures? Read the section on Inhibitors to Moving Forward in Chapter 16.

Use the previous chapters as a guide to the actions you can take to be more consistent.

LEVEL # 4 – SOLIDLY SERIOUS

At this stage, people exemplify my quote, "Success is an inside job with outside results." They know that "The only place success comes before work is in the dictionary" (Vince Lombardi). They are willing to put in the time, energy, and money needed to achieve their goals. Solidly Serious people have moved past Evidence of Effort (EoE) to Evidence of Results (EoR) or Evidence of Progress (EoP). The book you are reading is the result of my being Solidly Serious.

Earlier in this chapter, I wrote about my "journey" from the level of Not Serious to getting started, making progress and then sadly returning to level #1. My effort was inconsistent, pierced with doubts, and deferred by a lengthy break. Six months passed before I decided to pursue writing again. This time I was more committed to finishing. Early on, I got an editor, Steve Cohn, to do the proofreading and editing work required. I had two accountability partners who held me to making weekly progress. I met with colleagues to share ideas and brainstorm. My commitment to finishing this book meant accepting fewer personal invitations to social engagements and forgoing many fun activities so I could stay focused. It was not easy. But this time, I was serious about completing this project.

Being committed, overcoming the difficulties, making a personal investment of time and money, maintaining a strong belief in yourself and your ideas are characteristics of Solidly Serious people.

Thankfully, there are many level-headed, determined people to show us what it takes to be successful. They include people like Brad Crose, one of the Daring Dozen I profile at the end of the book. At age 32, Brad decided to go to law school. Having a wife and small child could have easily been an excuse for him to forgo pursuing his goal. Instead, he moved his family to Virginia to attend Regent University

School of Law. This was not an easy time for him, especially after his wife gave birth to their second child and later, their third child. Supporting a growing family and not having been in college for ten years meant achieving his goal required serious commitment, dedication, and focus. When Crose encountered major obstacles, he faced them and continued moving forward. Today he is a patent and trademark attorney. Read more of his inspiring story in Chapter 20 – Be Inspired.

Sometimes we need to get serious about overcoming challenges we have created. So it was with Jennifer Capriati. Playing professional tennis at 14 years old, she was an exciting and powerful player whose performances caught everyone's attention. Between 1990 and 1993, she won six singles titles, including the gold medal at the 1992 Olympic Games in Barcelona, defeating Steffi Graf.

After an early loss at the 1993 U.S. Open, Capriati decided to take a break. (Remember what I said earlier about "breaks" – be cautious of them.) During her time off, she became involved with questionable people, was arrested for possession of marijuana, and then shoplifting. She eventually entered into a drug rehabilitation program. She tried to return to tennis a year later but her loss to Anke Huber at the Philadelphia Tournament ended her plan. Capriati did not play on the tennis tour for 14 months.

> *Commitment is the enemy of resistance, for it is the serious promise to press on, to get up, no matter how many times you are knocked down.*
>
> David McNally – Author

In 1996, Capriati was determined to get serious about the game again. It was a long, hard journey that ended in a match many people feel is the best comeback in the history of tennis. Playing Martina Hingis in the blazing summer heat at the 2002 Australian Open, Capriati was losing 6-4, 4-0. No one felt she had a chance of winning. But she fought back, turning the match around to win 4-6, 6-4 and 6-2. The victory – achieved through her serious commitment – propelled Capriati to being #1 in the world of tennis.

Being Solidly Serious means standing the test of time. In the early 1980s, Lonnie Johnson had a successful career as an aerospace engineer working for the government. One day he was fiddling around in the sink working on one of his experiments when he accidentally caused a high-powered stream of water that shot across the room. The burst of water was so powerful it caused the curtains in the bathroom to start swinging. During a *20/20* TV interview, Johnson said, "At that moment I decided to design a high-performance water gun." The idea of the Super Soaker was born.

> *If you run into a wall, don't give up. Figure out how to climb it, go through it, or work around it.*
>
> Michael Jordan
> Basketball Super Star

However, the journey to success for Johnson would be a long and difficult one. He and his wife were raising three kids at the time; his marriage was in trouble, and he eventually ended up being $600,000 in debt. He recalls, "Along the way, there were lots of reasons to give up, but I always knew it was a great idea." After seven years of rejections, disappointments, and setbacks, he presented his product to the Larami Corporation, and they accepted it. Johnson's water gun was an instant success. Within two years, sales of the Super Soaker were well over $200 million and it was the number one selling toy in America. Over the years, retail sales of the Super Soaker have been close to $1 billion. His serious determination paid off. The royalties Johnson receives from his idea has made him an incredibly wealthy man.

You can become Solidly Serious and create EoR (Evidence of Results) or EoP (Evidence of Progress) by:

■ Becoming focused and disciplined.

■ Realizing success takes effort and lots of it. Be willing to do what is necessary to achieve your goals and dreams.

■ Regularly using Solidly Serious words and phrases such as will, absolutely, definitely, "I'll be there," and "Whatever it takes."

- Being open-minded and seeking the advice and direction of others.

- Moving beyond your previous mistakes and failures. Remember the past is the past.

- Staying on track with accountability partners and mentors.

- Asking for help from knowledgeable advisors, colleagues, and interested friends.

- Getting a coach to help you excel in your efforts,

- Understanding your dreams and goals will take time. So don't get discouraged. Instead celebrate your successes, both large and small. See progress as the path to your prize.

- Re-reading the chapters that will keep you on the path of progress.

LEVEL # 5 – SERIOUSLY SERIOUS

It has been said, "Nothing can beat the power of a made-up mind." This statement applies to level #5 people. "Must" is the word they use in their conversations as well as in their thinking and actions they undertake. Their dreams and plans are not optional, they are mandatory.

The difference between being Seriously Serious and Solidly Serious is the intensity of power and passion you need to reach your goal. Being Solidly Serious, you encounter and overcome *challenges*. Being Seriously Serious, you encounter and overcome *devastating events*.

I always say, "Many of us reach a point where we want to believe we are Seriously Serious, but in reality, we never really want to find out." Why? In being Seriously Serious, what individuals come face-to-face with is like "hitting a brick wall." It is so catastrophic everyone would understand if they decided to stop or forgo their endeavor. No one would think less of them because of the mental or physical pain they are enduring. Yet, they continue.

Grammy award-winning singer and songwriter, Gloria Estefan is such a person. She started singing professionally in the early 1980s as part of the band Miami Sound Machine. In 1988, Estefan decided to pursue a solo career. The following year, she released a top-selling album, *Cuts Both Ways*. The title track and "Don't Wanna Lose You" became a #1 hit. Her career was soaring. Then, in March 1990, she hit that brick wall. She was critically injured when a speeding truck hit her tour bus. Her spine was fractured. Two titanium rods were implanted into her back to stabilize her spinal column. Doctors feared she would never walk again.

> *Sometimes life is going to hit you in the head with a brick. Don't lose faith.*
>
> Steve Jobs
> CEO, Apple Inc.

Estefan was determined to return to the stage and to the career she was passionate about. She endured months of agonizing physical therapy so she could get her strength back to sing and entertain again.

Ten months after the accident, Estefan gave a stunning performance at the 1991 American Music Awards. Her singing *Coming Out of the Dark* brought me and many thousands to tears. Why was she able to return? Gloria Estefan was Seriously Serious about her dream of being an exciting and inspiring performer. Today, she is still performing at sold-out concerts throughout the world.

Other people have been Seriously Serious about their endeavors:

- Lance Armstrong, an award winning cyclist, overcame testicular, brain, and lung cancer to return to the world of cycling and win the prestigious Tour de France seven consecutive times.

- Marie Curie, devastated by the death of her husband, found the strength to continue the scientific research they had done together. She received a Nobel Prize in chemistry for her extraordinary work in radioactivity.

- Within 1½ years, Fran Drescher, Emmy-nominated actress, was hit with losses and brick walls. The TV show she created, *The Nanny*, was cancelled. She got divorced after 22 years of marriage. Her beloved dog died, and she was diagnosed with uterine cancer. Since her recovery, she launched Cancer Schmancer, an organization working to ensure women's cancers are diagnosed early.

- Tony Dungy's 18-year-old son committed suicide in December 2005. That is the hardest experience a parent can endure. Everyone would have understood if Dungy walked away from football, at least for a while. Everyone, but him. He continued as head coach of Indianapolis Colts and 13 months later, they won the Super Bowl.

And, let's not overlook non-celebrities who have shown Seriously Serious commitment. Recognize and draw strength from the people you know personally who hit a brick wall and climbed over it, crawled under it, or broke through it.

For me, such a person is Francine Ward. Like Gloria Estefan, one of her brick walls was a car accident. Doctors said she would never walk again. That is where the similarities end.

By the time Ward was 14 years old, she was an alcoholic and addicted to heroin. By age 18, she had dropped out of high school and was living on the streets of New York City, shattered and homeless. She was a continuing victim of the seedy side of life because of her poor choices and low self-esteem. Ward eventually moved to Las Vegas where she could work more easily as a prostitute to support her drug and alcohol habits. Run-ins with the law and arrests were commonplace in Ward's life. She attempted suicide several times to escape her misery.

As if Ward's life wasn't bad enough, one night she was struck by a car as she was walking the streets. She does not know who hit her, whether it was an accident or intentional. Whatever the cause, she ended up in the hospital in full traction and was told she would never walk again.

However, Ward did walk again. She walked out of the hospital with the accident being a catalyst for her thinking about changing her life.

Weeks later, Ward realized that she desperately wanted to live more than she wanted to die. She took the first steps in that direction by getting help to end her dependency on alcohol and drug. It was not easy, but it was crucial. Then at 28, she made the difficult decision to go back to school. Doing so meant facing the fear that she was too old, not smart, and unable to do the required work. And she faced her biggest fear of all – failing. She faced those fears, attended and graduated from high school, went to college, and found an interest in law. Then she faced the fear of not being able to become an attorney because she had a criminal record.

Anyone can give up, it's the easiest thing in the world to do. But to hold it together when everyone else would understand if you fell apart, that's true strength.

Anonymous

She also faced the ridicule of mean-spirited people who constantly brought up her past. They mocked her plans, saying women like her did not become lawyers but eventually returned to a life of having to pay lawyers to get them out of jail. Despite their doubts and cruel comments, Ward moved forward with her aspirations.

Today, Ward is a well-respected copyright and trademark attorney, sought-after motivational speaker, and author. Additionally, this woman who was told she would never walk again has run two marathons (at age 42 and 43) and has plans to run again in two years.

Ward beat the odds because she was Seriously Serious about changing her life. Her accomplishments and many accolades are a testament to what can happen when we decide to take control of our lives, get started, get help, make difficult decisions, stay focused, and be committed using the various strategies I've covered in the previous chapters.

You can read about Ward's remarkable story of transformation in her book, *Esteemable Acts: 10 Actions for Building Real Self-Esteem.* To find out more about Ward, visit her website at www.Dare2beExtraordinary.com.

If you find yourself facing devastating events, know you have the power to prevail by:

- Believing in yourself and your abilities to overcome any challenge.

- Seeking spiritual guidance.

- Getting the physical, emotional, and financial help you will need.

- Engaging relentlessly in your faith practices.

- Fortifying your mind with the knowledge of real people who have triumphed over unbelievable losses.

- Understanding you can and will win.

* * * * *

I have some questions for you. How serious are you about your goals and dreams? How serious are you about pursuing your passion? How serious are you about starting a business? How serious are you about writing a book? How serious are you about getting a promotion at work? How serious are you about losing weight, going to college, getting a new job, obtaining an advanced degree, being in a solid, committed relationship, or whatever else you say you want to do? Just how serious are you? I would like you to seriously consider that question and then complete the final exercise on the following page.

Just Get Serious® About Success
Chapter 18 Exercise

HOW SERIOUS ARE YOU?

The form below is the same one you used in Chapters 2 and 3 (Levels of Belief). That's because the similar thinking is needed. You can also download this form from www.JGSBook.com.

Column #1 Your Dreams, Goals & Plans (Short & Long-Term)	Column #2 Your Current Level of Seriousness	Column #3 Actions You Will Take To Increase or Maintain Your Level of Seriousness

In column #1, write your goals, dreams, and the things you want to have and do in life. (Use one line for each one.)

In column #2, write your current level of seriousness, based on the levels discussed in this chapter: (1) Not Serious, (2) Slightly Serious, (3) Sometimes Serious, (4) Solidly Serious, and (5) Seriously Serious.

In column #3, write what actions you will take to increase or maintain your seriousness. Use the ideas you just read about in this and previous chapters, as well as other ideas you may have.

Now, you have a plan to strengthen or maintain your levels of seriousness. Take action by adding what you listed to your daily routines or writing them on your to-do list. Act on them so your seriousness supports your goals and dreams. Periodically revise and update this form as your level and/or dreams and goals change.

Chapter 19

My Final Thoughts

I would like to leave you with this last story.

Within a few weeks of moving from New York City to Atlanta, I joined BNN (Black Newcomers Network). Six months later, I was on the committee making plans for the organization's fifth year anniversary celebration. At our initial meeting, members talked about finding a location, securing a DJ, holding a talent show, and presenting awards. At some point, I suggested having a motivational keynote speaker. The members said that was unnecessary. They never had such a speaker in the past, and they thought it would cost too much money. I insisted they consider my idea. I explained the speaker would motivate the audience with a powerful message and having one would add excitement to the event so we could possibly get more members to attend than in the past. I mentioned Dr. Dennis Kimbro (author of *What Makes the Great Great*) and several others as possibilities.

After a lengthy debate, the committee captain, James Hester, relented, saying, "If you want a speaker, you find one. Just remember, we don't have a lot of money." I believe he and the rest of the committee members felt I would not pursue it and they would not have to discuss the idea again.

The following day (Thursday), I decided to contact Dr. Kimbro. Since he lived in Atlanta, I believed talking with him would not be a problem. But, his phone number was unlisted. When I called Random House, the publisher of his book, I was told to send them a letter which they would pass along to him. With our event taking place in two months, I needed to reach him right away. Mailing them a letter to send to him would be wasting valuable time (this was before the Internet and email). I thought of several other ways to get his phone number but none of them worked, (today with Google, Facebook and other websites it certainly would not be a problem).

On Friday, I kept wracking my brain about how to contact him. Suddenly, I remembered he had spoken at my church. When I called there, the office manager was kind enough to give me the contact information for his PR representative, Gloria Gilbert. I phoned her and after a short conversation, she told me his fee was $3,000. I became disappointed because the group would never spend that much money. I thanked Gilbert for the information and started to hang up when she asked how I got her phone number. I explained Dr. Kimbro had been a speaker at Hillside Chapel & Truth Center and someone there gave it to me. She then said "Oh, that's one of Dennis' favorite churches. Since you heard him there, I will give you his special discount rate. It is $1,500." I instantly felt encouraged. I knew there was a remote possibility I could get the group to fund that amount. I told Gilbert I would get back to her.

I immediately called Ellen, the organization's president, to let her know the news and asked what she thought. Ellen was somewhat hesitant but suggested I talk with Hester, since he was heading up the committee. I spent hours trying to convince him. I explained with a speaker of Dr. Kimbro's caliber, we could have a black tie affair, charge slightly more than the previous year, recoup the entire fee and possibly even make money. He finally agreed with me and planned to call an extra meeting for the members to vote on expending the money.

The following morning, I lay in my bed reflecting on what had transpired over the past three days. I had suggested an idea that

316

sounded absurd to some and impossible to others, and now there was a good chance it would happen. With Hester on my side, I was certain the members would vote yes. I knew Dr. Kimbro would be an outstanding speaker and the event would be an incredible success. Those three things ended up being true.

As I thought about it, I realized, like everyone, I had the ability to conceive an idea, move forward ,and make it a reality. This was not a new revelation for me, but because everything had happened so quickly, it really hit home. Continuing to think, I became upset with myself as I remembered the many times I had dreams and plans but did not take any action because of being afraid, not knowing what to do, or letting others dissuade me from moving forward.

Does that sound like you?

I vowed not to let that happen again. Suddenly, a poem I studied in college came to my mind. In fact, when I first read it I found the verses to be so eloquent and so powerful I recited them to myself several times. Since I still find the message compelling I keep it on my bathroom mirror.

I've included it here for you on the following page. I hope it inspires you as it has inspired me.

Commitment
W. H. MURRAY

Until one is committed there is hesitancy,
the chance to draw back, always ineffectiveness.

Concerning all acts of initiative and creation,
there is one elementary truth,
the ignorance of which kills countless ideas and
splendid plans:
the moment one definitely commits oneself,
then providence moves too.

All sorts of things occur to help one that would never
otherwise have occurred.

A whole stream of events issues from the decision,
raising to one's favor all manner of unforeseen
incidents and meetings and material assistance
which no man could have dreamt would come his way.

(I end with my own words ....)

Whatever your dreams, goals, and passions are,
Believe they can come true

Then just get started – Just Get Serious,
and watch success unfold for you.

Wishing You Success
In All Your Endeavors!

Donna

Chapter 20

Be Inspired ... Stories of The Daring Dozen

The Daring Dozen are incredible individuals who are goal-getters, passion-pursuers or difference-makers. Their stories are based on interviews I held with them. As you read each one, I am sure you will be inspired to discover and pursue your passions, move forward on your goals, or make a difference in the lives of others.

Note: The traditional dozen is 12. The baker's dozen is 13 and you get one extra. This group is Donna's dozen and there are 14, so you get two extra.

BRAD CROSE

Brad Crose was selected to be one of The Daring Dozen because he had the courage to make a major career change after working for ten years in the Information Technology field.

Immediately after graduating from high school, Brad attended Purdue University, majoring in engineering. While there, he became interested in going to law school, but the thought never progressed beyond the stage of "that's a nice idea for someday." However, after ten years in the I.T. field, working long hours, having demanding support roles, and beginning to suffer "burn-out," he started to entertain the idea again. When dot-com crash hit in early 2000, Brad found himself without a job, having few opportunities for employment, and ready for something new.

Brad applied to and was accepted into the School of Law at Regent University in Virginia. At the time, the course of study was not taught as a distance-learning program, so he and his wife, Michelle, sold their house in Atlanta and moved to Virginia Beach, with Claire, their two-year old daughter. He was beginning a new three-year journey.

Many of Brad's fellow students were young, unmarried, recent undergraduates at the age of 22 or 23 years old. Other than school, they had no other major obligations. In an interview, Brad told me, "Being married and having a child did not make law school harder, but it meant balancing school and family life. In the beginning, I felt a bit disadvantaged because of my time commitments with family, which I valued as a higher priority. Also, while in law school, my wife and I had two more children. Although it was challenging, having family proved to be beneficial in that it provided me with lots of encouragement, support, and purpose."

While in school, Brad applied to take the patent bar exam so he could practice before the U.S. Patent & Trademark Office, not just in the state where he was admitted to the bar. Then he received a letter from the U.S. Patent & Trademark Office stating that the school would not accept some of his undergraduate engineering credit hours and he could not take the exam. This was a tremendous shock. He was already halfway through the program, working as a patent law intern, and planned to enter the field upon graduation. What was he going to do? After much thought and prayerful consideration, he decided to make up the credit hours to correct the situation.

So as if law school and having a wife and three children were not enough, Brad added 15 credit hours of science and engineering to his already full plate. "Not being easy" was an understatement. The additional classes meant longer days, much more work, and greater discipline to get everything completed on time. But Brad persisted. The credits were accepted and he was able take the exam, ultimately passing it to be a registered Patent Agent. As Brad told me, "I refused to give up despite the circumstances and it paid off. Had I let that hurdle trip me, I would not be a patent attorney today."

He went on to say, "I am passionate about my work because I enjoy working with inventors and entrepreneurs who have new, innovative ideas. Many of my clients are developing new technologies and launching new businesses. It is an exciting and positive area of law in which to work."

I asked Brad what he would recommend to people considering making a career change. He thought about it and replied, "I recall my hesitancies. It was certainly a high-stress decision. Mine was ultimately made to choose the path that moved me closer to what I was passionate about. Although I was burned out from my original IT career, I had no guarantee that a switch to law would be any better. But I realized I would not know until I tried." He went on to say, "The fear of passing up the opportunity and always second-guessing would haunt me. I would always be playing the 'what-if' game. So I just leaped into it. I would encourage others to make a decision based on what moves them closer to their passion, not merely a search for greener pastures or something to escape the current circumstances. When what you are clearly passionate about has been identified, and you are ready for the career change or life change, leap."

Brad's Favorite Motivational Quote

Never, never, never, never give up.
Sir Winston Churchill

* * * * *

CARLOS BARHAM

Carlos Barham was selected to be one of The Daring Dozen because his passion to serve makes a tremendous difference in people's lives every day.

Several years ago, I was providing customer service training to Atlanta firefighters. One day, I raised the question, "What made you decide to become firefighters?" One person explained how, as a child, he saw them subdue a blaze at a neighbor's house. The next described how they saved his mother's life. Several individuals talked about them visiting their schools on career day. A woman answered that her father was a firefighter and told how much she admired what he did. Suddenly, a man stood up and said something that has stayed with me ever since, "I am passionate about helping people and saving lives. Being a firefighter is my calling."

That was the first time I had heard the word "calling" used to describe something without having a church or religious reference, but it would not be my last time. As I presented other training classes to firefighters and asked my question about their career choice, many of them used words like "calling" or "passion." Carlos Barham is among that group of courageous and passionate men and women.

Growing up, Barham always wanted to be in the military to serve his country, as many members of his family had done. He also dreamed of traveling the world. By joining the Marines, Barham was able to do both. Along with being of service to the United States, he also experienced many diverse cultures, from poverty in Istanbul, Turkey to wealth and prosperity in Haifa, Israel. What he learned from his travels is "There's no place like home."

In 1996, Barham became a security supervisor and concierge manager at the Georgian Terrace Hotel in Atlanta. That position gave him an opportunity to use the teamwork skills, discipline, and sense of urgency he acquired in the Marines. However, he eventually missed the sense of purpose he felt in the military, as well as the camaraderie he shared with his fellow soldiers. So in 1998, he decided to become a firefighter.

When I asked Carlos what he liked best about being a firefighter he told me, "To serve the citizens of Atlanta with pride, honor, and diligence." Also, Carlos sees himself as a role model to young men and women. He does that on and off the job. In addition to fighting fires, he assists his community by hosting a summer leadership camp for 11- to 14-year-old young men. He proudly feels "If I can make a difference in one child's life by teaching him to love God, himself and others through leadership, while giving and growing, then I feel I have done my part. Our camp motto is to be 'Spiritually, Mentally and Physically Strong.'"

In his line of work, there are many sad occasions and challenges. Carlos said the biggest ones are witnessing the death of a fellow comrade and experiencing the loss of a child you're trying to save. Those are not easy things to face, but with a strong spiritual foundation, and indescribable support from the firehouse and his immediate family he is able to continue to press on. Along with these difficult times, there are incredible rewards by doing something great by saving lives.

Being a firefighter is more than a job for Carlos. Like many others, the passion to serve fulfills him. His job does not provide a luxury lifestyle or even pay all the bills. But the ultimate satisfaction and gratitude he receives from the citizens is far greater than money.

Working at his passion requires teamwork. One person cannot do all that is required to fight fires and rescue people. This teamwork starts long before the emergency. It begins with working together in the firehouse as a family. It comes from knowing and trusting what your partners are going to do before they do it. The result of the special training everyone receives enables them to work as one solid unit.

When I inquired about the three things that have contributed to his success as a firefighter, Carlos replied, "Being spiritually grounded, possessing a great work ethic, and having family support. For me, that means praying every day, approaching and completing work with a spirit of excellence, and being able to balance my passion to serve with the love for my family."

In closing, I asked Carlos what he would recommend for people who want to find their passions. He suggested, "Seek spiritual direction. Sometimes, you may not know what your calling is right away. Think about what makes you happy. Then, pray for wisdom and guidance."

Carlos' Favorite Motivational Thought

Life remains very simple by providing two choices, faith or despair. If you give up, there is an automatic loss. Only if you dare to struggle, do you dare to win.
From a speech by Dr. Jawanza Kunjufu

*   *   *   *   *

CINDY CANNON

Cindy Cannon was selected to be one of The Daring Dozen because of her determination to succeed despite the enormous health and personal challenges she faced throughout her life.

At age 12, Cindy's life began to be filled with pain, hospital visits, doctor's examinations, painkillers and misdiagnoses. That lasted for 28 years. It started with awful stomachache. Doctors thought she had ulcers and treated her for that condition. They also prescribed Valium and other medications to keep her calm, but all of them made Cindy drowsy in class.

Along with all her health complications, her home life was miserable. Her father was extremely verbally abusive and her mother was very submissive and lived in fear. Cindy's brothers were away at college. They knew what was going on but chose to do nothing. Other family members simply pretended that everything was OK in her home.

Despite being heavily medicated, missing many school days because of illness, and having a wretched home life, Cindy graduated from high school and enrolled in college. I asked Cindy with all her medical issues what made her want to further her education. Her answer was not what you typically hear, "I was motivated to go to college for two reasons. First, I was so miserable at home, I wanted to leave there as soon as possible. Second, my father said I was not smart enough to go and women should be barefoot and pregnant. I wanted to prove him wrong."

College was very difficult for Cindy. By now, she was in constant pain, continuously drugged with powerful painkillers, always fatigued, and missing numerous days due to being in the emergency room. Still, she pressed on by making arrangements with her professors to do extra work to keep her grades high. Cindy worked diligently and ended up on the Dean's List for most of her time at college.

After graduation, Cindy took a job at the Casual Male, a retail chain, as a trainee. Within a short time, she was promoted to manager and then district manager with responsibility for several stores. This was a difficult feat because all the other managers were male and they created a hostile work environment for Cindy filled with favoritism and intimidation. She persevered by being committed to doing the best work she could possibly do and most of the time exceeding the efforts of her colleagues.

Cindy eventually got into employment recruiting, where she became known for her tremendous success. She worked at OM5/Management Recruiters placing administrative support staff. For years, she was their #1 recruiter in Atlanta and #2 in the world. When she did not hold those slots, she was always in the top 10% in sales, winning luxurious vacations to places like Mexico and Hawaii.

During all these years, Cindy was still in pain, being misdiagnosed, having various surgeries and on painkillers. I asked her "How were you able to continue working?" Cindy replied, "I just keep moving. I was like the Energizer Bunny®. I knew if I stopped for too long I might not be able to start again. Being busy kept my mind off the pain, frustrations, and uncertainties. Also, I loved all my jobs. However, I was truly passionate about being a recruiter." I asked Cindy why that area was so special to her. Enthusiastically she answered, "I love connecting people and making them happy. In recruiting, you have a company that needs to hire an employee. It is my job to find the right person. It is such a high when you make a match and everyone is happy with the end results."

Cindy's medical misdiagnoses finally ended when, at age 40, Dr. Norman Shealy, MD, Ph.D., neurosurgeon, neurologist, and scientist found the cause for her years of pain. It was Idiopathic Eosinophilic Enteritis, a rare stomach disease that very few people contract. Recovery took quite some time. Today Cindy is 100% healthy and as always, she is only looking forward and staying busy.

Among her projects, Cindy is currently writing a book entitled (*Insider's*

Secrets to Interviewing). She explained, "It is based on my 25 years in recruiting and the thousands of interviews I have conducted. It has information to help people be better prepared for interviews. I go over the basic, intermediate, and advanced techniques. There are lots of secrets that readers will learn to be on top of their game. It will be available in a few months. Also, my husband, Roy and I will be working on a book about my health ordeals."

I asked Cindy, "What would you suggest to people facing difficult times, be it economic, health, or family crisis?" She thought for a few minutes and said, "Know there is a higher source. God is with you at every moment. Be positive and try to do the best that you can. Know everything will be OK, this too shall pass."

Cindy's Closing Thought

You can do and be anything that you want to be, no matter the circumstances; you just need to know how.

*　　*　　*　　*　　*

CINDY LIGHT

Cindy Light was selected to be one of The Daring Dozen because of her passion and courage to pursue new opportunities by moving to the United States without knowing our language or anyone here.

In 1997, Cindy spent two weeks in the United States, visiting 10 cities, as part of a business trip sponsored by her employer in China. During our interview, she talked about how that was a life-changing event for her. She described visiting San Francisco and finding herself connected to the land, to the sky and to the richness of this country.

Although Cindy had a good job as a Public Relations Director, upon her return to Hong Kong, she made a bold decision to relocate to the United States. Cindy told me she had a passion "for a better life, for opportunities to do more, and for 'bigger skies.'" She moved to Chicago, without a job, without knowing anyone, and without being able to speak any English. After a short stay in a hotel, she found a small apartment in China Town. Then through an association of alumni from Peking University, where she got her degree, she made friends within the Chinese community.

Cindy could have easily forgone learning English because where she lived, that is not necessary. Since she spoke both Mandarin and Cantonese, she could talk with everyone in her small community because they spoke either dialect. But she was not satisfied just being comfortable in her neighborhood. Cindy desired to learn English because as she explained to me "I came here for a bigger life. I wanted to be part of this great country. I did not want to live just in my small society. I wanted to have a real life in America and experience everything." She compared moving here to being reborn. "I was like a little child again in this new country. I had to learn how to speak … to listen ... to drive ... to read... to do everything."

This learning was interesting, frustrating, and difficult. But Cindy was determined. Along with her jobs, she worked for free as a server in Chinese restaurants so she could practice her English and observe American ways. It took Cindy several years to become somewhat comfortable in her ability to communicate in English and to understand our culture. Here for over 13 years, Cindy said she is definitely still learning.

When Cindy was five years old, her grandmother, a master-tailor in Shanghai, taught her how to sew. By the time she was ten years of age, Cindy was making all her own clothes and had found her passion. She used her skills to open Cindy's Sewing and Design Studio. She made window treatments, home décor, and clothes. She had a creative flair and a passion for making her clients happy. Word spread fast about her incredible work and within a short time, she had more business than she could handle. One day a client said to Cindy, "You are the best image consultant I know." Cindy had no idea what she was talking about. She had never heard of "image consultant" and did not know what they did. After doing research, she realized she was already using many of their techniques in her approach to designing and sewing.

Cindy was so excited about this newly found profession that she attended the next Association of Image Consultants International (AICI) Conference. She went to every class, soaked up all the information, and talked to all the attendees about what she was doing as a seamstress. Everyone was impressed with her passion for her craft, her vast knowledge, and her exceptional abilities - so much so that the following year she was invited to be a speaker at the AICI conference.

Today, Cindy is a certified image coach, inspirational speaker and Chinese etiquette consultant. She is currently writing two books, one on dressing for success and the other on Chinese culture from a business perspective.

I asked Cindy what advice she would give to someone who was

uncertain as to what they were passionate about. She suggested, "Consider two questions ... 'What would I do for free?' and 'If I had all the necessities of life, how would I spend my time?' Then compare the two lists for similar items and then rank them to determine the ones of most interest to you. That's a good place to start."

Cindy's Closing Thought

Be passionate about your passion.
Let it shine through in all you do.

*   *   *   *   *

ELLEN CROOKE

Ellen Crooke was selected to be one of The Daring Dozen because of her professional passion for journalism and her personal passion for motherhood.

Crooke's interest in journalism began with the Watergate scandal, which led to the resignation of former President Nixon. A nerdy ten year old, she was obsessed with knowing all the details. She read everything about the unfolding events, watched all the TV coverage, and intently listened to adults discussing the matter. She understood the impact of this national affair in ways most ten year-olds did not. She was fascinated with the power *Washington Post* reporters Bob Woodward and Carl Bernstein had in exposing the cover-up. She admired them and wanted to be like them.

That desire led Ellen to major in communications at the State University of New York at Geneseo. There, Crooke had a life-changing moment when one of her professors showed *The Harvest of Shame*, a TV documentary produced by broadcast journalism legend Edward R. Murrow. The film showed the plight of migrants working on American farms. Watching the film, Crooke knew she wanted to tell powerful stories that could make a difference.

Ellen started her career as a news producer who wrote, organized, and conceptualized the newscast and then moved into newsroom management. Her hard work as a News Director led her newsrooms to win three national Edward R. Murrow Awards for local news coverage. In news coverage, the Edward R. Murrow Awards are equivalent to the Emmy Awards.

Sometimes, pursuing our passions means we are among those that break the glass ceiling. That's what happened in 1993, when Crooke became the first female news director at the NBC affiliate, WNDU-TV in South Bend, Indiana.

Her passion for news caused Ellen to break another glass ceiling when she became a stay-at-home News Director. She had helped move her news station to top ratings in South Bend market. So after the birth of her second child, Ellen's general manager allowed her to work from home one to two days a week. That gave her a chance to do what she loved and spend time with her daughters, Erin and Emily, during their formative years. About the arrangement, Ellen says, "I have spent the rest of my career trying to pay forward that wonderful opportunity by helping moms who work for me balance their lives. My advice to mothers is to be courageous enough to ask for what you want, but while asking, also provide solutions and then show your boss you can do it."

Today, as the Vice President of News at the Gannett-owned NBC affiliate WXIA 11 Alive in Atlanta, Ellen is in charge of an entire news operation, picking the reporters and anchors and all the people behind the scenes. Most importantly, she sets the tone for the news team.

Along with being a news producer, Ellen is also a news viewer. And what she had been seeing prompted her to tell a college journalism class "TV news stinks." As the guest speaker for the day, she went on to say that much of the news was "boring, repetitive and depressing." This was nothing new. News Directors had been hearing that from viewers for years. What shocked people was that a local TV News Director was honest enough to admit it.

Crooke's feelings prompted her to change the direction of WXIA. "We have moved to provide local news that is not filled with every shooting, house fire, and car accident…but has real issues people truly care about. We are bringing news that helps. The late journalist Tim Russert said 'the best exercise for the human heart is to bend down and lift someone else.' I believe local journalism can lift the soul and heart of a community." Because of changes in their programming last year, WXIA received eight regional Edward R. Murrow Awards, one national Murrow Award and ten regional Emmy Awards. Ellen is the first to say these awards were the result of great teamwork with everyone being committed to the mission.

Crooke loves journalism because she sees it as the search for the truth. She said, "It is an exhilarating experience providing a voice for the voiceless and holding the powerful accountable." As passionate as she is about news and journalism, she is even more passionate about being a mother. Crooke feels, "My children come first. Anyone who knows me or works with me knows that. No professional accomplishment in life can compare to raising your children well."

I asked Ellen what insights she could share with those trying to pursue a workplace or entrepreneurial passion while raising their children. She thoughtfully replied, "I have always put my family first. I'd be lying if I said it has always worked out. When I am doing really well at work, I feel guilty I am not at home. When I am doing really well at home with my children, I feel guilty I am not spending enough time at work. I wish there was a magic formula. But I haven't found it, other than to say my daughters know they come first and I will always be there for them."

Ellen's Closing Thought

If you are looking to find your passion, be curious about the world around you. Venture into new areas and try different things. Passion comes from within. You will know when you have found it because you will feel it.

*   *   *   *   *

GENO EVANS

Geno Evans was selected to be one of The Daring Dozen because he proves the idea that it is never too late to pursue your dreams.

During his last year in high school, Geno spent time making and selling scarves. This was supposed to be the start of a fabulous fashion career he had envisioned for himself. To move in the direction of that dream, Geno got a job as salesperson at a men's haberdashery in Detroit. An unexpected meeting, however, took his life in another direction and put his original dream on hold for over 30 years.

One day a man by the name of Ivan Humphries came in the store to buy several suits. Amazed with the size of his purchase, Geno asked him, "How can you afford to buy five expensive suits, while I work in this store and cannot afford to buy one with my 40% discount?" Ivan simply replied, "I'm a hair stylist." As Geno told me during our interview, "I immediately found the nearest beauty school and signed up for classes. I wanted to make the kind of money Ivan was making. He took me under his wing and showed me the ropes, and I was on a new career path."

After beauty school, Ivan sent Geno to style the hair of his very special client, Ms. Gladys Knight. The famous performer was in town for a concert, and Ivan could not finish his appointments in time to see her before she was scheduled to perform. So he asked Geno to go in his place. When Geno finished Ms. Knight's hair, she looked fabulous! He knew right then that he wanted to be a star stylist and be famous in the industry. On that day, he found a new passion.

As Geno explained to me, "I started in this business because I was passionate about making lots of money. But very early on I became even more passionate about making women beautiful. I love the challenge of it all. Money is very important; however, it is not my main focus. And I love making and keeping my clients happy. That means having them look stunning, and that starts with their hair."

Geno's passion extends beyond his skills as a hairstylist. He shared with me that "If you had never met me and you walked into my salon, you'd know that I am a professional who is passionate about what I do. People have told me it is reflected in how everything looks and feels. The salon has a waterfall, fresh flowers, burning candles, chocolates, and waiting rooms that make you feel like are you in a special place. I set the tone at the front door by engaging the senses of smell, touch, feel, and sight. My clients are spoiled, and I love spoiling them."

I remarked that it sounds like an experience, not a salon. And Geno said something that I always remember, "I believe that when we are passionate about what we do, we want people to experience our passion in as many ways as possible."

Despite having an extremely successful business and being well respected in his community and his industry, Geno felt compelled to return to his original passion, fashion design, at 56 years of age.

Geno explained, "Two years ago, I decided to move my career to the next level by pursuing my original love. So I enrolled in a graduate program at the Academy of Art University. Age has given me the experience to make tough choices with a clear vision. I know how I want women to dress. I believe in the feminine edge in fashion: beautiful dresses, flowing gowns, and classy lines. Today, I am sketching ten to 20 designs a day. I am absolutely loving this! One bonus for attending the Academy of Art is that the graduate students get to premiere their collections twice a year during fashion week. I am excited about those opportunities. I am also making serious plans for a Geno Evans Couture Collection to premiere during the New York's Mercedes Benz Fashion Week in the future. I am definitely looking forward to that shot at the top."

I inquired about people's reactions when he tells them about his plans, especially at his age. He answered, "Other people can be a distraction to your belief factor if you listen to their bad advice, negative comments, or unenthusiastic remarks. One must always have a strong belief in self in order to achieve great success. If you don't believe in your dreams, why would you expect someone else to take you seriously?"

Geno's Closing Thought

Live your dreams. God gave you the gift of life; it's totally up to you what you do with your career or business. Find your passion and drive it past the limit. Your greatness is waiting on you; you must reach out and capture your own destiny. Stop thinking about the past, missed opportunities, or failures. You must take charge of your life today and create your own mindset for success.

* * * * *

JACQUELYN PAYNE

Jacquelyn Payne was selected to be one of The Daring Dozen because of her passion for service, which she demonstrated during her 30+ years as a flight attendant.

In 1972, Jacquelyn woke up one morning and decided to start looking for a new job instead of going to work at her desk job of only 3 months, which she found to be boring. She had three companies in mind and Delta Airlines was the first one. She arrived at their corporate office, inquired about being a reservationist, and was told there were no vacancies for those positions. The receptionist suggested that she apply to be a stewardess (the term used in the 1970s) since there were openings. With great hesitancy, Jacquelyn completed the application. Two hours and two interviews later, she had a new career. She planned to fly for about three years and then move on to do something else. She never imagined loving her job so much she would do it for 33 years.

A passion for serving clearly describes Jacquelyn. As a flight attendant, she received over 180 written compliments and thank you letters from passengers and co-workers. Yes, over 180! That intrigued me because I do not know of anyone else who had been recognized by so many people for their dedication for serving others. I asked Jacquelyn about her letters.

The first letter was from a man who was traveling with his 12-year-old daughter. Jacquelyn warmly recalled, "I noticed she seemed upset about something and asked why she looked so sad. She said she had broken the zipper in the back of her dress. I told her I would repair it and gave her my serving smock to wear, while as I was doing so. She was excited about getting her dress fixed but more excited about wearing a part of my uniform for a short time. Her father was impressed with my wanting to make his daughter happy."

The last letter arrived on the day she retired. It was from her supervisor,

Janet Payne (no relationship). Jacquelyn explained, "Janet wrote, 'You have been my role model.' She described how I was always impeccably dressed, how I was always professional, yet caring and concerned about everyone, and how she received only accolades about me from peers and customers. Those were the best compliments I received about my work as a flight attendant and about me as a person."

Jacquelyn also has many wonderful stories about passengers who she connected with during her travels. One really stands out in her mind. While helping passengers board a flight she heard someone calling her name over and over again as if she was desperately searching for her. Jacquelyn looked around and saw Elizabeth, an elderly woman she met a few weeks earlier. She recalled, "The woman was elated to see me. She introduced me to her sister and brother-in-law as if I was a long-time dear friend, saying she was praying I would be on the flight. Elizabeth explained that her husband had passed away earlier that week and how glad she was to see me because of the kindness I showed them during their last trip. Elizabeth became choked with emotion as she remembered how warmly I talked to her and her husband while escorting them to their next flight."

Elizabeth gave Jacquelyn a beautiful bookmark. She keeps it in her bible as a reminder of how seemingly small deeds can have a lasting impact on others.

I asked Jacquelyn what was it about caring for people and her job that she enjoyed so much. "First, it is easy for me. When you are doing what you love, it is not work. Being helpful, considerate, and kind makes me happy even when the person does not know what I have done or even acknowledges it." Later she said, "When I retired from Delta, I was searching for those wonderful feelings I had when I helped my passengers. Many people said I would never have them again. I refused to believe that. I knew God would not give me such an incredible gift and not provide me with opportunities to experience it once more. Then, I realized it was with me all along. I had used the gift in many aspects of life and I could use it on any job. So as a real estate agent, I show the same concern, kindness, and compassion to my clients as I did my passengers. That is so important, especially during these economically challenging times."

I asked Jacquelyn what she would recommend for those who wanted to serve others better at work, at home or in their personal lives. First, she suggested, avoid gossiping because that disconnects people. Instead, look to see the good in people and speak positively and pleasantly to them. Then she said, "Volunteer at a children's hospital, homeless center, or retirement home. Find ways to make life easier or more enjoyable for others, particularly those less fortunate than you. Don't do it looking for something in return. Do it from a place of genuine caring and concern, and you will find the emotional rewards are enormous."

Jacquelyn's Favorite Motivational Quote

What we do for ourselves dies with us. What we do
for others and the world remains and is immortal.
Albert Pine

*　　*　　*　　*　　*

JENNIE CAMPBELL

Jennie Campbell was selected to be one of The Daring Dozen because of her tenacity. At 85 years of age, she continues to pursue a passion she has had for over 75 years. By doing so, she inspires others to keep working at their passions during their golden years. By the way, Mrs. Campell is my mother.

At six years old, Jennie's mother introduced her to sewing. She remembers, "I had three brothers, and it was my job to sew the buttons back on the shirts when they came off." I asked how she moved beyond buttons. She smiled proudly and said, "I was inspired by my mother. She never bought any of her clothes. She made all of them by sewing free-hand, meaning she could look at a garment and know how to cut out the fabric and recreate it without a pattern. I was fascinated with her abilities and I wanted to sew as well as she did."

In high school, Jennie learned techniques her mother was not familiar with, such as using patterns and clothing conservation techniques (making women's blouses out of men's shirt and using men's pants to make women's skirts). Her home economics teacher, Mrs. Olsen, knew everything about sewing, and there was nothing she could not make. She inspired Jennie to broaden her talents and creativity which further fueled her passion for the craft.

When Jennie graduated from high school, all she wanted to do was sew. So working from home, she became a dressmaker. She had a couple of good customers who appreciated her work, valued her creativity and paid as promised. They would tell Jennie about all the compliments they received when wearing the clothes she made. However, Jennie found herself spending less time on creative sewing and more time doing alterations, such as adjusting hems and making garments smaller. To add to her frustrations, many people would pick up their items, promising to pay her on Friday, but she never saw them again. Jennie was only 18 years old at the time and found this very disappointing.

To further her skills, Jennie wanted to go to Traphagen School of Fashion in New York and become a fashion designer. She found out it was much too expensive. Since she loved sewing so much, she stayed in the field and got a job at Politi Imports working as an assistant for their designer. Jennie recalled, "Ms. Politi thought I did incredible work and called me her "little dress-maker." She was always praising me and telling everyone how amazing I was. I loved working there because all I did was sew. Everything was great until I asked for a raise. Then Ms. Politi started finding fault with everything I did so she would not have to pay me more money. So I quit because I wanted to work in a place where people not only valued my talents, but also respected me as a person. I figured with my passion and my skills, I would be able to find another job."

A few weeks later, Jennie was hired by Empire Trade School to teach tailoring to the veterans returning from World War II. Most of the men had never sewn before and Jennie found great pleasure in teaching them everything she knew.

Eventually, Jennie got married and stopped working when she had children. But she never stopped sewing. Jennie made pants, shirts, and jackets for her husband, and infant blankets and clothes for her baby daughters.

After a few years, Jennie and her husband separated. She moved back to her mother's house with her daughters and started working at New York Telephone Company as a telephone operator. Since financially supporting and raising her daughters was Jennie's sole responsibility, she never had the opportunity to go back to sewing professionally. Still, she never stopped sewing. She made all the clothes for her daughters, mother, and herself, including winter coats and raincoats. They never had to buy any outer garments from the store. She also ventured into making curtains, draperies, and upholstered items.

I asked Jennie what it was like to have a passion for sewing. She said,

"I love to go to fabric stores and spend hours just looking at materials, touching them, feeling the textures, visualizing what I can and will make. Then once I start working on something, it is hard to stop. Even today at my age, I can sew until 1:00 or 2:00 in the morning. And when I finish whatever I am making, I have a tremendous sense of accomplishment."

"When people compliment me on what I am wearing, it makes me feel so good. And even if they don't say anything, I know I have created something stunning. Many people are amazed when they ask me where I bought a dress or suit I am wearing and I tell them I made it. Then they ask about sewing – how did I get started; how long have I been doing it; how much time did it take to make whatever I am wearing. I excitedly answer all their questions."

Jennie's Closing Thought

Find something you love doing. Then you will experience the incredible joy I feel every time I have a needle and thread in my hands. And, believe me, that feeling can last you a lifetime.

*   *   *   *   *

JOANNE SMITH

Joanne Smith was selected to be one of The Daring Dozen because of her determination to pursue her passion of singing despite having a full-time job.

Joanne started singing when she was six years old and got the lead role in a play about Mother Goose nursery rhymes. All the clapping at the end of performance got her excited, and singing has been her love every since. During our interview, Joanne told me, "Once I got that high that comes from an audience's applause, I was totally hooked! A great show has my adrenaline so high that I have to get 'talked down' afterwards so I can go to sleep. I can't really think of any other way to describe the feeling. It's just the best feeling I know."

After one of her shows, a patron said, "I am so glad I came. I really enjoyed myself. I would hate to have missed the Joanne Smith experience!" Joanne decided to use what she said as the name of her band. She feels "'The Joanne Smith Experience' truly reflects what I endeavor to create – an evening of different styles of music (pop, R&B, country & western, and ballads) that take you back down memory lane or make you want to jump up and dance or close your eyes and just groove. Every time I step in front of a microphone, regardless of the audience size, my goal is to make you have a good time. So much so, that you are glad you had the "experience" and you will come see us again!"

Along with being a singer, Joanne is a Senior Executive Administrative Assistant at The Coca-Cola Company. This is the highest level you can achieve in the administrative field at this major corporation. Last year, Joanne attained her long-time desire of working in the Worldwide Sports & Entertainment Marketing Department. "In this area, there is never a dull moment. It is important for me to be on point because as soon as I am done with one project, another is waiting in the wings."

Joanne's two worlds of working and singing complement each other very well. She explained, "Many times my audiences are made up of co-workers and associates. I even perform at engagements for the company. The only challenge is when I have a gig on a work night. Then it may be a little challenging for me to stay awake the next day. But other than that, I can't think of anything that is too difficult. That is probably because I'm so happy to have the privilege of doing both."

Joanne added, "The biggest joy I get from having both a job and a passion is that my day job allows me to have a lifestyle and maintain the well being of my family. I sing because it's my passion, and though I get paid to do it, I'm not able to maintain my family from it – yet." She went on to say "I tried to stop singing when I thought it was just too much trying to do both. But I soon realized that I have the music in me, and I can't stop. So, I had to think of a way to do both. I knew I had to eat and have a home for my family and me. So working a 9-5 job was a must. So, I figured out how to do the music too."

"I got started by forming a band. Then I went to different venues and offered to 'work for the door' just to get my foot in and sing. Sometimes after paying my band members, I would go home without a dime. And I had already spent money on flyers, sound techs, outfits, hairdos, rehearsal spaces and the list goes on. But at the end of the day, it was worth it, because I was able to pay for all those things from my day job; I was able to hire the best musicians in town, and I was able to sing!"

At the end of our interview, I asked Joanne what she would suggest for those interested in pursuing their passion while continuing to work. Her insightful response was, "I recommend you take a realistic look at how much time your passion will take and decide if you have the stamina to invest in your dream, both financially and emotionally. Also, realize that things may not go exactly according your plan at first, so be prepared for those times and don't give up. If your dream is one that involves a large investment of money – carefully consider what those costs will be. You may have to budget differently in order to even get started."

She concluded, saying "At the end of the day, it will depend on how much you want to live your passion. If you do, then you will go after it from different angles if need be. With the economy the way it is now, no one can afford to quit a job, so be sure to take care of what's most important – the thing that puts food on the table, clothes on your back and a roof over your head. Be smart and creative, but don't give up on your passion either. It can be done! I'm proof."

Joanne's Closing Thought

My mother used to tell me, "Nothing beats a failure but a try." If you have a dream, don't be afraid to give it a shot. After taking care of your household, invest your time, your energy, and your money on your dream. If you don't try, you will never know what could've been.

*   *   *   *   *

JORDAN & EDITH DEAN

Jordan Dean was selected to be one of The Daring Dozen because of her passion for animals and for her ingenuity in finding a way to pursue it at nine years old. Edith Dean, Jordan's mother, was selected for actively supporting her daughter's dreams and being a role model of great parenting of a child with a passion.

I spent over four hours talking to both Jordan and her mother. I truly understand what passion looks like when it is embodied in a 12-year-old child – it is exciting, creative, unstoppable, and incredibly inspiring.

Jordan started showing a passion for animals when she was about three years old. Her mother remembers her being totally captivated with a big tortoise at the zoo. Her interest was so strong that within a few months, she gave Jordan a tortoise as a Christmas gift and her little girl was ecstatic. Her fascination with animals continued and the following year Edith bought her an adult dog encyclopedia. She recalls, "A friend of mine told me, 'Jordan is far too young to read that big book. It has over 300 pages!' But I felt she could at least look at the pictures. Over time, Jordan learned the breeds and characteristics of all 400 dogs in the book."

To continue nurturing her interest, Jordan was given different kinds of pets, including dogs, a chameleon, birds, and even a fire belly toad. Twice a week, Jordan's parents would take her and her brother to the Humane Society to play with the animals. Jordan always looked forward to the trips and asked if they could go more often. That led to her dog-sitting business.

When Jordan was about nine, she wanted to volunteer to work at the Humane Society, but kids have to be at least 16 years old to do so. As Jordan explained to me, "I would visit the center often to look at the animals and bring supplies for the pets and newspapers to line the pet cages. For a long time, I was very sad because I really wanted to volunteer so I could play with the dogs and cats on my own. Then one day I came up with the idea about dog-sitting."

Edith was not surprised with Jordan's idea because, even at nine years old, she was a very creative thinker and a problem solver. However, she never imagined that the following summer (seven months later) Jordan's business, Inn The Doghouse, would have a clientele of five dogs and she would make almost $500 doing what she loves.

Today, Jordan's clientele has grown to 15 dogs. Her dogs range from a tiny Chihuahua to a huge Samoyed and include the controversial Pit Bull breed. The longest stay at Jordan's home was three weeks, when the owner went to Haiti and left his Yorkshire Terrier with Jordan. Most frequent are overnight visits. Because of Jordan's consistent care and concern, one of her customers calls six months in advance to make sure Jordan will be available to care for her Teacup Poodle when she takes her annual vacation.

Jordan's dog sitting business has become a family affair. Edith won't schedule family vacations or make other plans around the holidays. Why? As Edith cheerfully explained to me, "That's when Jordan's clients really need her services and when she does most of her dog-sitting. During holidays, we are at home and Inn the Doghouse is open for business."

Talking with Jordan, I was impressed not only with her knowledge of dogs but also with her concern for them as well. She held a bake sale at school and raised $350 for an organization committed to closing puppy mills, places where dogs are housed in shockingly inhuman conditions to breed puppies. Jordan has volunteered for special programs with the Atlanta Humane Society, PetParade, and other events. She enjoys being part of a pet therapy project where volunteers take dogs and puppies to senior citizen homes so the residents can interact with them. Because her heart is truly in animal rescue, recently Jordan teamed up with two other girls who share her passion to form an organization that would actively find homes for abandoned animals.

Jordan reminds me of another Daring Dozen selectee, Linda Hall, who told me that she is "consumed with every aspect of jewelry design." Jordan is consumed with every aspect of caring for animals.

Not surprisingly, Jordan wants to be a veterinarian* when she grows up. She described to me that her dream is to "have a big dog-sitting business with 50 clients (dogs), several people assisting me, and a built-in spa for the dogs. It would be a Hollywood version of the best dog-sitting place ever, where dogs are pampered and happy."

Jordan's Closing Thought

I believe what my grandfather would always say to me, "If you think you can, you can. If you think you can't, you are right."

Edith's Closing Thought

It is important to steer children in the direction of their natural bend, to encourage, and support the development of the gift they were born with, not the one we wish we had or the one we think is best. That is what I have done with Jordan, and I know it works.

*   *   *   *   *

* In June 2011, Jordan was one of fifty students (8th and 9th graders) accepted into Purdue University's Boiler Vet Camp for Juniors. She found attending the hands-on program was a confirmation of what she wants to do for the rest of her life. Her passion and commitment was quickly recognized by the instructors and counselors; so much so, that Jordan has already been invited back for the senior program (10th – 12th graders). She will be eligible to attend it in two years. Jordan is well on her way to fulfilling her dream of being a veterinarian.

LINDA HALL

Linda Hall was selected to be one of The Daring Dozen because she represents what is possible for all of us. She literally stumbled on her passion, and within a few months, she was excitedly pursuing it.

On July 25, 2009, Linda Hall was attending an 11-year-old's birthday party, where a family friend was helping the children create colorful magnets using polymer clay. As Linda watched the children, she became fascinated by the clay's brilliant colors. Although she had never made jewelry, she started to wonder whether the clay could be used for that purpose.

Once Linda got home, she decided to research polymer clay. She was shocked to find out not only could it be used to create jewelry, but there was an entire industry of people already doing that and more. They were also creating vibrant and decorative picture frames, vases and bowls, game pieces, toys, holiday ornaments, and various household items with the clay. Linda was absolutely amazed because she did not know anything about this at all.

Then Linda realized there were organizations of people who worked with this colorful and versatile medium, including the International Polymer Clay Association, and the Greater Atlanta Polymer Clay Guild. The latter had a chapter that met in Tucker, Georgia, about 30 minutes from Linda's home. In September she attended their meeting. The next month (October), she took her first clay class, which was making bangles. By the end of the session, Linda had found her passion – working with polymer clay. Two months later, she was selling her beautifully handcrafted bangles as holiday gifts.

When I interviewed Linda, I asked her to describe how she felt about her newly found endeavor. She excitedly told me, "I am consumed by every aspect of polymer clay; from reading articles, researching new techniques, taking classes, experimenting with color, looking for new creative ideas. Ideas for using the clay run through my mind several times a day. My friends tell me my eyes twinkle and my whole face glows when I talk about what I am working on."

Linda continued "When working with clay, I experience the feeling of eating my Aunt Ethel's homemade bouillabaisse – overjoyed and intensely immersed by the essence of color, texture and spices serenading my taste buds. When I finish the first bowl, I want more." Later she told me, "I prefer not having conversations about my clay projects late at night because I end up with ideas running through my mind and I am unable to sleep. Eventually, I get up and start working on pieces until two o'clock or three o'clock. And then I have a hard time going to my day job in the morning."

Like Joanne Smith, a jazz singer, Linda has a full-time passion and a full-time job. She is currently working at an insurance brokerage firm as an employee benefits administrator. I inquired what it was like doing both. She said "The challenge is not getting too excited about my jewelry endeavors while talking to my co-workers and managers at work. I have noticed that can make people uncomfortable because they don't know what they truly want to do. Or they have never ventured out to follow their dream. So I try to be somewhat low key when mentioning my jewelry. This can be difficult because sometimes I feel like I am trying to keep a volcano contained!"

I asked Linda what suggestions she could share with people who were interested in pursuing their passion as a business while continuing to be employed doing something else. She explained, "You have the best of both worlds. As you consider and research your passion, get your bills in order and start putting money aside to invest in your endeavors later on. This is a good time to understand if you have the makings to be an entrepreneur. Go to the Small Business Development Center, Small Business Administration, and other such organizations in your area to take classes to see if you are cut out for the hard work and discipline it takes to start, maintain, and grow a business. There is a lot to consider. So do it now while you are currently employed. With the uncertainties of today, don't wait until you lose your job. Get prepared in advance."

Linda's Closing Thought

"Most of us know the sayings 'Tomorrow is not promised' and 'Never put off till tomorrow what you can do today.' That is true of so many things in life. I think of my mother. She always dreamed of doing volunteer work when she retired. I remember all the years she worked so hard as a nurse and then she died at age 65 without having the opportunity to live her dream. I don't want that to happen to me or to you. Each day that goes by is one day less we have. So if you have something you want to do, don't just sit around thinking about it, instead start it today!"

*   *   *   *   *

MARGARET JOHNSON

Margaret Johnson was selected to be one of The Daring Dozen because of her determination to pursue a childhood passion at age 33, despite her parents' opposition.

Growing up in the 1950s, Margaret dreamed of having one of three careers – being a police officer or a firefighter because they helped and saved people, or being in the military because they defended our country's freedom. Her love for these professions started when she was about four years old and watched movies where people were being rescued or protected. Despite the nobility of her dreams, her parents did not think highly of them. In our interview, Margaret explained, "They pretty much said, in no uncertain terms, that they would disown me if I did anything that stupid. You see, my Daddy was in the Army during WWII, and he had an extremely low opinion of women in the military."

So to prevent a rift with her parents, after her graduation from high school, Margaret took various jobs working at a printing firm, a business consulting company, AAA Motor Club, and the U.S. Department of Agriculture.

One day Margaret was at an air show held by the United States Army Golden Knights at Dobbins Air Reserve Base. Since she still had a yearning to be in the military, Margaret found herself talking to a representative from the Georgia Air National Guard. He mentioned knowing a recruiter who could get people into the Guard who could not get in the regular military. Margaret was excited to know she may not have missed her opportunity to pursue her childhood passion.

Margaret interviewed and passed the physical. She enlisted on September 20, 1976. The day she was sworn in, Margaret called her parents and told them what she had done by asking them one question, "What have I wanted to do all of my life?" Her father immediately said, "Join the military." They swallowed loudly and said, "Well, that is what you always wanted to do." They accepted Margaret's decision and supported her.

When she enlisted, most of the men and women were between 18 and 29 years old with the average age being in the mid 20s. Margaret, at 33, was definitely the oldest in her class. I asked Margaret what was that like. She replied, "I was somewhat intimidated. But it was exciting just being there! At the same time, I was very worried that I might not be able to keep up with them physically."

Margaret recalled, "When we did the calisthenics, I was in way over my head. I was never able to run the mile in the time they wanted us to complete it. And when we had to cross over the swimming pool upside down hanging onto to a rope (ankles over the rope and using your hands to pull yourself along), I scared my Drill Sergeant because my legs turned black with bruises. But I did not fall in the pool. Several of the younger women did. So I was proud of myself for staying out of the water."

Despite the physical challenges, Margaret said, "I loved it. I have always believed everyone should have to be in the military for, at least, three years. I have always felt women should be drafted the same as men. Look at Israel and Greece. Their women all serve, or at least back then, they did. The United States quit drafting at the end of the Vietnam War and, at first, I was upset about that. But it has turned out well after all. Just think, all our military is volunteer. True, different people have different reasons for enlisting, but everyone comes out as mature adults and that is a good thing. Yes, I believe the military would be good for everyone."

Margaret loved the Guard's camaraderie and the summer camps, as well as her job, which was reading a radarscope and tracking aircraft (similar to what air traffic controllers do). For several years, she was in charge of evaluating the troops in Radar Operations and later became responsible for keeping everything in the center running smoothly. She made all her promotions when she became qualified and retired with the rank of Technical Sergeant E-6. Margaret pursued her childhood dream and loved it!

I asked what she would recommend for people who have not found their passion. Margaret replied, "Consider what means the most to you, what you are most interested in doing. That is what will make you the happiest and give you the most pleasure in life. Once you know what those things are, then start doing them."

Margaret's Closing Thought

Remember it is your life; no one can live it for you any more than you can live for someone else. Life is too short to be unhappy and feel unfulfilled. So find what brings you joy and pursue it.

*   *   *   *   *

PAM WILLIAMS

Pam Williams is the 2011 Georgia Teacher of The Year. She was selected to be one of The Daring Dozen because of her passion for teaching and changing lives.

I knew Pam Williams was a special person when I read what one of her high school students wrote about her. "Ms. Williams has an amazing ability to break down difficult concepts into simple lessons for students to understand. Her enthusiasm and passion for the subject she teaches radiates throughout every word she speaks." Wouldn't you want to have a teacher like that? I know I would.

There are people who know what they are passionate about early in life (as a child or teenager) and then there are those who stumble onto it as a young person or an adult. Pam falls in the latter category. She remembers being like lots of little girls and playing teacher as a child. At the time, she had no real aspirations for the profession. In fact, during her senior year in high school she was thinking about pursuing a career in physical therapy. She told me, "The doors simply seemed to continue opening for the field of education." She believes the great teachers she had inspired her to become a teacher.

Today, Pam could think of doing nothing else. She says, "I have the opportunity to make a real difference in children's lives life every day. I consider my profession second only to parenting, and truthfully, I often spend more time with my students than some of them spend with their own parents. What an awesome responsibility!"

I asked Pam how she knew that teaching was her passion. She said, "I find myself teaching in every area of my life. If I see a child in the grocery store trying to read a label, I pause to help him or her sound out the words. Recently, while I was waiting in line to complete absentee voting, I observed that the adults in front of me were very nervous about voting because they had never done it before. Without even stopping to think, I found myself 'holding class' in the hallway with many eager faces looking on. Teaching is as simple as breathing to me." She went on to say, "Being passionate about teaching feels exciting and challenging. I go to teach every day and it rarely feels like work. I do not think of teaching as my job… it feels more like a calling from within."

When I asked Pam why should people consider being a teacher, she passionately answered" Why NOT be a teacher? If you love young people and feel a need to help them traverse the rocky road of growth into adulthood, then teaching is a perfect opportunity. No two days are alike, boredom is rare, and learning can be as imaginative as you dare! The rewards are endless because the seeds of success that you help plant can go on to create untold success for many people."

Although having a passion means a sense of extreme personal pride and pleasure, there can be stresses and disappointments, as well. I asked Pam to talk about those times. "My greatest frustration lies in my inability to level the playing field for all of my students. For some, no matter what strategies I implement, learning remains a difficult task for them. Then many of my students have baggage that follows their every step. Whether it is economic disadvantages, poor parental support, peer pressures, teen pregnancy … these teens have far more obstacles that stand in the way of them achieving what seem to be impossible dreams. It is my desire to help them find the stepping stones to make the paths more navigable."

There are many success stories Pam shared with me, including a 14-year-old girl whose mother was prostituting her, and an eighth grade boy, who wrote in his journal that in ten years he would be dead or in jail for murder. Thankfully, both of these young people turned their lives around and, years later, came back to thank Pam for believing in them when few others did. Of those experiences, she says, "Year after year, my students return to thank me for caring and making a difference. Often times, I am so humbled because I simply had no idea that my impact had even existed. These moments have made me even more keenly aware of the influence that teachers possess."

Pam feels her success as a teacher comes from "Making a real investment in my students beyond just imparting content knowledge, but also helping them see themselves differently. Next, it is important for me to be a team player with others in my profession and not be afraid to ask for help. I don't have all the answers, and I realize there are people with more wisdom than me that I can go to. And lastly, flexibility is key. Times change, people change, and plans change. But the one thing that must remain constant is my focus in providing the best learning environment and opportunities for my students."

Pam's Closing Thought

I always tell my senior students that when they find what they love doing, they will find their passion in life. Many people think success is about money. I believe true success is achieved when people find their passion, because then they will work harder, fight longer, and reach higher for their success. So find yours, and success will surely follow!

*　*　*　*　*

Selita Victoria

Selita Victoria was selected to be one of The Daring Dozen because of her passion for hospitality and entertaining, which lead her to open the Omni House, an upscale event rental facility.

Located in Covington, Georgia on four acres of land, The Omni House is a unique blend of elegance, excitement, inspiration, eclecticism, and tranquility. The interior and exterior were created to be an experience in comfort, fun, and enjoyment for guests who attend events and the clients who host them.

The path to Selita's passion began as a conversation she had with friends about not having saved enough money for retirement. That led her to taking a financial planning seminar. During the class, the facilitator asked the participants to close their eyes and think about what they love to do. Selita immediately thought of entertaining. For years, she had hosted many barbecues and parties at her home. The facilitator then asked them to imagine how they could make a living doing what came to their minds. Over the next several months, Selita continued to ponder the question.

Selita's thoughts lead her to consider opening an event rental facility. She explained to me, "You need to have a vision and a plan or nothing will happen. I started to picture the place I wanted to own (the location of the property, the number of rooms, the type of kitchen, patio, and dining areas). I wrote down everything I thought was needed. I showed my plans to people in similar businesses and they added items I had not thought of. Next, I decided to pay off all my bills and get my credit in order. I stopped buying anything that was not an absolute necessity. I began telling close friends and family members about the concept I had for a place with exciting décor, a warm welcoming feeling, a large outdoor area with a gazebo, lots of nice comfortable furniture to relax in, a water fountain, and an atmosphere where guests could meet wonderful people. Those who attended my many parties in the past had a sense of what I wanted to create, and they were excited about it."

"Next, was finding the right house with plenty of space for parking, several acres of land, and two levels (one for living and one for entertaining). The location needed to have zoning which would permit me to move forward with my business plans. All of this had to be at a price I could afford. Real estate agents constantly told me what I wanted was impossible. But I did not give up. I continued to talk to agent after agent and, eventually, found one who felt she could possibly find such a place. She said I would have to be in a position to move fast because what I wanted would not be readily available. Within two weeks, she called to say she had the ideal house. When I looked at it, I knew she was right. It had everything I wanted. It was perfect. Within month, I moved in."

Once Selita purchased the property, the real work began. Because she had a full-time job as a Property Manager, Selita had the funds to initially invest in her dream. However, she did not realize how much she would spend in additional expenses beyond her original investment. Selita explained to me, "My dream is like a newborn baby that needs all my love and attention to grow. It requires lots of time, energy, talent, and money. There are ongoing expenses for upgrades, repairs, and new equipment; things like an industrial oven, microwave, wide-screen TVs, a stage and microphones. I want the very best for our guests and clients. I want everyone to thoroughly enjoy themselves so that each event creates opportunities for more business. It always feels like there are never enough hours in the day to do all that's necessary. This is especially true on the day of an event. Fortunately, I have great friends who are more than willing to help out. But everything starts and ends with me."

Selita continued, "There are many challenges working a full-time job and pursuing a full-time passion that require catering to clients' needs for events that are often once in a life-time affairs, such as weddings, retirement parties, baby showers, and anniversary events. Everything needs to be perfect, or as close to perfect as I can make it. I want my clients and guests to have an experience that they will never forget. That takes lots of planning, meetings, phone calls, and contact with many people to make an event come together the way my clients and I envision it. This is definitely hard work. But the best rewards for all my efforts are when my guests tell me 'we had a fabulous time' and clients give me hugs and say 'Everything was wonderful and you exceeded our expectations.' It's moments like these that I am so happy I made up my mind to pursue this passion."

I asked Selita what advice she would give to people who are searching for their passions. She suggested, "Ask yourself what do you love to do. Ask your friends what they think you are good at. Ask for spiritual guidance and direction through prayer and meditation. Just keep asking until you find an answer that you can move forward on."

Selita's Closing Thought

Passion has no boundaries. Passion is audacious.
Passion is total commitment. Passion is an
unstoppable energy. Passion is not about you;
it is about the universe and your impact on others.

Glossary

ABC	Always Be Celebrating
ACT	Assist, Congratulate, Thank
ATIP, ITIP	Avoid Taking it Personally, Instead Take It Professionally, Positively or Proactively
C-Zones	Comfort, Confining, Convenient, Costly and Crippling Zones
D & D	Delay (your response) and (get the) Details
D-Blocks	Doubts, Disruptions and Distractions that hinder our progress
EoE	Evidence of Effort
EoP	Evidence of Progress
EoR	Evidence of Results
GAP	Goal Achieving Partners
KIP	Keep It Positive
JDI	Jordan Dean Idea (Thinking big like Jordan Dean and many other children)
JGS	Just Get Serious
LTL, LTL	Lose the Loot, Learn the Lesson (Loot is anything of value.)
PE Principle	Recognizing the Parallels or the Exceptions between ourselves and others
PPC	Passion Pursuit Cycle
QYA	Question Your Assumptions
SMARTER	Formula for setting and achieving goals: Specific, Measurable, Ambitious, Real aspirations, Time, Energize, and Review
START	Start Thinking, Appreciating, Respecting, and Thanking
STOP	Stop Treating Others Poorly

About Donna "Serious" Satchell

Donna "Serious" Satchell is an Achievement and Business Speaker, Success Skills Trainer, Life Coach, and Author. Just Get Serious® is her trademark and business philosophy. She is serious about developing, designing, and delivering presentations and coaching to organizations and individuals who are serious about getting results.

Donna has presented programs at AT&T, The Coca-Cola Company, The Home Depot, City of Atlanta, Centers for Disease Control (CDC), Clemson University's Conference for Women, Chapters of International Association of Administrative Professionals (IAAP) and American Business Women's Association (ABWA), as well as other organizations, schools, and conferences.

As a member of the National Speakers Association (NSA), Donna is the past recipient of the NSA Georgia Chapter's Spirit Award for her outstanding commitment and contribution. She is also a member of Speakers Roundtable, an advanced chapter of Toastmasters International, and has competed in several of the organization's speech contests. Donna received her training certificate from the American Society for Training and Development (ASTD) and has taken classes on advanced training and presentation skills through Langevin Learning Services and other companies.

With over 25 years of corporate, marketing, and category management experience, Donna was the first administrative assistant promoted into a management-level marketing position at Clairol. There she received numerous individual and team awards and was recognized as one of the company's experts in field-based promotional analysis and category management.

Donna earned a bachelors degree in business administration from Mercy College in New York where she graduated summa cum laude.

Her collegiate memberships included the Alpha Chi Honor Society and the Delta Mu Delta Honor Society.

A past recipient of "The Best Motivational Speaker in Five Minutes or Less", Donna also won "The Two Minute Adversity Challenge Speech", both sponsored by The Twinkie Awards, which honors small business creativity and excellence.

Passionate about personal development, Donna co-founded Women Aspiring Together To Succeed (WATTS) with a business colleague, Lynda Shorter, in 2000. For more than 10 years, they have organized, and facilitated regular meetings and special events for the members and guests. Under their leadership, WATTS continues to inspire, motivate, and empower women. Donna is also on the Advisory Committee for DeKalb Technical College in Georgia and actively participates in their planning sessions.

Donna has co-authored several books, including *The Power of Motivation, 303 Solutions to Accomplishing More in Less Time, 303 Solutions for Communicating Effectively,* and *303 Solutions to Developing the Leader in You.*

If you would like information about Donna's services as a keynote speaker, success skills trainer, or life coach, you can contact her office at:

Donna Satchell
STARR Consulting & Training
770-498-0400
Donna@JustGetSerious.com
www.JustGetSerious.com

Continue To Just Get Serious®

Now that you have finished reading Just Get Serious® About Success, you can:

Stay Motivated

Sign up for a free membership in the JGS Book Club. You get a free teleseminar, free monthly motivational newsletter, and free life assessment. You will also be notified when new exercises, stories, and inspiring videos are added to the book's website. Everything is designed to keep you excited and motivated about your life aspirations. Sign up today at www.JGSBook.com (click on JGS Club).

Be Inspired

Read additional information and watch videos about many of the people featured in this book at www.JGSBook.com (click on Daring Dozen).

Keep On Track

All the exercises in the book are available at www.JGSBook.com. Download them from the JGS Club webpage and update them as your life or circumstances change, so you can stay on course to achieve your goals.

Get Coaching

To find out about the Platinum JGS Coaching Program, please send an email to Donna@JustGetSerious.com, and all the details will be sent to you.

Share Your Story

If you have an inspiring story of pursuing your goals or passions and want to be featured on the book's website, please send details to info@JustGetSerious.com. A representative will contact you.

Improve Your Leadership Skills by Becoming an Active Member of Exciting Organizations

Check out your local chapters of:

- Toastmasters International – www.Toastmasters.org

- American Business Women's Association – www.abwa.org

- International Association of Administrative Professionals www.iaap-hq.org

Also use the Internet to find out about associations focused on your field or area of interest.

Expand Your Knowledge and Increase Your Business Success
(For Entrepreneurs and Business Owners)

Investigate the services and seminars offered through your local offices of:

- Small Business Development Centers (SBDC) - www.SBA.gov (click on Counseling and Training)

- Service Corp of Retired Executives (SCORE) - www.score.org

- U.S. Small Business Administration (SBA) - www.SBA.gov

Also use the Internet to search for business-focused associations in your area.

Recommended Books & Audio Programs

- *A Setback Is A Setup For a Comeback*
  Willie Jolley

- *Attitudes of Gratitude*
  M. J. Ryan

- *Brag, The Art of Tooting Your Own Horn Without Blowing It*
  Peggy Klaus

- *Breakthrough Networking – Building Relationships That Last*
  Lillian D. Bjorseth

- *Esteemable Acts*
  Francine Ward

- *Forgiveness: How to Make Peace With Your Past*
  Sidney B. Simon and Suzanne Simon

- *It's Not Over Until You Win*
  Les Brown

- *Kick Your Excuses Goodbye*
  Rene Godefroy

- *Mayday!: Asking for Help in Times of Need*
  M. Nora Klaver

- *The Seven Habits of Highly Effective People*
  Steve Covey

- *What Makes The Great Great*
  Dennis Kimbro, Ph.D.

- *You Deserve More*
  Jewel Diamond Taylor

Index

www.ingramcontent.com/pod-product-compliance
Lightning Source LLC
Chambersburg PA
CBHW060238100426
42742CB00011B/1565